*Blessings Beyond View
via The Love Palace*

Another Vantage Press title by the author:

Establishing a Board of Christian Education Ministry within a Local Christian Church

Blessings Beyond View via The Love Palace

Excitement—Humor—Suspense—
Enlightenment and Love

Marvin O. Riddick

VANTAGE PRESS
New York

FIRST EDITION

All rights reserved, including the right of
reproduction in whole or in part in any form.

Copyright © 2009 by Marvin O. Riddick

Published by Vantage Press, Inc.
419 Park Ave. South, New York, NY 10016

Manufactured in the United States of America
ISBN: 978-0-533-16114-0

Library of Congress Catalog Card No.: 2008907070

0 9 8 7 6 5 4 3 2 1

Contents

Introduction		vii
I	Foundation (Getting Settled)	1
II	Father	6
III	Mother (Phase I)	18
IV	The Tragedy of Uncle Henry and Aunt Malverda's Untimely Deaths	36
V	Growing Up with Grandparents O'Hara and Viola Riddick aka Mamma and Grandpa Dock and Several of Their Children	101
VI	Mother (Phase II)	146
VII	The Joy of Being Able to Search for and Recognize Blessings Even through Pain	159
VIII	The Planted Seed that Contributed to My Narrow Escape Provides Secruity As Well for My Soul Even in Times of Trouble	179
IX	My Response to Two Important Questions Relative to the Title and Me	191
X	My Perceptions of This Book Being Helpful to Many People	205
Annex A		239
Copies of Death Certificates:		
Henry E. Riddick		240
Malverda S. Riddick		241

Copy of new articles (*News & Observer*, Raleigh, NC, March 25, 1939)	242
Annex B	243
Photographs	244
References	258
About the Author	259

Introduction

It has been a rewarding experience for me writing this book during lengthy intervals over a period of seven years (2000–2007). I have never before experienced such mixture of love, joy, happiness and pain as I did in reliving and/or reiterating much of the contents herein. The love, joy and happiness that I experienced in growing up with my grandparents O'Hara and Viola Riddick proved to be dominant over the pain of not being with my biological parents that I experienced at intervals.

Believe it or not, much of my hidden pain from childhood did not surface until after I had grown up to be an adult. By this time my world had expanded significantly beyond the home where I grew up; ''The Love Palace'' and its local environmental village in that it takes a ''village'' to raise one child as the saying goes. The ''village'' concept was truly a reality in my growing up on a farm in the South (Wake County, NC near Raleigh) in that parents in the local environment rendered discipline, care and concern for the children of one another.

Although I felt loved and blessed having been brought up in the manner that I had been, it took more biblical education, many years of training and experience (including military) for me to realize the extent of how God has truly blessed me. The more my interest in the study of God's Word expanded, I discovered the more my spiritual vision expanded, enabling me to gain a clearer view of myself as well as gaining a clearer view into the hearts and minds of others (a gift from God—a discerning spirit). While I was forced to go to Sunday school **with** my grandparents (my aunts and uncles were like my siblings) growing up, I didn't feel forced at that time because such was the "norm."

Additionally, all the real happenings were at the church but not necessarily of or within the church in my then-world of reality. Hence, now in my later years, I can really appreciate having been **taken** to Sunday School, as opposed to **being sent.** I view it now as appropriate Christian spiritual guidance by my grandparents, exposing me to the source of spiritual strength that I would need in my adult life in the normal scheme of life years after they would have been called from labor to reward as they have been. Truly I praise God today for blessing me through my grandparents during my early childhood.

Therefore, in deep appreciation for Grandpa Dock and Mamma (Viola) being obedient to the will of God by taking on the awesome responsibility of providing a home for me as a less-than-two-year-old toddler, providing love, care, Christian training and nurturing to the best of their ability as I believe, I truly praise and thank God for such wonderful and loving grandparents whom I love and honor for their having fulfilled the role as my parents during childhood. While Grandpa Dock was called to eternal rest January 29, 1946, I thank God for Mamma (Viola) whom I never knew as Grandmother, but Mamma in that she had the lion's share of the parenting responsibility in my growing up to age eighteen. Also, I will forever be grateful and thankful to God for seeing me (especially as a child) through the difficult times and yet allowing me to enjoy the good times associated therewith plus allowing me to see and experience the events that are mentioned within this book, through which He further allowed me to envision its title, *Blessings Beyond View via The Love Palace.*

I feel especially blessed and thankful to God that I am now able to realize that it is AGAPE love (brotherly love) together with a mixture of hope and belief that while I pursue the truth about the untimely deaths of my biological Uncle Henry Edward Riddick and his wife Malverda Riddick (March 24, 1939), I can do so without malice or hatred within my heart toward anyone. Therefore, I am blessed in feeling free to live expectantly each day believing that there probably are some former officials of the city of Raleigh, North Carolina and state of North Carolina or their relatives still among us who know the real truth involving the untimely and brutal deaths of Henry and Malverda, who may reveal such truth under the appropriate investigative circumstances. I am also extremely blessed to be able to spiritually look beyond others' faults and see their needs just as God looks beyond my faults and sees my needs. If someone knows the truth, it is my prayer that the contents herein will stir up their souls to come forth and reveal such truth. Further, it is my prayer that the same soul-stirring effect will grip the hearts, minds and souls of county, city, state and federal officials that are currently in office, to the extent that they will be moved by the power of AGAPE love together with their "oath of office" responsibility, combined with their respect for truth and justice, to review and/or investigate Henry and Malverda's deaths so as to remove what appears to be a cover of injustice for sixty-eight years (1939–2007) and let truth and justice now finally prevail.

Although I now know that I have been extremely blessed as far back as I can remember, I really didn't understand the true power of AGAPE love until I was well into adulthood. For this, I praise God for my mother (Rev. Juanita Hoke) whom I also love and honor. She is very special indeed. In reading this book, you will better understand God's plan as to why I was with my grandparents and not with my biological parents. In Mother's adult later years, she became a powerfully learned ambassador of God's Word. She is still preaching and teaching but mostly now teaching God's Word at the ripe and blessed age of ninety. In that she received her college education obtaining four (4) degrees (associate, bachelors in elementary education, bachelors in theology and a masters in Christian education), all of which were earned after reaching age sixty, her knowledge and teaching skills, especially biblical, have made a significant contribution to my literary endeavors. Having been one of her students in the course "How to Read and Study the Bible," made me realize how important it is for us to seek and obtain biblical knowledge in that such knowledge contributes immensely to our achieving success in any legal life endeavor if we apply such knowledge thereto. In that many of America's enemies are here within America, I hope this book will, to some degree, encourage American citizens to realize the power of the above-mentioned biblical knowledge by simply observing how America's enemies are constantly striving to remove the presence of power in the word "God" by removing the word "God" from all of the basic pillars of America's foundation in their ultimate goal of trying to completely destroy America which obviously includes America's freedoms and power.

In addition to my dear mother being my chief spiritual mentor (CSM) is another important mentor in my adult life, her baby sister, (my aunt) Mrs. Sadie Fields. Aunt Sadie, creator and proprietor of the fashion label "Laurina Togs Created by Sadie Fields," created the label in honor of her mother (my grandmother) Laurina Barnes (deceased). Sadie constantly makes "deposits in my spirit" to use her terminology. To know Sadie is to admire her, plus she is an aged senior citizen who is a top-of-the-line professional seamstress and businesswoman, still functioning daily, as of this writing, in her profession. The high quality of her creations, some having been exclusively created for several notable professional personalities resulted in her being honored with a "citation" from one of this nation's First Ladies who was at that time Mrs. Jaqueline Kennedy. One can easily feel the sincerity and true Spirit of AGAPE love when Aunt Sadie tells you, "I love you more." Certainly a special "thank you" goes out to all of the relatives, friends, teachers and schoolmates, many of whom are mentioned herein, who are among the living and to the memory of those who have been called home for their "deposits made within my spirit." I view the dividends derived from such deposits as contributions that have added flavor to this book.

It is my hope that each page of this book will grip your reading interest, allowing you to reap the full benefits that can be derived from being entertained by humor, suspense and enlightenment through reading pleasure. I feel confident that once you have read this book, you will gain a deeper appreciation for the Christian educational training concept that my previous book advocates, *Establishing a Board of Christian Education Ministry Within a Local Christian Church.* This is especially pertinent regarding spiritual leaders and members of Christian churches.

While you may not have experienced growing up during your childhood on a farm in the South with a portion being in sharecropping as I did, many of you can identify with some childhood experiences herein but through different cultures, environments and at different stages and spiritual levels in life. I also feel assured that this book will help many of you to look back from whence you came and feel a sense of accomplishment being where you are today and be inspired to strive for higher heights. Likewise I feel assured that this book will also help many who started out on the positive road of life, who have been tricked by the enemy and fallen by the wayside to be inspired to get up and gather the strength from God to break the chains of whatever personal addictive entrapment that may have enslaved you, symbolically brush yourself off and get back on the "good foot" telling yourself "with God's help, I can make it."

While we view and experience worldwide violence, terrorism and one-on-one violence within our environments, witnessing the hatred that many people carry within their hearts for one another seemingly being on the rise, it is my prayer and hope that as one reads this book, more compassion for one another will be gained and the need for AGAPE love to become more prevalent among mankind will be realized and sought after from God Almighty. I feel assured that this will help all of us to take a deeper look within ourselves as we look through our individual lens whether they be of riches, poverty, tragedy, sickness or addiction entrapment/enslavement and see what a great contribution that each of us could make individually and collectively toward world peace through AGAPE love. Further, it is perceived and believed that such will allow the revelation of many previously hidden "Blessings Beyond View" being revealed to us while being reminded that regardless to the highest of heights that we may reach in this life, we must be very careful not to glorify ourselves. Instead, **TO GOD BE THE GLORY.**

Marvin O. Riddick

*Blessings Beyond View
via The Love Palace*

I
Foundation (Getting Settled)

Early Sunday morning January 6, 2002, I had awakened rather early as usual in our modest home in Westchester County, New York. The lamp on the night table by the bed was on and the light seemed centered upon the large family Bible (King James version) that remains open at all times. I enjoy researching scriptures and reading the Bible frequently. It is truly the greatest book ever written. Although the television was on and turned down low, I wasn't really watching it. Now that I am retired, I have to remind myself to watch the time on Sunday mornings for I still have an obligation as church organist on Sundays. While going over some matters in my mind somewhat casually that Sunday morning, a gospel group came on television singing an old hymnal in a gospel rhythm that caught my attention and stirred up my emotions spiritually. The song they were singing was "The Lord will make a way somehow." The words of the first verse and chorus are:

Like a ship that's tossed and driven;
battered by the angry sea
when the storms of life are raging
and the fury falls on me
I wonder what have I done
that makes this race so hard to run.
But I say to my soul take courage,

The LORD will make a way somehow.
CHORUS: The LORD will make a way somehow
when beneath the cross I bow. He will take away your sorrow,
if you let Him have your burdens now. When the load comes
down so heavy; the weight is shown upon my brow.
There's a sweet relief in knowing
the LORD will make a way somehow.

    I began to think back through my early years (1937) realizing how blessed I am today. Although the major purpose of this book is not designed to be a tear-jerker, tears of joy began to fall from my eyes and I began to rejoice, thanking and praising God. Further, this book is not a biography of my life. However, there are some events and circumstances in my life that I am not ashamed to share with others, because these events and circumstances, in time, turned out to be blessings in disguise. This has caused me to become a firm believer in the concept that in the worst of situations, blessing(s) can be found if we look long enough and deep enough, even though it may take years to find the blessing(s).
    In order for you to get a clear view, I must take you back to the infant stage of my life for you to see the strong foundation upon which my life was molded. In the building trade industry, blueprints are prepared and followed in laying the foundation of a particular building. It is my concept the higher the building is planned above ground level, the deeper the foundation has to be for strength purposes. The picture of the house on the front cover of this book appears to be a typical old Southern shack that many American blacks called home. Believe it or not, this one, even though an eyesore, was a mansion in comparison to many others that were also eyesores along the major routes of travel on Southern highways. This one was located at that time just a few miles outside of Raleigh, North Carolina city limits on Louisburg Road. Just imagine how some of those looked that were deep into the

woods off the highways. Even so, the foundation of the lives that were housed in many of these eyesores that we called houses and homes to many were very comparable. Therefore, this book is not just about the author nor any one particular individual. It is hoped that many individuals will be able to see himself or herself at some crossroads of their lives and be made aware of blessing(s) found that they were not previously aware of. Hence, in my case, we have *Blessings Beyond View via The Love Palace*.

    I was born in Raleigh, North Carolina (St. Agnes Hospital), Wake County, May 17 and grew up in the St. Matthew township. My mother's maiden name was Juanita Barnes and my father's name was Johnny Marvin Riddick (deceased). I only remember a few things about my father because he died a couple of months prior to my fifth birthday. It is my understanding that due to my parents' unwed status and their economic situation at that time, my father's older brother, Henry Riddick, wanted me to live and grow up in a supposedly well-established home with him and his wife Malverda. I am told that my Uncle Henry wanted to adopt me. My mother, with a limited elementary education at that time and sleep-in domestic employment with a white family seemingly thinking about what was best for my welfare, consented to such adoption. Although my father, probably out of fear of losing pride together with other possible selfish reasons and probably without considering what was best for me, his child, would not consent to such adoption. Shortly you will be able to see what I perceive to have been the hand of God working in both of my parents' decisions.

    Through the years, I have found some humor in my father's decision. Such humor is not relegated to his being a black man. Tradition in the South at that time focused upon any man holding on to his title as "father" would probably be in the forefront of a black or white man making the same seemingly irresponsible decision. Where is the humor? Here is a man with no money to clothe and feed his child, no home to take his child, no secure employment, very limited education and faced with an economically bleak future being presented with a golden opportunity that would seem to be in the best interest of the child and yet he takes a supposedly courageous last stand, holding on to his father "titleship" of the child even if it means the child being without the basic necessities of life.

In order to see the humor in the foregoing, you may need to put on your intellectual imagination hat and imagine a one- or two-year-old baby son talking to his father as follows: "Hey Dad, that was a mighty courageous decision you made about not giving me up for adoption to your close brother and all. I really appreciate what you did because it makes me feel loved. In the meantime, Dad, I'm a little hungry and need a little milk and I need a couple of diapers until I get old enough to take care of some personal needs. Oh, I seem to have a problem in that I sleep a lot while I am growing up. Until I get a little older to provide for myself, I need a little comfort like somewhere to lay my head where I can get the sleep needed. Dad, do you think you could help me get these things?"

Readers, please don't think for one moment that I am making fun of my wonderful father whom I love very much because I am not. I am trying to point out the realities of life. He was just one young man among millions of black or other men who would have probably made the same decision under the same circumstances. Notwithstanding the foregoing concept, there is a hidden blessing in my father's seemingly irresponsible decision probably unbeknownst to him. It's truly amazing how God can take man's good intentions but unsound judgment, and integrate and mold them into His master plan, resulting in a positive outcome and certainly blessings beyond view. I stayed with my Uncle Henry and Aunt Malverda for a short duration as I am told. I was too young to remember them. Listening to different views of relatives regarding my stay with Uncle Henry and his wife Aunt Malverda, I have formulated some perceptions of my own. I perceive Uncle Henry as a man who loved children and wanted one of his own very badly. I am told that he spent a good deal of his personal time with me during that time. He was the one who was there to catch me when I was making my first steps beginning to walk. He was a family man and loved his wife dearly. My being with him and Aunt Malverda would have a major impact upon their lifestyle, especially in Malverda's case, as he probably thought.

I am told that Aunt Malverda was a very pretty woman. She was full of life and enjoyed living. Although she seemingly loved me dearly, she did not seem to be endowed with or demonstrate the motherly attributes in caring for a small baby at that time as would be expected of one in the role of mother. After a few unintentional injuries that I suffered while in her care, it is my understanding that she realized that she was not "cut out" so to speak to be the type of mother that was normally expected of mothers during that time. She was a good friend of my mother and she talked very honestly with my mother regarding what my mother should consider regarding my well being. Malverda was a person with a wonderful personality as I am told. Such, combined with her natural beauty, caused her to be focused upon her being viewed as a lovely person.

From several different sources, I have heard she and Henry were two very wonderful and lovely individuals. However, as we all have, they too, had their shortcomings. Based upon different sources of information including that which I have researched, it is my perception that Henry and Malverda's respective shortcomings contributed to their young and untimely deaths at the same time, March 24, 1939. More light will be focused upon this area later. During that same period, God's Will would have it to be that my father's parents (O'Hara Riddick and Viola Malone-Riddick) would take me as a toddler and bring me up in their household which is the same house on the front cover of this book. That was a God-sent blessing for my life.

II
Father

My father, Johnny Marvin Riddick, was born May 17, 1915. From as much information I am able to gather, he attended the St. Matthew school. Any additional information regarding his education beyond that is not available to me. As you have probably noticed, my father and I were born on the same day of the same month (May 17). Being very practical, I was probably and unwanted birthday gift to my father. I am told by many people, relatives and friends who knew him, that I am his double in looks and in some of my ways in that he was a very lovable person full of life and energy, especially humor. Humor, to me, is a very important tool in our daily living. The appropriate selection of humor used at the appropriate time and in the appropriate manner can be very helpful in getting others to view a very serious matter from a clearer and more positive perspective. Humor will also aid in others' acceptance and appreciation of something that will be beneficial to them which was previously unacceptable due to an unclear negative perspective. As far as I can determine through close relatives of my father, it would appear that his formal education did not extend beyond the seventh grade at St. Matthew's Elementary School. I am told that his closest buddy was his cousin, Theolphus Jones (deceased) whom we called "Thee." Thee lived with his parents (Rev. Millard Jones and Anner Horton-Jones) up the road just a little piece across the road from the St. Matthew Baptist Church and St. Matthew Elementary School.

During the time that Johnny and Thee were pals hanging out together, so to speak, there were two very popular cowboy characters in the movies named "Buck Jones" and "Tim McCarver." As custom would have it, almost everybody at that time was given a nickname. "Theopholus" became known as "Buck/Thee" and Johnny became known as "Tim" and/or "Sweetmeat." At a very young age, my father became ill and had to be taken care of by his parents (Dock and Viola). The real burden was on his mother Viola whom we all called Mamma. Families were very secretive at that time regarding what illness a family member had. I perceived families as being ashamed of certain illnesses of other family members and everything was handled in somewhat of a hush-hush manner. Most black families had to use "home remedies" to care for loved ones at home because of economic conditions. The families were poor and had no money for hospitals and doctors. I am told that Johnny contracted tuberculosis from another woman he was dating at that time who had a reputation that was unacceptable to Johnny's family or the church community. She had cut several people and was known to keep her razor with her at all times and bragged about what she would do to others with her razor. Because of her track record in actually harming others with her razor, most folks who knew her were afraid of her in that she was very sneaky and cunning in the way she attacked the person she had targeted. I am told that one could never see her pull out her razor until it was too late. She kept it in a silk handkerchief and when she touched one with her handkerchief, they were being cut without knowing it right away. Based upon the different sources of information, I perceive that my father became involved with her for pleasure and convenience but could not get away, as she would have killed him even if she had to do it while he was asleep. Therefore, he was stuck with her as I perceive. Even so, he kept the type of relationship with my mother "Juanita" that was perceived by her, his parents, siblings, relatives and friends including the church community, as the woman he would eventually marry.

Getting back to Johnny's illness, tuberculosis at that time was viewed by many as "consumption" and was very contagious. Johnny's illness left him no choice but to turn to his parents who would do their best to take care of him. The living space, what some would view as a shack, is viewed by me as a mansion from God. Although space was very limited, space was found for this prodigal son "so to speak." Learning later in life how major decisions were made in the household, I am confident that Mamma was at the forefront of the decision to let Johnny come home so she could care for him, notwithstanding that he had a contagious disease.

Even though basic living facilities such as running water, electricity, plumbing and bathroom necessities that we take for granted today were not available, especially to most black families at that time, it is amazing how Mamma, without any formal medical training, organized standard operating procedures (SOP) for hygiene rules within the large number of family members in the limited household space to be followed. Without exception, these rules were followed and obeyed to a "T" unless a family member wanted Mamma to symbolically kill them meaning with a whipping for the younger children and a stick, broom handle or stick of stove wood for the older children. She wielded love, respect and power and none in the household dared to challenge her authority. Those in the household who were old enough to understand, realized that she was an intelligent woman and had their best interests at heart. In order for you, the reader, to get a clear mental picture of the living scenario and thoroughly understand life and living at that time under the conditions, I must provide a description of the house that is pictured on the front cover and family members within the house at that time. The kitchen was the log house (unseen in picture) to the left of our house (The Love Palace). The kitchen was also semi-detached but joined by the porches. One could walk from the porch of the living quarters of the house to the kitchen porch and into the kitchen etc.

In the kitchen, there was a large iron cooking stove with a ''warmer'' at the top part of the stove to keep certain cooked foods stored that were leftovers such as biscuits, cornbread, fried salt pork, fried country cured pork shoulder and occasionally country cured ham. Boy, did I love that country ham, Mamma's hot biscuits, ''Grandma's molasses'' with hot ham gravy poured over the molasses and a cold glass of buttermilk. Considering the basic daily diets (loaded with animal fats) of most blacks at that time, it's amazing that some of us have lived as long as we have.

The fireplace in the kitchen was our major source of heat to keep warm in the kitchen during winter months. The heat from the kitchen stove was not enough to keep the kitchen warm, especially considering the filling between the logs were filled in with what we called ''white dirt'' mixed with water that had the appearance of cement. Over a period of time after this had dried, pieces would fall out, leaving a crack that air would come through. In the kitchen was a big round table that would seat the family. This was accomplished with a few homemade chairs and homemade benches. By the door was a little ''wash stand'' where the washpan remained for washing hands and faces and then we would discard the water so it would be ready for use by someone later. A clean wash towel hung on a nail just above the wash stand daily. Next to the wash stand was what we called a ''safe.'' The dishes were kept in the upper portion of the safe and two or three pails of water were kept on the platform portion of the safe just a little above waist height of an adult. Whenever these pails were nearly empty, the remaining portion of the water in them would be poured into the kettle on the stove and the reservoir on the right hand side of the stove. We would then have to take the water pails across the field down to my great-grandfather's house (Edward Malone) where the well was located and draw water to bring back up to our house. This is where we had to also take the mule and cow to give them water that we had to draw from the well and put into the water trough for them. Watering the livestock had to be done three or more times daily, especially during summer months. The well water was so cool and tasty, especially when there was hot weather. Now you have a good mental view of the kitchen. The pantry was attached to the kitchen. This is where certain supplies that were mainly associated with kitchen needs such as a barrel of flour for cooking biscuits and other cooking needs, a barrel of corn meal for cooking cornbread, a large can of lard for cooking etc. from killing hogs the past winter and some canned goods prepared during the past summer. Let's move on to the other portion of the house.

Adjacent to the kitchen was the living room with a door from the outside and a door on the inside that opened to the one large room of the house. Believe it or not, there was legitimate living room furniture in the living room (couch and two chairs). An iron heater stove, dresser, victrola and guest bed were in the living room. In comparison to many other blacks and poor whites at that time, we were "cooking with gas and living in class" as the old slang statement goes. We were so poor that we didn't realize we were poor. The real blessing is that we were not taught to think or feel that we were poor. We were taught that we were not inferior to anyone. We were also taught not to look down our noses at anyone.

Let's complete describing the household. It was a rare occasion or event that the living room was used. The only other room in the house was a large room to the right as you face that portion of the house with the kitchen to your left. This room had two large beds, one smaller bed, a tin-lizzie stove near the corner, a dresser, two or three trunks, and several guns in the corner by Mamma and Papa's bed. By the way, I called Papa "Grandpa Dock" more often that I called him Papa, but I didn't call Grandma Viola "Grandma." I called her "Mamma" and I called my mother 'Mother." Mamma and Grandpa Dock slept in one bed; their son Clyde slept in the smaller bed. Sometimes when Ivory (Bro), an older son was there, he and Clyde slept in the smaller bed. Sometimes when another Cousin (Julius Jr. called June) was with us, he slept with Clyde and Bro in the guest room (living room). Four (4) of us (three daughters and I) slept in the other larger bed. Thelma (deceased), who was the older among the four of us, slept with me at the foot of the bed. Ruby, the next older daughter and the youngest daughter, Viola, slept at the head of the bed. Viola, the youngest daughter, was named Viola after ''Mamma.'' Johnny, my dad, slept on a cot in the kitchen, in the corner by the side of the fireplace as he was still with tuberculosis.

Just a few times in the early stages of his illness while other family members were in the fields, he and I would be home alone. I remember he and I shooting marbles together but I don't remember him winning nor do I remember our ever completing a game as we started talking with him; asking me questions that would make me talk or him telling me something that was fascinating to me. Although I can't remember our specific conversations during those times, I remember him having me laughing. It was during those few times that he and I developed a father and son bond. I could feel he loved me dearly and I loved him dearly, not really understanding the father and son bond as I was only four years old and for all practical purposes, Granpa Dock was Daddy. I remember very vividly the one spanking that my father gave me. It was a bright and sunny Sunday morning in the fall of the year. Everyone was doing his or her respective chores and or getting ready for church. Grandpa Dock was across from the barn with the shovel putting some extra dirt on the stored sweet potato hills that looked like pyramids. I was down there with him and I soon decided to go across just a little ways to the side of the barn and sneak me a little smoke. There was a good deal of loose dried-up corn leaves and corn storks that we referred to as "farter." If you break a corn stork at one joint and break that piece again before the next joint, you could light one end and draw smoke through the other end. It would be like smoking a big cigar. My smoke break was not an impromptu situation. I had planned it because when I supposedly was being with Grandpa Dock, I had sneaked a few long-stem matches and put them in my pocket. I hadn't figured on the little breeze upsetting my plans.

I had planned to take my smoke and go back across where Grandpa Dock was at the sweet potato hills. I would have myself a nice smoke and everything would be all right. It didn't work out quite that way. When I struck the match to light my smoke, it wasn't the match that caused the problem. It was the sparks from my puffing to keep my smoke burning at the lighted end that got out of control. The next thing I knew, the barn was going up in flames. I remember Ivory (Bro), Mamma and all the family coming out of the house getting water and screaming. Even my daddy Johnny came out on his crutches, I said to myself, "Oh Lord there goes all the peas that Mamma, Thelma, Ruby and Viola had picked 'on half' during the week." I was so scared that morning because I knew that I was almost facing death knowing what Mamma was going to put on me. Mamma was fast. Before I knew what was really happening, Mamma had reached up in one of the maple trees and with one of two strokes had taken the leaves off a "switch" and gone to town on my rear end. It seemed like I didn't have a friend anywhere that morning. The whole crowd seemed to be against me as I thought. Grandpa Dock was very funny about anybody beating me other than Mamma. I kinda thought that he would come to my rescue as it seemed to me that Mamma had beaten me enough. After he didn't say or do anything, I said to myself, "Why don't Grandpa Dock do something? Can't he see that this woman is trying to kill me?" You would be surprised to know the thoughts that go through the minds of four- and five-year-old children. I really loved Mamma and knew that she loved me. But that morning when it looked to me as if she was never going to stop beating me, I asked myself, "How can this woman claim she loves me and be beating me like this?" While she was whipping me, she and I were engaged in seemingly repetitive dialogue that would make one think today that Mamma had a problem understanding the English language. The dialogue was basically as follows:

Mamma: "Whatcha do it for, huh?"

Me: "Awe Mamma, I don't know Mamma; I ain't gon do it no more Mamma."

Mamma: "You gon do it again, huh?"

"Me: "Awe, awe Mamma, I said I ain't gon do it no more Mamma."

Mamma: "You sassing me boy? You talking back to me youngun?"

Me: "No mam Mamma; I ain't sassing you Mamma; I ain't talking back Mamma."

Mamma: "You gon do it again huh? You gon do it again, huh?"

Well, by this time I was convinced that anything that I said would be the wrong thing. So I just cried and hollered and stopped trying to communicate with Mamma while she was beating me. After she finished whipping me, I was still crying and she threatened to whip me some more if I didn't stop that crying. Anyone who has experienced a severe crying state realizes that you just can't abruptly stop. However, I realized that I was already in serious trouble and would be in more trouble if I didn't stop. It had to be the Lord that helped me to put on crying brakes. It seems that the moment I stopped crying, my dad, on crutches, stated, "Come heh boy; go git me a switch." I was obedient but shocked. He had just seen how Mamma almost seemingly tried to kill me and now he was going to beat me too for the first time in his life—that would later prove to be the only time in his life that he would beat me. Under my breath I cursed to myself "these d— people is crazy." Disregard grammar as that is exactly what I said to myself. I secured a good switch for him. Somehow or other something came to my mind. As I stated previously, I was going to be five years of age in just a few more months. It seemed that somebody was inside of me talking to me saying, "He doesn't really want to whip you; he just wants to show that he is your father by whipping you." I gave him the switch and even as a small child, I felt sorry for him standing there sick on crutches with a switch to whip his only child that he would ever have, a four-year-old son whom he had just seen be whipped seemingly mercilessly.

I didn't try to duck or get out of the way of him hitting me with the switch, which I could have easily done, as he wouldn't have been able to catch me. Instead, I stood there where he could reach me and hit me two or three soft licks with the switch. Even though I was a small child, I knew that his whipping me was more painful to him than it was to me. Now that I am a man with a better understanding of God's love, I further realize the depth of some of his pain at that time. His illness gave him time to think alone. I can imagine now that he regretted over and over again having gotten involved with the woman from whom he contracted his illness. He was a young man and would never realize the beauty of seeing his child grow up. He would never experience the wonderful feeling of being responsible, respected by his parents, wife, children and peers. My mother and I had become very important people in his short life that was left. My mother remained close to him with hope in the forefront showing love even until this day. She truly loved him. The few times that he and I were alone shooting marbles in the yard would be the only times that he and I had together. Mamma would not allow me to be with him for the most part when all the family would be in the household because his illness was contagious. His eating utensils were boiled in a separate pan and washed separately from the other dishes and stored separately. Even though there were times that he wanted to give me something such as a piece of candy or chewing gum, as a father would give to his child, even now to show love and to see the glow on the child's face, Mamma would not allow him to give me anything nor allow me to take anything from him.

At that time, it was painful to me, a little child, and to him, as my father. Even though I didn't understand then, years later I fully realized that it was in my best interest and understand that Mamma was exercising good medical hygiene precaution for the benefit of the entire family. Mamma took my mother under her wing and treated her as if she was actually married to my father as my parents were engaged and would have married had my father recovered. I discovered years later that my mother and father had gone for blood tests to be married but the blood tests results for marriage would not allow approval for them to get married because of his contagious illness. If my father had ever gotten well, he and my mother were to be married, notwithstanding the danger to his life and my mother's life from the other dangerous woman with whom he had been involved.

Mamma made mother welcome to the home. She could come and see us when she could or so desired. The other woman was not allowed to "darken our door" per Mamma's rule. His condition became worse instead of better and he was finally taken to St. Agnes Hospital, which was the hospital for Negroes in Raleigh, North Carolina at that time. Recounting now the conditions and circumstances at that time, it is my perception that my father knew that the disease had engulfed his body and he was at his end. It was really useless to take him to the hospital at this stage of his illness. Unfortunately, economics dictated that home remedies, which were very effective for many illnesses, be tried. It wasn't long after he was taken to the hospital that the Lord called him home. Although I do not remember the actual "Home Going Service" in the St. Matthew Church, I remember very vividly the activities at the gravesite. During that time, at the gravesite for funerals, the casket would be slowly let down into the grave, which made loved ones left behind feel as though their hearts would burst. I remember someone holding my arm while I was trying to pull away, seemingly trying to get them to stop putting my dad in that ground. I was screaming and hollering, "Don't put my daddy in that ground."

I have often thought about how life might have been with Dad, my mother, me and possibly ten or twelve more brothers and sisters. Certainly our lives would have been much different and for better or worse, who knows? I am convinced however, that God's guiding angel was there to guide my mother and me even though I did not grow up with my mother. I will elaborate later. Many sons, in all probability, would not think very highly of their father under the same set of life's circumstances as those of my father and me after they had grown up and became men. I, too, would probably not think highly of my father were I looking back as many or maybe most men would look back while drinking from the cup of bitterness and blame. I am blessed to be able to look back while drinking from the cup of love and understanding—looking beyond my father's faults and seeing his needs as well as viewing God's love. While my father probably didn't know so at the time he made the decision, he made the best decision that he could have ever made for me by not consenting to my being adopted by his brother and sister-in-law, Henry and Malverda. They died young, unexpectedly and under circumstances that family, friends and many others know that were much different than those supposedly of the official nature that were given at the time of their deaths. This will be further discussed later on as it is very important to me and other family members to clear the name of Henry Riddick, as he did not kill his wife Malverda nor did he commit suicide as official sources would try to make us believe in the South almost seventy years ago.

Getting back to my father's decision not to let me be adopted, I could have perished along with Uncle Henry and Aunt Malverda had they received legal custody of me. Even if I had survived their fate, had I been in their legal custody, my disposition after their deaths under the laws of North Carolina might have been in an orphanage or foster home or with family members other than my grandparents wherein my life could and would have been much different than it turned out to be with my being in the custody of my grandparents, in the environment of a strong Christian home. I am convinced today that such decision by my father was a blessing then and now far beyond the view of my father or mother at that time. Therefore, such a blessing from God overshadows any bitterness that I might have been allowed to harbor within me. Instead, I love my father as a child and as a man now that I have grown up because his personality was one that any adult or child could not help but love. He was filled with fun and laughter.

Additionally, when we look through the rubble of life with God's love in our hearts, we will always be able to push the unpleasant portion of life aside and focus upon the good wherein God's blessings, that may have been previously hidden, will then be found. I should point out that my father was the fifth of eleven children. They are, in order of their birth: Julius Riddick 1908 (deceased), Maude Riddick-Dunn 1910 (deceased), Henry Riddick 1912 (deceased), James Louis Riddick 1913 (deceased), Johnny Marvin Riddick 1915 (deceased), Ivory Riddick 1917, Edna M. Riddick-Perry 1919 (deceased), Thelma Riddick-Counts 1922 (deceased), Ruby Riddick-Brooks 1924 (deceased), Viola Riddick-Jackson 1927 and Clyde Riddick 1929 (deceased).

III
Mother (Phase I)

My mother, Juanita Barnes, was born in a little small country area known as Eureka, which was out from Freemont, North Carolina near Wilson, North Carolina. Her mother was Laurina Lewis-Barnes and her father was Rev. Amos Barnes. I will focus upon my mother in two phases in order to provide the reader with a clearer view of how she is integrated into the events that I am focusing upon herein that relate to my life, since I did not grow up in the household with my mother. The first phase will focus upon her early life at home, my birth through my graduation from DuBois High School, Wake Forest, North Carolina. Juanita was the seventh child of eleven children born to Laurena and Rev. Barnes. Listed in order by birth, they are: Eleanora Barnes-Coley 1908 (deceased), Leora Barnes-Harris 1910, Pauline Barnes-Artis 1912 (deceased), Rev. Dr. Estella Barnes-Mack 1914 (deceased), Rev. Cleophas Barnes 1915 (deceased), Sissy Barnes 1916) (infant death), Rev. Juanita Barnes-Hoke 1917, Gladys Virginia Barnes-Woodward 1920 (deceased), Thadis Epimetia Barnes 1922 (deceased as of December, 2008), Mary Magdaline Barnes-Williams 1924 (deceased) and Sadie Bell Barnes-Fields whose date of birth is not known. The land that Amos and Laurena raised their children was land inherited by Amos and his sister Hattie; from their parents Perry Barnes and Louisa Reed-Barnes. Amos ruled his household with the type of authority that was well-respected during that time frame by blacks and whites. His style of living close to God and making his family "tow the line" so to speak, at that time would very probably be comparative to a home being a prison in today's society. Even so, he was viewed as an upstanding respected citizen in the black and white communities. He made sure the family was well fed and clothed. He handled all the money and paid all the bills. He did not throw away his money gambling or anything of that nature; he handled the family income rather wisely at that time. When other blacks needed to borrow food or money etc. they would come to Rev. Amos Barnes. I'm told he kept copious records (his account books).

In his view, one's character, which he pronounced as (care-rack-ter) was very important. Since I didn't know or meet him until I was about cleven or twelve years old, everything that is stated herein about him is what was told to me by his children and some of his other grandchildren who were there with him at that time. Any community neighbors who might have been short of money or food could and would come to Rev. Amos Barnes even those whose (care-rack-ter) was not the best. He would never turn them down for food. However, he would issue instructions to Laurina and/or to his children as applicable, to hurry up and give certain undesirables the food they needed so they could quickly leave his premises. He would let such people know that he didn't particularly want them on his premises. Amos let his children know that they could leave home if they desired when they reached the age of eighteen. Until that time, it was clearly understood that you belonged to Rev. Amos Barnes. If the children had any idea of running away from home, the local sheriff would find them and bring them back to Rev. Amos. Of course, they would get the beating of their life from Rev. Amos. Amos, as many other Southern black parents at that time didn't want the child "spoiled," so they made sure the rod wasn't spared. As far as many black parents felt at that time, it was biblically correct to beat a child (sometimes mercilessly) in order to save the child.

Most of Rev. Amos' children called him "Pa." Grandma Laurina called him "Unsey." I haven't found anyone in the family as yet who has knowledge of what "Unsey" meant. Generally speaking from what has been told to me, most of his children were afraid of him. In just about any situation, there will be at least one exception. In this case, the one child who could and would openly defy him and very often get away with it was Gladys Virginia (the eighth child). At that time, Gladys was the frailest of the children and yet she would break his rules, knowing that she would be beaten for doing so. Somehow after breaking a rule she would often find a way to manipulate her father's mind to the extent that he couldn't beat her.

One Saturday afternoon when many other local neighbors would cease from the regular farm work until Monday, Rev. Amos did not choose to take the Saturday afternoon off. After the noon meal at around one P.M. when it was the usual time to go back to the field, Rev. Amos gave out the usual call sign to the children that it was time to go. In the interim, Gladys had already stated to some of the other siblings that she was not going back to the field that Saturday afternoon. She started making quiet grooming preparations such as secretly straightening her hair in the back room with the straightening comb & curlers. Grandpa Amos didn't sanction the use nor presence of these items being in the household. While Grandpa Amos and the other children were on their way back to the field that Saturday afternoon, he looked over his brood and discovered that Gladys was missing. He always called her by her middle name, "Virginia." He then asked the other children, "Where is Virginia?" Seemingly in an unrehearsed chorus, they all simultaneously responded "she's in the house, Pa; she say she ain't going to the field 'cause everybody else is off and ain't nobody working but us." Armed with this information, Grandpa Amos called her and stated, "Virginia, come on out of that house girl rat now."

Her non-fearing and defying response was, "I ain't working this afternoon, Pa; everybody else is off 'cept us" or words to that effect. Grandpa Amos couldn't believe what he was hearing.

Using one of his favorite expressions, "Well gin-til-men," he again called her and asked her, "What did you sey?"

Again, in an unfearful and calm voice, she responded "I said I ain't working this evening, Pa; everybody else is off 'cept us."

By this time the other children practically held their breath in fear that he would probably beat Gladys nearly to death. Grandpa reached up in one of the trees and broke off a limb that was a strong switch and started in the house after Virginia. The foot race of the century was about to begin. Gladys was a natural runner and could run with the speed of a young deer. When Grandpa went in one door, Gladys went out the other door and the race was on. They were headed across the field to the woods with Gladys leading the way to the "maw hole" which was very familiar territory to Gladys but somewhat unknown territory to Grandpa Amos. Although Grandpa Amos knew the layout of his land, he didn't know about some of the little secrets about certain areas that the children were knowledgeable of. The maw hole was a little stream of water slightly adjacent to the main part of the pond. The foot path led one to the maw hole where you had to jump across the maw hole to get to the other side. After a brief rain, the water in the maw hole would be slightly up, probably knee or waist deep. When the water was down after a draught, the maw hole would be muddy. Either way, one had to jump across the maw hole a certain way to keep from getting wet or muddy by not falling in the maw hole. The children were very familiar with the maw hole as they traveled on foot to go to the road where their Aunt Winnie lived, as well as other relatives and neighbors. The children would practice crossing the maw hole by getting a good running start on an uphill portion of the land leading to the maw hole and begin their leap at a specific spot in order to successfully make the jump across. Grandpa, using the mules, horses and wagons for his travels at that time had to use the route established for that type of travel. Therefore, he was unaware of the specific requirements to successfully jump across the maw hole. Gladys knew exactly what she was doing by leading her Pa in the direction of the maw hole. The race ended at the maw hole because Gladys knew what to do and she successfully crossed over to the other side to safety; symbolic to spiritually crossing over the Jordan River that we so often sing about.

Well, Grandpa Amos wasn't so fortunate. He didn't know how to do the special maw hole jump. In addition to landing in the maw hole, he busted the ball of his big toe. With all the other children having watched the main event of the day and seeing Grandpa lose the race, he was humiliated and injured in facing defeat. He hobbled back to the house which was the starting point of the race and called on Grandma Laurina, (Renna) as he called her to practice her medical skills on his big toe. Gladys went to wherever she had planned and enjoyed herself. Of course she knew that it would be best if she didn't come home that night and she didn't. During that time Grandma's sister and brother-in-law (Aunt Winnie and Uncle Abram) would let their home be a temporary refugee camp for those children of Laurina and Amos who would occasionally run away from home for an overnight stay, or just a short duration until the local sheriff would bring them back to Rev. Amos, as they were under eighteen. Gladys stayed over at her Aunt Winnie's that night and came home the next day crowing like a rooster (whistling). Whistling by a female was unladylike according to Grandpa's assessment of one's care-rack-ter and he didn't allow his daughters to be whistling in his presence. Not only did Gladys defy him by staying out all night, she came home whistling which was open defiance of his rule. She had the audacity to appear unafraid even though she knew that she was going to get a beating. She was often able to fake repentance by telling him, "I did wrong, Pa; I deserve a beating. You're doing the right thing to beat me, Pa; I don't blame you." When she did this, he would often say, "Gin-til-men, can't whup a youngun penting like that and fessing up to huh sin." As fate would have it, the rod would not be spared when she came home that day. Believe it or not, in spite of Gladys' occasional defiance, Grandpa had the utmost love and respect for Virginia, as he called her, even though he was slightly afraid of her. She played so many games with his mind until he really didn't put any scenario beyond her capability.

To further demonstrate this theory, Grandpa had gone to Eureka one day and heard some news about a local but distant neighbor who was chasing his teenage daughter to chastise her for some wrong she had committed. When he caught up with her and was about to beat her, she had a knife, unbeknownst to her father. Being very determined that she was not going to be beaten by her father, she cut him in the face. This was startling news in that area during that time. When Grandpa returned from Eureka that night as he, Rena and the children sat around the heater in the house, he broke this startling news to them. Everybody seemed startled except Gladys, who stated, "I don't blame her; I woulda cut 'im too thin to fry and too thick to boil." Grandpa was somewhat shocked to hear such response.

He stated, "Gen-til-men, Rena, we are raising a murderess heah." Later on, being somewhat concerned for his own safety, Grandpa told Rena, "Maybe you better get them knives and put 'em up in a safe place." One night thereafter when Gladys had a run-in with Pa and anticipated a beating, she put all the knives in a bag and took them to her bed in the dark with the lamp light out. She gave Grandpa a warning by shaking that bag of knives and stating, "Pa, don't come in here." It is my understanding that he listened and took heed.

Although none of the other siblings would dare defy Grandpa Amos the way Gladys (Virginia) did, there were some isolated incidents, but none as defiant as those by Gladys. One such incident after Juanita and Gladys had both moved away from home was instigated by the older brother Cleophas whom everybody called "Buddy." Grandpa was sitting at the dining room table seemingly dozing. Although Buddy was a grown man, he was in the kitchen one night with the other younger siblings and stated, "I'll give anybody a dollar who will slap Pa up side the head." One of the younger siblings, Mary Magdaline, who was about thirteen at the time, boldly stated to her brother Buddy, "Hope God ma kihme I do it fah a dollah." Mary was rather sharp-witted and after she had determined that her brother Buddy was serious about the deed and dollar, Mary put her plan into action. She walked up to her Pa while he was lightly dozing and slapped him up side of the head pow! This frightened him and woke him up. Immediately, Mary said, "Pa, dare was a spider on yo hed" and she started squishing her foot round and round on the floor as if smashing the spider with her foot. Her Pa's response was, "Gin-til-men, Rena, we got to do some sprang cleaning and git rid of these spiders." The other children were in a semi state of shock and it took all of their strength to keep from laughing out, for they knew if Pa found out the truth, he would have beaten Mary half to death at that time. After Mary had convinced her Pa that it was a spider on his head and that she had killed the spider, Mary quietly went back in the kitchen with the other children and told her brother Buddy, "Gimme my dollah." Being a man of his word, Buddy gave her the dollar and to my knowledge, Grandpa never found out the real truth.

Grandpa Amos had made it very clear to all the children that they could leave home when they reached age eighteen. He also made it very clear to the girls that they better not get no babies while they were growing up at home and not to bring back no "bastard" after they left home at age eighteen. In other words if you became pregnant and not married, don't even think about coming back home to him. However, until you reached age eighteen, you belonged to his household under his rules and he could and would beat you half to death if you broke his rules. Whenever the farm work was caught up to the point that Grandpa could hire the children out to large white plantation farmers, Grandpa would collect the money and make all the financial decisions. The children were clothed, fed and had a roof over their heads and their necessary needs were taken care of by Pa, who had control of the money. When my mother, "Juanitus," as he called her, had reached her eighteenth birthday, Grandpa had hired the younger children out to a large, local white farmer to harvest tobacco. Juanita and her pa had discussed her being hired out but she made it clear to her pa that she was now eighteen and could handle her own money. Grandpa made it very clear that if she stayed under his roof, she would abide by his rules, including him collecting the money if she stayed there and was hired out. Juanita was eighteen so she left home and went to the Barnes children's temporary refugee camp which was Aunt Winnie and Uncle Abram's house across the woods.

    Now that she was on her own needing work and money, Juanita went to the local white plantation farmer where her sisters and brother had been hired out by Pa. Juanita wanted work and inquired as to whether he needed any more hands. He responded, "Ah sho do but ah can't hire yu One netus. Yu Pa came and told me if I hire yu, he would haf to pul dem oter chilun back." Juanita went back to her new temporary home with Aunt Winnie and Uncle Abram. Within a short time, Grandma Laurina put Juanita's few clothes in a sack and took them to Juanita as Grandpa Amos viewed the situation as Juanita having left home because she was eighteen years of age. This was the beginning of Juanita being on her own in the world.

After suckling tobacco for Uncle Abram, he paid her a few dollars. Uncle Abram promised to take her to her older sister Leora's house in Raleigh, N.C. in about two weeks as Juanita had requested him to do. As he promised, Uncle Abram drove her to Raleigh to her sister and brother-in-law Leora and Garland Harris. The time was around midsummer. Within approximately two weeks after her arrival at Leora's, her other sister Pauline was also in Raleigh and she was working and living in at a boarding house. Pauline was older than Juanita but younger than Leora. Within a few weeks, Pauline was instrumental in getting Juanita a job at the same boarding house where she was working. However, Juanita was not able to live in at the boarding house yet. She resided with her sister Leora and her family. Although Juanita, along with her other sisters and brothers, attended their father's church, which was Turner Swamp Primitive Baptist Church in Eureka, N.C. at that time, their attendance was not on a regular weekly basis. Rev. Amos Barnes was a prominent member of that church for some time until a domestic incident conflicted with the doctrine of the church as I am told. It is my understanding that Rev. Barnes, while in the process of administering corrective measures to his son Cleophosis (Buddy), he used the aid of a piece of wood that proved to be a little too harsh as Buddy's jaw was injured to the extent that he had to be taken to the local doctor. This resulted in the local law becoming involved. Hence, Rev. Barnes was fined for using such harsh measures. Being disobedient to parents during that time was rather dangerous thing for a child to do. Such measures today are viewed as "child abuse." During the era mentioned, corrective measures as those cited above were viewed by the parents as "training a child to walk upright." When you saw a youth walking strange as a result of some type of injury, it was often perceived that the child had difficulty adjusting to "upright" training.

Anyway, getting back to Rev. Barnes, it seemed that if a church member had any problem with the local law wherein the member was fined by the legal system, the church would also take some type of action as well. The member would have to meet some type of established requirement(s) by the church in order to remain a member. I guess Grandpa Amos felt that he had satisfied the requirements of the local law and that should be sufficient considering the ideology of "separation of church and state." He probably felt that he should be "cut some slack" since he was a prominent preacher locally. I understand that he prided himself in being knowledgeable and somewhat "up to date" in governmental affairs, so to speak. I don't know if Grandpa left Turner Swamp Primitive Baptist Church on his own or if the elders saw the need to implement an old church song that states, "If there's a preacher in the church, and he won't do right, whatcha gonna do? Just take him by the hand and lead him to the door; take your foot and kick him out and let the church roll on."

I don't know exactly how it happened but I was informed that the church doctrine prevailed and Rev. Amos Barnes moved on to another church. I am told that he was rather strong in his convictions, right, wrong, or indifferent. Juanita was not a member of a church. Her sister Leora, as I understand, was concerned about Juanita's salvation. Juanita went to a small local Baptist church in Raleigh, North Carolina with her sister Leora and family. It was during the church's revival. During revival at that time there was a "mourner's bench" up front. Revival during that time consisted of singing, praying, and preaching while the unsaved sinners were seated on the mourner's bench. After the preacher would finish preaching, those that desired to do so would gather around the mourner's bench, singing and praying over the mourners. Once a mourner felt that his/her sins had been forgiven and he/she had accepted Jesus Christ as their personal savior, the mourner would get up, often in an emotional manner, rejoicing and shouting, signifying that they had been saved. Of course, some mourners became tired of sitting on the mourner's bench and got up to give the preacher their hand to signify that they had been saved. There was a little catch in getting up from the mourner's bench. The old, seasoned, praying Christian warriors, who were usually the senior citizens, had to feel that you were saved. Otherwise, if you got up from the mourner's bench and if they didn't feel that you were saved, they would quickly and boldly tell the mourner, "Sit back down on that mourner's bench, you ain't got nothin." In most cases, the mourner would be obedient and sit back down.

Juanita had never been in a revival before and therefore had not been to the mourner's bench. That night, Leora encouraged Juanita to go the mourner's bench. Juanita, following her sister's advice, went to the mourner's bench. During that portion of the service where the church congregation gathers around the mourners singing and praying etc., Juanita was on her knees supposedly praying as the congregation gathered around. While the singing and praying were taking place in a congested fashion, a man stepped on the heels of Juanita's feet and she screamed. Immediately, someone shouted out, "She's got the Holy Ghost," and the congregation began rejoicing and shouting loudly. In the interim, Juanita didn't move because she was hurting. The man that stepped on her heels, knelt down beside her and asked her, "Do you have it?"

Juanita responded, "Have what?"

The man said, "The Holy Ghost."

Juanita said "I ain't got nothing; you stepped on my heels and hurt my ankles."

The man took her by the leg and heel and snatched both ankles. At the conclusion of the service with the congregation assuming that Juanita was saved, people left church rejoicing. On the way home, Leora was very happy about her sister being supposedly saved. She asked Juanita, "How do you feel now that you have the Holy Ghost?"

Juanita responded, "What Holy Ghost? I ain't got no Holy Ghost. That man stepped on my heels and it hurt."

Prior to this, while Juanita was at home with her parents, her ankles had been out of place. Well, her ankles were sore and hurting to the extent that her sister Pauline sent her to the doctor. Juanita explained to the doctor what had happened at the church and how her ankles had previously protruded out. The doctor explained to Juanita that what the man had actually done was jerk her ankles in place as they had been out of place prior to that incident. The doctor fixed her ankles up and told her that they would be sore for a few days but would be all right afterwards. Although Juanita didn't become saved at the revival, she actually received healing which was a blessing to her as she later stated.

While Juanita was still staying with her sister Leora, she met a young neighbor named Annie who lived across the street from Leora at that time. Annie was dating Theolphus Jones (Thee Buck) who lived in the country with his parents, Rev. Millard and Anner Jones, just across from St. Matthew Baptist Church. This was just up the road from Deacon O'Hara and Viola Riddick, who were the parents of Johnny Marvin Riddick (Tim/Sweetmeat), Thee's cousin and buddy. Annie and Juanita became friends. On an occasion when Thee came to date Annie, Johnny came with him and Annie introduced Johnny to Juanita. Johnny and Juanita seemed to like one another and they had more double dates. During one date, they went to St. Matthew Baptist Church on a Sunday night. Johnny and Juanita sat together. During that era in most Southern black Baptist churches as I recall, men and women who sat together in church as husband and wife or boyfriend and girlfriend, the general custom was that the man would give his hat to the woman to hold in her lap after they sat down. She would hold it until service was ended and dismissed. I guess the woman holding the man's hat had some significance to other single men and women to let the other men know that this woman is taken and let the other women know that this man is taken. Even though we as humans are upper class animals, I guess this concept is just another animal way of marking off your territory as the lower class animals do. Certainly the relationship between Johnny and Juanita was steadily getting closer and closer.

As I understand it, Johnny was beginning to take the relationship to another level in order to carry out his obvious agenda. He asked Juanita to be his girlfriend, which implied at that time, to be his one and only. Sad to say, Juanita being brought up further back in the woods (country life) than Johnny and therefore didn't quite understand what he meant. Johnny was her first boyfriend and she was somewhat backwards in the area of boyfriend and girlfriend relationships at that time. So she asked him, "What's a girlfriend?" meaning what are the requirements and duties so to speak of a girlfriend. With Johnny in the obvious position to be her teacher or mentor, he probably felt like a fox would feel being left to watch over the chickens. From my understanding it would appear that Johnny took a very calm and persuasive approach to such a serious matter. He began to explain about how girlfriends and boyfriends kiss. Although Juanita's vocabulary did not contain any form of the word "pregnant" at that time, she knew that there was some relationship between kissing and a woman's stomach getting large quickly and a baby being on the way. Therefore, she immediately stated, "That's the way you get big," meaning pregnant. Therefore, the kissing requirement to be a girlfriend would have to be put on hold for a while. In the interim, they continued to date each other. Obviously the relationship was growing stronger and almost ready to resume course number 101 in the kissing requirement to be a girlfriend.

During that time, most houses (even shacks that we called houses) had a front porch. It was very fashionable to have a two-seat swing on the front porch. Also, there would be single chairs on the porch. During a date, the boy and girl would sit on the front porch in the swing together if they were on good terms, and where they could be seen by parents or guardians or by whoever had been delegated the responsibility of watching the dating couple during a date. It was generally a standard procedure that the dating couple was always aware that somebody had been designated to watch them so that there would be no kissing course instructions (course 101) or smooching instructions (course 102) taking place during a date on a Sunday evening or Wednesday night. I guess parents and guardians felt that if they could prevent the kissing and smooching from taking place, they wouldn't have to worry about the girl becoming pregnant. Believe it or not, with all the standard operating procedures (SOP) for watching a dating couple in place during that time, there would always be that one occasion when a designated watcher would fail to carry out their responsibility and the dating couple would bypass courses 101 and 102 and proceed directly to (course 103) sex that usually developed into big problems nine months later. Although Juanita was not under all of the restrictions that she would have been under had she been at home with her parents in Eureka, North Carolina, she was still under the watchful eye of her big sister, Leora as she was living with Leora and her husband, Garland. Leora had met Johnny and he seemed to be a very nice fellow from a nice family so to speak. Johnny was very personable and conducted himself in a manner that made a parent or guardian feel that he could be trusted with an innocent teenager female who really hadn't learned the facts of life about the birds, bees, nature and people. Wrong! Wrong! Wrong! As I understand, Johnny didn't really force the issue of the kissing course 101 upon Juanita. Instead, he just "marked time" and concentrated upon him doing the things that would allow her to let him into her mind and heart. It would appear that he was rather patient.

It came time for church revival at the Cotton Street Baptist Church, a local church that Leora and Garland attended occasionally, especially during this special week of nightly services. Juanita didn't go with them to revival services this particular night and she stayed at the house while they went. Johnny just happened to come by. Whether this was coincidental or a well-thought-out plan by Johnny, none of us will ever know as such secrets went to the grave with Johnny a few years later. In any event, Johnny showing up to see Juanita and discovering that Leora and Garland had gone to the church revival, there was no better time than now to resume the girlfriend duty instructions with Juanita being his student per his thinking. Time was of the essence and he didn't have any to waste. Therefore, a pictorial scenario seems to have been that Johnny conducted a brief refresher review of the kissing course 101. Afterwards, he moved swiftly on to courses 102 and the advance course in dating troubles at that time which was course 103 previously described. It was then or shortly afterwards that the unplanned but expected entry of this writer into the world became a reality. By this time, Johnny and Juanita were married in their hearts to one another but not according to man's laws. Juanita was still working at the boarding house. On one occasion during mealtime for the boarders, one gentleman politely requested his dessert. Juanita stood in a chair in the cooking area looking in the cabinets trying to find the dessert. Another employee friend came in the area and asked Juanita what was she looking for. When Juanita responded indicating what one of the boarders had requested, the inquiring friendly employee explained to Juanita that the pie on the counter was the dessert.

Sometime later on, Pauline, Juanita's older sister, had a fight with the boss lady and Pauline quit. Well, Juanita, although pregnant, quit as well. Before this, however, Juanita had informed Johnny that she was "big," meaning pregnant. She didn't know exactly just what she should do.

Johnny stated to her in supposedly an assuring manner, "Go ahead and have the baby; you are not the first woman to have a baby."

Since his statements did not include the phrase, "We'll get married" or the word "marriage," Juanita asked Johnny, "You gonna help me take care of the baby?"

His response was, "A way will be made," or words to that effect as furnished by Juanita. Although Juanita and Johnny didn't break off their relationship, the dating was somewhat put on the back burner especially since the word marriage had not surfaced. Johnny's next new relationship could only be termed as "physical convenience" since the woman he was involved with was known to be extremely violent. Her reputation was very notable in the violent arena as she had harmed many people with her main weapon that she carried on her person at all times (a straight razor). For obvious reasons I cannot mention the name of the lady even though she is now deceased. She was very jealous of Juanita and had threatened to kill Juanita even though Johnny and Juanita were not seeing each other at that time. The woman that Johnny was seeing, as I am told, was very skinny but very attractive. It was speculated that she had tuberculosis, which was incurable during that time. Johnny contracted the disease from her.

In the interim, Juanita had found other temporary domestic employment. Juanita's pregnancy was at the stage that she now had to start thinking about the birth of her baby (yours truly). Her sister Pauline had previously told her about a program for unwed mothers at St. Agnes Hospital (Raleigh, North Carolina). Juanita applied for that program and was accepted. Unwed mothers would work in the hospital and be given room and board until about six months after their baby was born. They would receive a very small amount of cash as most of their pay was retained for their room, board, prenatal care, delivery and baby food during their stay at the hospital until the baby was about six months old. When Juanita and her baby boy had to leave the hospital, she and the baby were staying with sister and brother-in-law (Leora and Garland). Juanita's father (Rev. Barnes) had previously stated when she left home that she would be pregnant within a year's time. Therefore, his prophesy was true. His policy was: none of his daughters could come back home to live in his house with a baby unless they were married. Juanita could not go back home nor did she want her mother and father to know that she had a baby. In spite of trying to keep this information away from her parents, it seems that God has a special "hotline" for praying mothers when something is not quite right with a mother's child, regardless what age that child may be or where that child resides.

One day when Juanita came home to her sister's house after getting off work, she noticed that Leora had dressed me in my best Sunday outfit and had put me in the middle of the bed. Juanita immediately inquired as to why she had used my best Sunday clothes. At that moment before Leora answered, their mother (Laurina) stepped from behind the door. She had come to Raleigh, North Carolina to see about her daughter Juanita and me, her grandchild. The Spirit of God had revealed it to Grandma Laurina. Grandma Laurina picked me up in her arms, kissing and playing with me while stating the old familiar phrase that is typical of grandmothers throughout the world, "Oh, what a beautiful baby," regardless of what perception others might have regarding the baby's beauty. She gave Juanita her blessings as praying mothers will do and counseled her to do her best in taking care of me, her grandchild.

Grandma Laurina, Juanita and her other siblings were successful in keeping the secret of my being in the world withheld from Grandpa Barnes until a few years later. I am told that I was somewhere in the age category of four to seven years of age when he found out. Grandpa Barnes was in the hospital in Durham, North Carolina with a spell of sickness. He engaged in conversation with a female employee who had previously worked at St. Agnes Hospital during the same time that his daughter Juanita (my mother) had worked there. When he mentioned his daughter's name, the employee remembered Juanita's name. She stated, "I know a Juanita who had a little boy and worked at St. Anges." Grandpa informed her that it must be another Juanita because his Juanita didn't have a child. The employee began to question him if he was sure because the Juanita she knew grew up in the Fremont, North Carolina area which would seem to be too much of a coincidence. When he was released from the hospital and went home, he asked "Rena, you know anything about 'Juanitus' (his pronunciation) having a baby?" Somehow Grandma (Rena) was able to sidetrack providing him full confirmation but responded in a manner that would include the possibility of Juanita having a baby being a reality. The inquiry ended and who knows what his beliefs were at that time. My inner feelings tells me that he suspected what was a reality.

IV
The Tragedy of Uncle Henry and Aunt Malverda's Untimely Deaths

I stated in chapter one that I would focus more on my father's older brother (Uncle Henry) and his wife (Aunt Malverda). I feel the need to remind the reader of the time frame surrounding our focus in order for the reader not to lose the image of conditions during that time, especially for Negroes (as blacks were called at that time). It was around the end of 1937 or early 1938, before my first birthday. A permanent home for me had not been established. Therefore, to use an old Southern expression I was "from pillar to post." Uncle Henry loved children but was not blessed to have children of his own. By the way, I include Uncle with Henry because I do not want the reader to confuse him with his grandfather Henry Riddick (my great-grandfather) after whom Uncle Henry was named. Uncle Henry stayed on his brother Johnny's case about his responsibility to my mother and me. Since my father Johnny was not providing the care that he should have been providing for me, Uncle Henry wanted to adopt me, as I am told.

In trying to get this accomplished, a symbolic ping-pong scenario is about to take place with me (the baby) being the human ping-pong. The scenario begins by centering upon an adult birthday party at Uncle Henry and Malverda's home. My mother Juanita had asked her sister Leora to look after me for a while that late evening and early night as she wanted to attend the birthday party at Henry and Malverda's home. Juanita had found out that Johnny would be there and she wanted to talk with Johnny about support for me as she states. Something inside tells me that Juanita wanted to see Johnny for her own purposes as she was probably still in love with him in spite of his failure to meet his responsibility in providing financial support for me. Leora agreed to keep me for a while and Juanita went to the party. Sure enough, Johnny came also. I guess Juanita stayed at the party too long for Leora. The party was going good as birthday parties went a that time. Leora dressed me in my little ''Sunday go-to-meetings outfit'' and carried me to Henry's home where the party was going on at it's peak. Leora put me in a chair in the middle of the party where all attention was focused upon me, this little baby. Leora left, indicating that she was not going to take care of someone else's baby while they party.

After Leora left, Henry, Johnny and Juanita had a discussion, which was rather heated between Henry and his brother Johnny. Henry didn't feel that Johnny was living up to his responsibility as a man and father. Juanita, probably being upset with Johnny, decided to take me to Johnny and Henry's mother (Viola Riddick). She hired an acquaintance to take her and me from Raleigh, North Carolina out to the country (St. Matthew) area where Mamma Viola resided. When she left me at the Riddick's homestead that night, there are several versions as to how this was done depending upon who is providing the version at any given time. The one thing that I am sure of is that the reader will eventually see the involvement of the Hand of God before the scenario ends.

Obviously, Mamma Viola was not willing at that time to take on the responsibility of rearing me from a baby. Therefore, she took me back to Leora's in Raleigh, North Carolina where Juanita was residing. When Mamma Viola arrived with me, Juanita was at work and Leora would not accept me. However, she gave Mamma Viola the phone number to where Juanita was working. If the reader puts on an imagination cap, you can imagine that temperatures were probably very high that day. Although Mamma Viola was not accustomed to using a phone, she used one that day and called Juanita at work concerning what to do about me, the little baby that was the center of so much confusion and seeming hostility at that time. Juanita's response to Mamma Viola at that time, "You tell your son Johnny that he had better find a place for that baby and I mean PDQ." (PDQ at that time meant pretty damn quick.) I would imagine that the phone conversation ended with the existence of an unpleasant atmosphere between Mamma Viola and Juanita.

My mother Juanita did not take me back that particular day. I beg of you, the reader, please do not come down so hard upon my mother Juanita because you still have not seen the "long arms of God" in this scenario. I know it would appear that a mother should take her baby regardless to what the circumstances might be. It has been this writer's observation that God's long-range plan in a specific situation does not necessarily follow the logical sequence and manner that man might perceive as normal. Just what happened next that particular day, I don't know and probably will never know because those who know are either gone to eternal rest or the memory of the few who are still around as pertains to specific details in this scenario have failed. I don't know how soon thereafter but Uncle Henry called Juanita and wanted to adopt me. Henry and Malverda took me, hoping to adopt me. I am told that I made my first walking steps in the custody and care of Uncle Henry and Aunt Malverda. I have heard that scene described several times expressing the joy Uncle Henry received when he had me taking my first steps alone coming to him. It is my understanding that Malverda was a full time mother at home with me.

Through the years I have been made aware or led to believe that the quality of care I received from her was not the best because of some medical problems that developed with me. The evidence of one such medical problem is still with me today as I am told that she accidentally dropped me or allowed me to get my foot in a burning fireplace. Keep in mind that I was still a small baby while with her and Uncle Henry. Taking care of a little baby without ever having any children of her own was indeed a new experience for Aunt Malverda. The decision to adopt me was Uncle Henry's decision and may or may not have included any input from Aunt Malverda at all. Uncle Henry, as I am led to believe, wanted a child in his home. His love for me as his nephew who needed a stable home environment was a fitting opportunity to achieve his desire. In addition, his other motive for wanting to adopt me may have included his desire to tie Aunt Malverda down caring for me, and she would not be able to be free to get out as she was accustomed to doing, as per my understanding.

    Keep in mind that Aunt Malverda was a very beautiful lady with a rather charming personality as I am told and as I have concluded from viewing her photograph. Uncle Henry and Juanita went uptown in Raleigh for the purpose of my being adopted. Johnny, my father, was not with them. They were informed that Johnny's signature was needed in order for Henry to adopt me. Later Uncle Henry and Johnny had another heated argument regarding Johnny's refusal to sign for my adoption. My understanding is that Johnny didn't want to give up his rights. Considering the fact that Johnny was not providing any support for me, his reasoning would appear to be the most humorous and yet irresponsible pattern of thinking that any reasonably thinking person could be confronted with. However, unbeknownst to Johnny, Henry and Juanita, God's plan was working. Although Uncle Henry tried to convince Johnny that he could see me anytime he desired to do so, Johnny still didn't want to give up his rights. It's my perception that God didn't want me adopted by Uncle Henry and Aunt Malverda because of what would be happening in the very near future. Although Uncle Henry did not own a car, as I understand, Aunt Malverda could drive and had access to a pretty car. I do not know who owned the car that she had access to. Further, I do not know if Uncle Henry knew about this. However, it is my perception that such could not be kept a secret in a black environment at that time. I am told that Aunt Malverda would dress me up and put me in the "rumpseat" and we would hit the road. Where we went, I do not know and at that time wasn't the least bit concerned. Anyway, after I was with Uncle Henry and Aunt Malverda a few months their marriage foundation began to crumble. Rearing a child is a huge responsibility and somewhat an unfair responsibility to place upon Aunt Malverda with my having a mother and father alive, irrespective of Uncle Henry's personal desires and motivations. However, God's plan was still working.

It is my perception that Aunt Malverda was an up-front person if she was your friend. After the marriage began to fail, she went to Juanita and explained to her that she could not continue to keep me. She also explained to my mother Juanita that, "You ain't in no position to take care of this child by yourself. Johnny's people got money and they can take care of this child. Johnny's mother is the only one who can make him support this child. I am gonna take this child out there to them and I don't care how painful it is to you, don't you go and git this child from them."

This was a bold move for Malverda as everybody knew that Viola Malone Riddick was a seasoned and tough Christian that you didn't fool around with. Even her grown children feared her. I later found out that the main reason she was feared is because she was under the power of God in dealing with the huge problems of life at that time. Therefore, she had to remain in God's protective habitat to make it in life, especially as the matriarch of the Riddick family. When Malverda was telling Juanita that she was taking me out to the Riddicks, she really meant that she was taking me to my grandmother, Viola Malone Riddick.

Knowing what I know now, this took a lot of guts by Aunt Malverda to do this. In the same breath, when one is being led by the Spirit of God, nothing is feared. Aunt Malverda may not have known at that time, but she was being led by the Spirit of God to take me to my grandmother as that was God's plan. God knew that my mother, father, Uncle Henry and Aunt Malverda were not prepared to provide me with what I needed outside of the food, clothing and shelter arena.

Although the worn planks, logs and assorted discoloration of tin that made up the unsightly shack called a house where Mamma Viola's crowded family resided, the home within was built on a firm foundation. This is what Aunt Malverda meant when she said, "They got money." Although money was a scarce commodity, there was plenty of food, as everything was raised by the family. The spiritual environment was indeed rich. This is what created the false perception that the Riddicks were financially wealthy. God was first priority in the lives of Viola and O'Hara Riddick. Had it not been so, they would not have been able to successfully raise eleven children at that time and under the conditions that existed. Yet, they were about to have to take on number twelve, me. Although Aunt Malverda followed through with her plan to take me to the Riddicks in St. Matthew, I don't know the details and will probably never know. I was told many times through the years of one humorous episode when I was brought back to Mamma Viola.

It must have been in late summer or early fall of 1938 as Mamma (Viola) was holding me in her arms in the yard with her husband O'Hara, her daughters Edna Mae (whom we called Eddie Mae), Thelma, Ruby, Viola (a daughter named after Mamma Viola) and a son Clyde who was the baby. Clyde was seven years and a few months older than I am. At that time he was eight going on nine. He asked, "Who's gonna take care of that baby?" I, a little baby not quite two, responded as if I didn't quite get his question and as if to indicate that he should repeat the question, I said, "Uh?" They all thought that this was the funniest thing in the world. I am told that Grandpa Dock (O'Hara) could not stop laughing. God fixed it so that their hearts were captured and my being shuffled from household to household was over, for I now had a permanent home arranged by God. That event was retold throughout the years even up to now in my senior citizen status.

Juanita, in the interim, had followed the wise counsel of Aunt Malverda and didn't make any contact with the Riddicks. Poor child, even now I feel so sorry for what she might have been experiencing at that time. Here she was with a limited elementary education, cannot go back home because of her father's rule about unwed mothers, with little or no training about God's Word even though her father was a minister. She had to depend on the counsel of friends such as Uncle Henry and Aunt Malverda. Of course taking me to the Riddicks was not Uncle Henry's idea; it was Malverda's idea, probably unbeknownst to Uncle Henry. Notwithstanding the circumstances at that time which might seem to suggest otherwise, there is no doubt in my mind about my mother Juanita's love for me then or now. Again, for weeks she went without seeing me and scared to confront Mamma Viola to inquire. Knowing her as I do now, I am sure that was a living hell for her at that time. God can heal wounds and restore relationships to the extent that they will be better than before if we only allow Him to operate in our lives.

From this point on within this book when I refer to Mamma, I am talking about Mamma Viola, my grandmother. When I refer to Mother, I am talking about Juanita my biological mother. Afterwards, Mamma was in Raleigh one Saturday shopping and she saw my mother on Hargett Street by the grove which was the main location that you would see blacks during that time. Most blacks, especially from the country, could be found on Hargett Street. The supermarket was there where only certain staples were purchased because most food items were raised at home on the farm. Incidental farm items that were needed could be purchased on Hargett Street as well as certain livestock feed for the chickens, cows, mules and hogs. Anyway, God had prepared Mother and Mamma for this face-to-face meeting. Mother was scared, not knowing what to expect. Mamma approached Mother in a manner paraphrased as follows: "Hy you doing? I have your child now and I am going to raise him. As long as I have something to eat, he's got something to eat. My doors hang on the hinges of welcome and you welcome to come and see him any time that ya can. As far as I am concerned, you're my daughter and I'm gonna treat you as my daughter. Don't go out here and mess yourself up; take care of yourself and hold yourself up respectable."

Well, that meeting ended in tears of joy and hugs between Mamma and Mother. God's plan was being manifested. As is stated in the gospel song *I won't complain,* "He knows what's best for me." I will pick up from this point in a later chapter focused upon my growing up. By this time Uncle Henry and Aunt Malverda's marriage had completely crumbled. As I understand, they had separated or rather Malverda had left Uncle Henry. I say the latter because it would appear that he loved her to the extent that he almost worshipped her.

Before I go further it is necessary that I provide the reader with a mental sketch of Henry and Malverda's respective personalities, together with some insight as to conditions in the South at that time, especially as they relate to race. This will become a very important factor very soon herein when we began to focus upon the main topic of this chapter. Henry was known to be a well-mannered young man who was very lovable to those who knew him. He did not have any history of being abusive to his wife or anyone else. Although he provided counsel when needed, he was not perceived by his other siblings as one desiring to be bossy. I am told that he was dependable and didn't mind work. He was honest and desired to live a clean life as I am told.

Nothing in the history of his growing up or young adult life would suggest otherwise. In my years of growing up, in all the conversations I heard about Henry and Malverda, I never heard anything about him beating her or her accusing him of beating her. He was a quiet type of person and a replica of his father, O'Hara.

Malverda, as I am led to believe, was basically the same type of person. She had a heart of gold and to use an old familiar Southern expression, she would give you the "shirt off her back" if she was your friend and you needed it. Malverda was a people person who loved life. She was an outgoing person who loved and enjoyed freedom. This is not to be confused with promiscuity as is often done. Yes, I am told that she had men friends; yet I do not know if these male friends were intimate. I do know that it was a general custom at that time if a man knew his wife was seeing other men, he would whip her from time to time and nothing was done about it from a legal perspective as I am told. Yet, I say again, that I never heard of Henry beating Malverda for seeing another man or for anything else. Based upon what I have heard of him, it was not within his character to be beating upon a woman. I repeat, he was the spitting image of his father O'Hara in this respect. Although I will get into living with Mamma and O'Hara (Grandpa Dock) later, I never saw Grandpa Dock raise a hand to Mamma or even act or appear as if he wanted to whip Mamma, even at times when her fussing seemed unbearable to the extent that had he placed a strip of duct tape over her mouth, it would have seemed justifiable.

I'm injecting this now for the reader to get a clearer view of Henry and the type of person his character depicted him to be. When Malverda left Henry, his heart was torn to shreds so to speak as I am told. Of course he tried to get her to come back with him to no avail. I have heard nothing in all the years of my life that would seem to suggest that Malverda didn't love Henry or provide a clue as to why she left him. We must keep in mind that black folk especially in the South at that time didn't have much say so even about their own destiny, when it conflicted with the desires of the white male ruling class in the South during that period. Keep in mind that most rural black families were ''sharecropping'' which is what Mamma and Grandpa Dock were doing. Most of the other blacks who were not sharecropping were laborers or doing domestic work for white folk. Also, keep in mind that in 1939 even though slavery had ended approximately seventy-four years earlier, most black families in the South were still tied up in chains of economic slavery. They still had to depend, in some way from an economic viewpoint, upon the white man in the South to gain access to employment to make an honest living. In the 1930s there was very little difference in the attitudes and actions of some Southern upper class white males as pertains to their sexual desires for a black female than those attitudes and actions in general of white Southern slave owners during slavery. Black females were sexually used and abused by their slave owners during slavery. During slavery, the black female had no choice whatsoever and she understood this fact regardless of what her personal desires might have been in such matters. In the South during the 1930s, the black female still had very little or no say in such matters if the upper class white male was determined and if she valued her life. Further, failure of a black female to be cooperative with a supposedly upstanding white male could result in some type negative accusation against her. Hence, any accusation of a black female by such white male, regardless to its validity, would be sufficient grounds for a black female's life to be ended by the hate mentality of a white supremacist group; operating openly in the South at that time. Sad as it may be, there was very little or nothing that the black male could do about it if he wanted to continue living at that time.

It is so pathetic in my opinion the way evil can play tricks with an ignorant mindset. I say ignorant because to hate people for any purpose is ignorant in my view. One may hate another's ways but shouldn't hate the individual. Further, hate definitively conflicts with love which is the command that JESUS left with us. An individual's ways can and may change but not the color of that individual's skin. Perceptive example of tricks evil plays with ignorant mindset: A white slave owner could sleep with his black female slave (his property) and other white males had no problem with such during slavery. Yet, in the late 1930s, years after slavery ended, when an upstanding white male (by their standards) through forceful persuasion would sleep with a black female, other white males hated it to the extent that they would be ready to lynch the black female (and might have) for sleeping with a white male and feel justified in doing so.

Keep what I just mentioned in mind as you will see the identical concept emerge through the events about to unfold. As I stated previously, Malverda was a very pretty woman in the eyes of many males, black and white. At some point after she left Henry, she was employed as a "cook" working for Attorney William H. Yarborough whose residence was situated on Cambridge Road beside the Boone's Pond Dam.[1] Malverda's residence was listed as Cambridge Road on her death certificate,[2] which is the same address as her employer William H. Yarborough. Tragedy struck on the night of March 24, 1939 when Malverda was killed in her home, which was the servant's quarters within the Yarborough residence. Her standard certificate of death shows that she was "killed by Henry E. Riddick, shot in chest and back." Tragedy also struck on that same night as Henry was also killed. His standard certificate of death shows that his death was by "Suicide."

Although I will discuss in more detail my growing up in the home with Mamma later, I must inject certain aspects now in

---

[1] *News & Observer.* March 25, 1939.
[2] Standard Certificate of Death—Certificate No. 16 North Carolina State Board of Health Bureau of Vital Statistics, filed 3-28-39.

order for the reader to understand how I arrived at the conclusion that Henry and Malverda's deaths were not accomplished by Henry when I discuss in detail their death certificates, the *News & Observer* article both of which have already been mentioned and piecemeal information gathered. Although I just recently reviewed their death certificates and the referenced newspaper article, I didn't just conclude that Henry did not kill Malverda or himself; the Holy Spirit has revealed this to me years ago through Mamma. The information that I will point out regarding the above-mentioned documents will merely be supportive evidence that clearly points out very reasonable doubt through conflicting information presented by the two documents mentioned. Although I have not, do not, and will not participate in any procedural activity, scientific or otherwise, to establish contact with the dead, the Spirit of God revealed to me long ago that I was the one chosen by God to pursue this matter by gathering the necessary information to initiate the process to eventually prove that Henry and Malverda were both victims of foul play, beginning the process with the information presented within this book.

When I was a little boy, I became very interested in family history. Mamma was the family historian. Although I don't remember the exact date that Mamma informed me of Henry and Malverda's death, I was a little boy when I found out. From that time, I have never been satisfied with the official versions of their deaths; neither was Mamma. On rare occasions when she and I would be alone and she was washing dishes or doing something in the kitchen and I would be with her, Henry's death seemed to bother her to the extent that she would be talking to herself stating, "That boy didn't kill hisself, that old white man killed him." At other times in the same type of setting, she would say, "They killed him" or "Them old mean white men killed him." On the occasions that she would bring it up, I would ask her questions about Henry and Malverda. She might answer one or two of my questions and then she would shut me up abruptly sometimes in a scolding manner as if I had done something wrong in asking questions. She made it crystal clear to me that I was not to be asking anyone questions about Henry's death. Even though fearful, children at times will be disobedient. When I would be in the presence of some of her other children (my aunts and uncles) whom I later referred to as my sisters and brothers because of our closeness growing up in the household, there were times when I felt that the time was ripe for me to ask them a question or two about Henry and Malverda. They, like Mamma, would answer a question or two and then realize that they shouldn't be talking to me about Henry and Malverda and shut me up in the same fashion as Mamma did. I began to conclude within my mind that we all were thinking the same thing without stating that the white supremacy group KKK, operating in the South at that time, was the focal point within our minds. As years passed, I realized that Mamma had indoctrinated her children and me for our own safety not to be discussing this matter. After growing up and moving to New York, I was still plagued by Henry and Malverda's untimely deaths. I was never afraid of the KKK; I was afraid of Mamma if I didn't do what she said. Almost each year at vacation time, I would go back home to visit Mama and other relatives. Occasionally I would ask Mamma and my brothers and sisters, as we referred to one another, about Henry and Malverda. Even though at this time I am a grown man, they still didn't want to discuss it. Knowing that they are no longer fearful of the KKK, I couldn't figure out why they didn't want to discuss it until a light went off in my head which made the reason very clear to me. They knew Henry as a peaceful and lovable person. I was a baby when he died and therefore didn't know him. For him to be murdered, as we all believe, was very painful to discuss or focus upon for those who knew him. Further, for their own safety at the time in our Southern society, their minds had been indoctrinated that this matter was not a conversation piece. It seemed like an unwritten law within the family not to discuss it.

I made the commitment to myself as a little boy that I would one day vigorously pursue finding out the truth about his and Malverda's death, not realizing at that time that such commitment was given to me by God to take on this task. Now that Mamma and most of her children have passed on, I still make my frequent trips back home to see some of my grandchildren, one sister and brother (again as we refer to each other), cousins and friends. My cousins, like me, are of a different mindset than that of the generation(s) before us. Some of my cousins didn't know anything about Henry and Malverda until I told them. My first cousin James Robert Riddick's father Julius (deceased) was the oldest child of O'Hara Riddick and Viola Malone Riddick (both deceased) and therefore Henry's older brother. Julius' second wife was also named Viola, which was the same name as that of his mother and sister. My first cousin James Robert Riddick, whom we call Robert, is the son of Julius and Viola (wife of Julius with same name as Julius' mother Viola and sister Viola).

Julius had maintained among his photographs over the years a picture of Henry's wife Malverda holding me when I was a baby. Robert obtained that picture and loaned it to me in 2001 to have a copy made. After all these years, that photo was my first glimpse of Malverda and seeing just how beautiful she looks in that photo. She is even more beautiful than the beautiful mental picture that had been painted in my mind years past. That photo is also the first and only photo of me as a baby that I had ever seen. Owning a camera was a rarity among black folk during that time, probably because of economic conditions. Of course I had several copies of the photo with Malverda and me made, including a large copy framed in my home now. I have looked at that photo and even studied it an unlimited number of times since I've had it. It seemed to me that the photo was constantly talking to me. Yet I wasn't able to decipher the message that was supposedly being given to me. Of course I didn't dare mention this concept to anyone, including my family and friends, for fear of them thinking that I might be showing beginning signs of Alzeimers or rapidly becoming a candidate for the nut house. Although I had concluded some years ago that I would write a book during my retirement, I had not come up with a blueprint acceptable to me within my mind. Yet, that photo constantly talking to me was beginning to disturb me but not from an anxiety or fearful viewpoint. I wasn't getting the message that the photo was trying to give to me even though I felt a message was there. Finally a light went off in my head revealing the message that the photo had been trying to get across to me since I received it from Robert. The message was as follows: "This photo is the 'magnetic master key' to open the first door where some official information can be examined, which will reveal that there were lies and cover-ups about the deaths of Henry and Malverda Riddick. Further, this key will hopefully and ultimately lead to a thorough investigation resulting in Henry's name being eventually cleared, thereby confirming my belief for years and the belief of many blacks and whites for years that Henry Riddick, Son of Viola Malone Riddick and O'Hara Riddick did not kill his wife Malverda Riddick nor did Henry commit suicide. Further, the information and conclusions presented by officials of the City of Raleigh, North Carolina seems to be supportive of one probable theory that they were both most likely murdered, probably by a jealous white male lover and covered up by white officials. Symbolically, this magnetic key may cling to the minds and hearts of individuals or relatives of individuals who know the truth to open the door to their hearts to come forward and reveal the truth, thus relieving themselves of a perceived tormenting burden." Hopefully anyone having knowledge of the truth or information that will lead to the truth concerning the deaths of Henry E. Riddick and his wife, Malverda Riddick, will do the right thing by reporting such to the source that you deem appropriate.

After I received the message that the photo was revealing to me, I felt such a mental relief. It seemed as though a heavy burden had been lifted from me. Before I started the search for official records pertaining to his birth, marriage and/or death certificates, I casually contacted family members who were living at the time of Henry and Malverda's deaths. Believe it or not, I could not pinpoint the year from any of those I spoke to as their memory appeared to be blocked even though they were teenagers, and in some cases adults in 1939 at the time of Henry and Malverda's deaths. For some strange reason as a child growing up, I memorized the year each of Mamma's eleven children was born but couldn't remember the month and day for all of them. Henry was the third child, born 1912. When I inquired through a phone call to an agency in Raleigh, North Carolina about Henry and Malverda's death certificates, I was informed that I would need to know the year they died. Based upon other information I had received through the years from Mamma, Mother and others in association with my age being around two months from my being two years of age when Malverda and Henry died, I was able to establish a broad time window between 1938–1940. I called my cousin Cassandra whom we call ''Kay'' or ''Kay Kay'' and discussed with her that I was writing a book and why I needed to obtain Henry and Malverda's death certificates. By the way, I am glad we did not call her ''Kay, Kay, Kay.'' Kay is the generation after me. Her mother Marion (deceased) and I are first cousins. She and her sister Marilyn were excited about my project and rendered rather helpful suggestions that led to my being able to obtain the death certificates of Malverda and Henry. Once death certificates were located for Henry and Malverda, we could then start looking for something in the newspaper archives for an article about their deaths.

    We didn't know Malverda's maiden name. Believe it or not, Kay was discussing my project with one of her close friends. Lo and behold it turned out that her friend was a distant relative of Malverda. We discovered that her maiden name was either Scott or Stickland. Coincidentally but shortly afterwards, piece-mealing information led to determining the year of Henry and Malverda's deaths and eventually the month and day which turned out to be March 24, 1939. The next direction was to start looking for an article in the local newspaper regarding their deaths the next day after their deaths (March 25, 1939). Bingo! An article in the *News & Observer* in the March 25, 1939 edition was located. Certainly we were excited. Near the end of July, 2002, I obtained the newspaper article and the two death certificates for Henry and Malverda. I carefully reviewed them over and over. It was bad enough that the picture of Malverda and me kept talking to me for months. Now I have the newspaper article and the two death certificates seemingly talking to me since the end of July, 2002. Although I am laughing now because it is somewhat humorous to me and probably to you as well, there is a deep sense of mind-provoking thinking patterns associated with what I just stated about the newspaper article and death certificates talking to me. What is really happening per my spiritual belief is that God is allowing me to open my mind, void of anxiety, to review and analyze these documents in an objective manner similar to that of a trained professional, who has no biological or friendship connection therewith, even though I am not professionally trained in this specific area.

Accordingly, the Spirit of the Almighty allowed me to see through and beyond that which is written within the referenced documents, and see what should have been written, but wasn't written, and why it wasn't written, all of which is being very clearly revealed to me. You will see later on that what I previously stated about the article and death certificates talking to me holds more truth, which when revealed, results in more sadness than humor. It is so sad that what clearly appears to be the real truth is that two young lovely people died undoubtedly painful and unmerciful deaths. What is equally as sad is that those who had the responsibility to seek the truth through following established procedures in such cases failed to do so, according to the information in the article and the death certificates. Such failure, intentionally or unintentionally in my opinion, contributed to some degree to the real truth being covered up for whatever reason(s). Keep in mind that the information within this book only begins the process that will pave the way to initiate the procedural actions that will ultimately lead to the undisputed truth about Henry and Malverda's untimely deaths, as their civil rights were (in all probability) violated which may be determined if an appropriate investigation were initiated and thoroughly conducted. I am about to share with you some of my thoughts in challenging some of the information recorded on the referenced death certificates and that in the newspaper article. I solicit you, the reader, to put on your ''objective and unbiased'' thinking cap as I point out certain conflicts, inconsistencies, actions and omissions, etc. that are clearly ''out of the norm.'' Your being made aware will allow you to review and analyze these documents very closely and draw your own conclusions. A Xerox copy of both death certificates and a copy of the newspaper article are located herein for your review and examination purposes (Annex A). From a layman's perspective, let's start examining the documents as follows:

Malverda's Death Certificate

(1) My first observation in items 1 and 2 is that the place of Malverda's death and her residence are the same, which is Cambridge Rd. This address is also that of her employer who is an attorney. (2) My second observation is also in item 2 in that her last name (married name) Reddick is incorrect. The correct spelling is Riddick in that there are Reddicks unrelated to Riddicks. (3) My third observation is the date in item 18 regarding burial, cremation, or removal which is shown as ''3/27/1939.''

This was listed as a "homicide" death, which we are supposed to presume that no one was present at the time of death except the homicide victim, (Malverda) and her assailant, supposedly Henry Riddick. I say this because in the two referenced documents examined it is not shown that anyone (eyewitness) was present at the time she was supposedly shot. Since it is indicated in a latter section item 23 that she was "shot in chest & back" without showing what type weapon she was shot with, wouldn't it seem out of the norm to release the body so soon for burial or whatever reasons without an automatic autopsy being performed to determine the cause of death, and if it were by a pistol, what type? Further, since this was a homicide, it would seem that the officials should required an autopsy to be performed following normal procedure for a homicide case. An automatic autopsy is a requirement for homicide cases in most states today and probably at that time as well in the state of North Carolina. With no one supposedly present but Malverda and Henry, how could the officials automatically conclude that Henry shot her, without an autopsy and without knowing the type of weapon that actually shot her? How could such basic crime procedure be omitted or viewed as unimportant by the officials? Maybe they didn't realize how important this detail would become sixty-eight years later, now. Even though we may conclude that their omissions appear to be intentional to some of us, an investigation would be needed now to support such conclusion depending upon what the investigation reveals.

While I am convinced that the officials knew that no person (black or white) in North Carolina would dare question the word or intent of a Southern white man (official) about his official action(s) or statement(s) regarding the death of a "Nigra" or "Colored" as blacks were referred to at that time by many whites, they probably didn't envision that such would be questioned sixty-eight years later as well. This referenced detail might have been considered to be minor by a white man (official) in

1939 concerning the death of blacks. I am confident that it was a major detail in 1939 as well as now if the victim(s) would have been white. Therefore, we are given no choice but to question the intent of the officials' actions. I suppose the officials probably felt since their word would not be questioned, they had no real need to be concerned with referenced omissions and deviations from standards. (4) My fourth observation is how clear the time is indicated "10:30 P.M." When I analyze Henry's death certificate, you will understand how significant it is to clearly understand what time Malverda was killed and not be able to understand the time entered on Henry's death certificate. I will get back to this again when I go over Henry's. (5) My fifth observation is item 23 in responding to where the injury occurred, the written response shows "in home." This lets us know that Cambridge Road (her employer's address) was her home as also indicated in item 2. (6) My sixth observation is also item 23 in responding to manner of injury, which shows "killed by Henry E. Reddick." Since no one has been named that was there to witness the tragedy but the victims Malverda and Henry, we must presume that the information furnished to the coroner was furnished by police/sheriff's department men along with that furnished by Attorney Yarborough (Malverda's employer). If this be the case and again, without anyone being present to see it happen and without an autopsy and therefore without knowing the weapon used, where is the evidence to substantiate that Malverda, without a doubt, was "killed by Henry E. Reddick?" The back of my mind and my inner feelings keep telling me that at least one other person actually witnessed Malverda and Henry's deaths, as I sincerely believe that they both were murdered.

The term "killed by Henry E. Reddick" without the revelation of any type of "normal" investigation to show how such was concluded seems to be a convenient term since no one, especially a black person who valued life and freedom at that time, would dare question those who made such determination.

(7) My seventh and final observation for now, regarding Malverda's death certificate is also in item 23. In responding to nature of injury, the following is entered, "Shot in chest & back." It would appear that she was only shot twice, once in the chest and once in the back according to the information recorded on the death certificate. This is a serious conflict from the information quoted in the *News & Observer* which states, "Deputy R. L. Atkins quoted Yarborough as saying that he first heard the sound of the door crashing in, then three shots as the husband wounded his wife in the chest, side and back . . ." In response to the foregoing quote and if the quote is correct, how could Yarborough know and state the three (3) areas (chest, side, and back) where she was shot if he didn't witness her being shot? The quoted statement indicates that she was shot three times while the death certificate indicates that she was shot only twice, i.e., once in the chest and once in the back. Therefore, would the truth reside in what was quoted from Yarborough or does it reside with what is entered on the death certificate? In addition to the obvious conflicting information just pointed out, there are many unanswered questions associated with the way the deaths of Malverda and Henry were handled by the authorities that must be pursued for answers even now, sixty-eight years later. By the way, please make a mental note of a portion of the *News & Observer* article that quotes Yarborough "door crashing in." There are some very important and unanswered questions associated therewith. An appropriate investigation would most likely bring forth answers to many such questions. If the results of such investigation conclude the omissions and conflicting information were intentional cover-ups, such would constitute injustice, in my opinion. Although in many instances the wheels of justice have been known to turn rather slowly, there is some comfort in knowing that they do turn. Unless there are pursuits that I am unaware of, it has taken sixty-eight years to begin the process of pursuing the truth

in Henry and Malverda's deaths. I do believe that the truth will eventually be found.

Henry's Death Certificate

(1) My first observation is item 2 which shows his last name incorrectly as ''Reddick'' instead of his correct last name ''Riddick.'' (2) My second observation is that his residence is shown as ''1310 Poole Rd.'' Yet, in item 23 of his death certificate, it shows that his injury (supposedly suicide) occurred ''in home'' which could be misinterpreted as his residence at 1310 Poole Rd. The information in the newspaper shows that his death happened in the garage seemingly adjacent to basement living quarters of Malverda, which was in the home of Yarborough located on Cambridge Rd. This is obviously conflicting information as to where the supposed suicide occurred. (3) My third observation is item 22 regarding the time of Henry's death. As well as I know how to tell time, I cannot decipher the numerical time or time language that is entered on Henry's death certificate and I doubt if anyone else reading this would be able to decipher it either. I find this very strange especially since the time entered on Malverda's death certificate is very clear and easily determined and both death certificates bear the same name signatures in items 20 and 24 in Malverda and Henry's death certificates. Yet, it cannot be determined by what is entered on Henry's death certificate the actual time of his death. This appears rather clear to me to be indicative of a person or persons trying to cover up the truth trying to make lies appear to be truth regarding the deaths of Malverda and Henry when, in reality, they both may have actually been murdered by another person.

Accordingly, it appears that after Henry's time of death had been written on the death certificate, it was altered afterwards, whether immediately or at some time later, we do not know. In my mind, the alteration brings forth the question, "Why was it necessary to alter the time that had already been entered?" Another question comes to mind. "Was the time altered so as to have Henry's death occur after Malverda's death?" In reality it wouldn't make any difference as to whom was shot first in relation to whom died first. However, the individual making the alteration may not have been thinking in the arena just mentioned. To me, the alteration appears to be either 10201 P.M., 10301 P.M. or 10801 P.M. I don't know what time any of these times represent. Do you? It is very obvious to me that the actual time of Henry's death cannot be determined from the information entered on his death certificate in its current form. It is my understanding that many or most cities and states prohibit death certificates being filed with cross-outs, white-outs, strike-overs and alterations, etc. If corrections, as I understand, are required after a death certificate has been filed, it has to be done by legal process by the city where it was originally filed and appropriate notation indicated on the death certificate that such correction was made.

The alteration on Henry's death certificate disturbs me deeply in that I can't help thinking that the purpose for such alteration is to support the conclusion by the officials which I feel is inaccurate. Therefore, human nature mandates that I question the mindset of the individual(s) who entered the time and altered the time, which cannot be determined as written. Since it would appear that the time was normally written as time would be written in its original form, what factor created the necessity to alter the time especially to the extent that it cannot be determined? Was it in the mindset of the individual(s) who altered the time to do so to make it appear that Henry supposedly shot Malverda first and then shot himself to support the allegation that he killed Malverda when in fact he probably didn't kill her? I am suspicious of Henry having been framed. A lie needs cover and supporting props; the truth does not need cover nor props as the truth will stand on its own. Again, if it were actually the truth that Henry shot Malverda and then shot himself, it wouldn't make any difference at all what time he actually died whether before or after Malverda died. I say that because it is a possible reality. It would be very probable that after he supposedly shot her and then himself, he could have died immediately and she could have lived minutes or hours after he died. Although Henry could have been shot last, if that had been the case, he still could have died first. Therefore, if the truth had prevailed regarding the actual truthful time that Henry's death (more likely murder) occurred, such time would have been entered on his death certificate without the necessity of any alterations whether the actual time of his death occurred before or after Malverda's death. Often when someone is trying to cover up the truth, their actions, instead of covering up the truth, actually leads to and reveals the truth. It appears that the suicide concoction needs supporting props. If we focus carefully upon what appears to be the original time entered on Henry's death certificate, it seems to coincide with an originally intended time of "10:01 P.M." Again, why was it necessary to alter 10:01 if that was the actual time of Henry's death? Remember what I said a moment ago about untruth needing props? The question comes to my mind, "Was it felt that a time should be entered after Malverda's already recorded death of 10:30 to serve as a prop to support the suicide concoction when such wasn't necessary at all in reality?" We don't know but a thorough investigation now may reveal the answer. Again, I reiterate that it would have made no difference whatsoever as to whom was shot first in its relationship to whom died first; the truth needs no props. I am convinced that there is a link between the "outer limits" non-comprehensive time on Henry's death certificate and the manner in which he and Malverda went to their deaths.

Before we go into the link, let's complete our observations on Henry's death certificate. It is perceived necessary to remind the reader(s) of the true powers of the Holy Spirit and how He (Holy Spirit) will reveal matters through His Word (Holy Bible)[3] to those who believe and seek Him. Being the staunch believer that I am, there is no doubt in my mind whatsoever that God has chosen me among the Riddick family members to bring this matter to the surface where one day the truth can eventually be revealed to us all. For sixty-eight years since 1939, it is my belief that the voices of Henry Edward Riddick and Malverda Strickland Riddick's blood have been crying unto the Lord from the ground and God has revealed such to me. (See Genesis 4:10.) My fourth (4) observation on Henry's death certificate is the response in item 23 relating to manner of injury ''shot with pistol.'' Although Henry may have been shot with a pistol, it doesn't sound as if Henry shot himself. Wouldn't it seem expected from a procedural perspective to indicate the caliber of pistol and who did the shooting, even if Henry had shot himself? Thus the response would have seemed more in accordance with procedures had it been stated similar to the following example: ''shot himself with 38 cal. pistol.'' My fifth (5) observation is in the same area pertaining to the response in regards to nature of injury ''shot in head.'' Was the person who made both referenced entries being intentionally evasive by not fully stating what should have been stated? Yes, he was probably shot with a pistol and yes he was probably shot in the head but who did the shooting, himself or someone else? I don't believe that he shot himself and I don't believe that he shot Malverda. Let's examine some pertinent factors that are obviously missing, seeming to be intentional, and yet omitted for the purpose of persuading others to supposedly assume and focus upon the concocted ''suicide'' version.

Cameras were available in 1939 and were supportive as a tool to be used in the initial investigation of these types of cases in taking photos of the crime scene. Why weren't pictures taken

---
[3] KJV Holy Bible.

and shown? Where was the pistol found? Was it found in Henry's hand? If not, was the pistol tested for Henry's fingerprints? If not, why not, since fingerprints would have been part of normal procedures? Why wasn't the caliber of pistol mentioned? Surely it had to be available if he actually shot himself. If it wasn't available, did Henry shoot himself and then dispose of the pistol? Maybe so, since "Nigras" were capable of assorted miracles according to some whites during that time in the South. Was the pistol officially retained, as it should have been, as evidence? I don't know but I have a feeling it is available but not **officially.**

Local Newspaper Article

In the March 25, 1939 edition of the *News & Observer*, Raleigh, North Carolina, the article was entitled: ***"Negro Kills His Wife; Turns Gun on Himself.*** W. H. Yarborough's Basement Scene of Murder and Suicide." Any and all references within this book wherein I refer to Attorney William H. Yarborough or just Yarborough, I am referring to that William H. Yarborough referred to in the *News & Observer* newspaper article March 25, 1939 indicated above.

Now as we go into the link, there is a theory or possible scenario that seems to keep coming at me that would seem to shed light on this case. I will share it with you a little later on. In the interim, according to the calendar, March 24, 1939 was Friday, which was the night Henry and Malverda met their deaths. Keep in mind that we do not have any knowledge of any abuse or violence having taken place between Henry and Malverda, either before or after they were separated and living in different households. It is my perceived opinion from what information that I was able to gather piecemeal over the years is that Henry truly loved Malverda and wouldn't harm her.

It is my perception that the article is supportive of the officials' conclusion. Therefore, the question in my mind is, "Was it constructed to do so?" While we don't know, we certainly can draw our own conclusions. Based upon the omissions and deviations by the officials, another question is raised in my mind: "Was Henry being framed to protect the possibly white person(s) that may have actually murdered Malverda and Henry?" I can't seem to get away from the omission of photographs not being taken or not made available to the public regarding a crime scene such as this case. Being redundant, I can't understand there being any valid reasons why such basic information relative to a crime scene is omitted including the omission: Where was the pistol found? Was it found in Henry's hand or near Henry's body? If it wasn't in Henry's hand, were Henry's fingerprints on the pistol? Why wasn't the pistol tested to confirm that Henry's fingerprints were on the pistol? What caliber was the pistol? Also, I can't seem to comprehend why the sheriff wouldn't personally go to a major crime scene such as this one, unless he didn't want to be a part of a "cover-up" that he probably knew or suspected was taking place or would have to take place in order to protect the real murderer(s). Again, getting back to photographs, it would have seemed a part of standard operating procedures for any crime scene especially this one (two people dead) to have photographs of the scene. Being somewhat redundant again, the only reason that I can conclude as to why photographs were not taken or made available is that the photos might have revealed something that would not support the officials' conclusion regarding the deaths of Malverda and Henry. In other words, photographs might have made it more difficult to make us believe such conclusion as many or possibly most of us don't believe anyway. Therefore, considering these circumstances, I feel confident that many of you probably feel as I do, in that I am somewhat suspicious of the responsible officials' intentions in their omissions and deviations from what would appear to have been standard operation procedures (SOP) mentioned above.

If what the officials concluded were true, it would seem that photograph(s) of crashed door, the position of Malverda and Henry's bodies and of the pistol as to where it was found, confirmation as to whether Henry's fingerprints were on the pistol etc. would have all been information to support the officials' conclusion, in my opinion. I truly believe that a thorough investigation even now after so many years would provide some answers leading to the truth and possibly disprove the officials' conclusions.

Let's look at a portion of the first paragraph of the article. I quote, "A basement in Budleigh was the scene of murder-suicide last night when the husband of Attorney William H. Yarborough's Negro cook broke down the door of the servant's room and shot her three times before applying a pistol to his own head shortly after 10 P.M." Probably "Budleigh" is a typographical error intended to be "Raleigh." Anyway, getting to the quote, anybody who has any knowledge of racial conditions during that time, especially in the South, would never believe that a black man broke down the door of a white attorney's house, especially while people were in the house. Again, why wouldn't pictures have been taken of the "broken-down door" so to speak, to at least provide some support? It's my perception that the white powers at that time couldn't care less what blacks believed or even the few whites who may have desired justice prevail in the cases of black victims. From what I can gather and perceive, Southern justice for a black man within the Southern judicial system during the time frame in question seems to have depended upon the economic value such black man was to his white employer if he had a white employer. If the black man wasn't employed by a white employer that valued the black man's worth to the employer's benefit, the black man, in my opinion, was in serious trouble seeking justice within the Southern white judicial system during 1939. Therefore, white officers of the law didn't seem to demonstrate any concern about any conflicts within what they stated because what they stated was law for all practical purposes, and no black or white person at that time would dare to question the words of a white official.

Let me pause here and inject an important personal note along with some realities. I certainly hope that not one reader of this book will misinterpret what I am writing and conclude that I am putting all Southern whites at that time in the same barrel because I am not. There have always been good and bad people in all races even during slavery. Further, it is my sincere belief that there have always been some good in the worst of us and some bad in the best of us. It wasn't a picnic at that time for some whites living in the South, especially those who desired to do what was right or desiring to see right and justice prevail. Many of us believe that the first law of nature is self-preservation. Therefore, those whites who knew certain actions by other whites were wrong also knew they would be jeopardizing their own families if they spoke out against them. The whites in the South at that time who were economically sound enough to go against the word of another white in support of a black man were few and far apart, in my opinion and experience. The other whites had to go with the flow if they didn't want big troubles. Generally, it was a custom, a tradition, and a way of life for one white man to support the word of another as far as it related to a black man. Therefore, as I write, I do so under the influence of God's divine love for my fellowman regardless to race or gender and feeling blessed that God has elevated me beyond the level of drinking from the fountain of hatred. Although I cannot condone or dismiss the evil mean-spirited actions of some of my white brethern and the pain that they brought to my people and my family in this case, I still I thank God that He has blessed me spiritually to the extent that I can look beyond the faults of their demonically motivated actions and see their needs.

Now we can get back to the article. Let's look at another disturbing portion of the article as it relates to procedures. I quote "Coroner Roy M. Banks and members of the sheriff's department agreed that the deaths were clearly murder and suicide." Considering the omissions and deviations already mentioned, I am confident that many of you feel as I do and cannot accept such agreed-upon conclusion as truth. I see no evidence whatsoever concerning any type of procedural investigation being conducted to support the agreed-upon conclusion by the officials indicated above. If nobody was there to witness the actual shooting of Malverda and Henry with no information presented as to whether the believed-to-be weapon used was still there in the hand of Henry or near his or Malverda's body, especially after W. H. Yarborough supposedly having heard the door being broken down, wouldn't it make sense to conduct a thorough investigation before drawing such a conclusion? Wouldn't the circumstances warrant an investigation prior to such conclusion? Further, wouldn't an investigation be required as standard operating procedure? Also, as you will see later on in the article, Henry's body was in the garage and Malverda's body was in her living quarters in the basement. Further, the agreed-upon conclusion does not reveal any input in the finalized decision from the sheriff himself. Wouldn't it be a normal expectation to expect the sheriff and not the sheriff's deputies to make the final decision? Speaking of the sheriff, here were two deaths (where one or both could possibly be homicide) and yet the sheriff did not go to the crime scene as we can determine. I find this very strange and it raises critical questions.

This was a major crime scene that should warrant the sheriff's personal attention notwithstanding the victims being Negroes and probably not significant in his realm of thinking. Even so, why wouldn't the sheriff go to the scene himself? Did the sheriff already know or suspected that something wasn't quite right and decided to distance himself from this case? It would appear that the sheriff should have at least required some type of investigation to determine how what happened actually happened. Does such common logic seem farfetched, especially from a responsibility perspective associated with his position as sheriff? It would seem to me that the sheriff, if he was interested in the truth, would have conducted an investigation to provide answers: What is the complete description of the pistol? Where was the pistol found at the crime scene? Where is the pistol now? Wouldn't it be considered normal for a sheriff to desire an autopsy at least of Malverda (homicide) and ballistics testing and fingerprinting (in this case) to be accomplished and the retention of such pistol and results all be a pertinent part of such investigation? Ballistics testing was operational at that time. It would appear that all of the foregoing would be required in order for the officials to arrive at the "clearly" conclusion that the officials so "clearly" concluded. Were these procedures intentionally omitted even though they were probably normal requirements? In my being redundant, notice that there wasn't any information as to where the pistol was found or if it was found or any other descriptive information provided about the pistol. Yet the newspaper article referred to the weapon used in Malverda and Henry's deaths as "a pistol." In examining Malverda and Henry's death certificates, we find in item 23 of Malverda's death certificate that there isn't any reference to "pistol." Yet the same area of her death certificate indicates "shot in chest and back." In Item 23 of Henry's death certificate we find two seemingly skillfully stated phrases "shot with pistol" and "shot in head."

Carefully reviewing the newspaper article and both death certificates, I find very significant information about "pistol" is being omitted. I am very suspicious and led to believe that it was probably intentional not to provide any information about the pistol in the newspaper article or the death certificates. Also observe that the referenced news article does not mention anything about Yarborough seeing the bodies or being in the basement prior to the arrival of Deputies Atkins and Joe Partin. Further, since it would appear by the newspaper article that the deputies were the first to visit the scene of the deaths, the only things that are mentioned that they found initially are the bodies of Malverda and Henry; plus Deputy T. S. Rhodes was quoted, "We found an extra round of shot and a razor in his pocket," referring to Henry. It would seem so elementary to provide information about the supposed "pistol" used if, in fact it was a pistol that the officials concluded. In opposition to what were clear to Coroner Banks and the sheriff's deputies, it is very clear to me that both Malverda and Henry were brutally murdered.

Another quote, "Deputy R.L. Atkins quoted Yarborough as saying that he first heard the sound of the door crashing in, then three shots as the husband wounded his wife in the chest, side and back, and finally another shot as the husband staggered into the adjoining basement garage and ended his own life." It is somewhat humorous and yet so sad how this group of officials (sherrif's deputies, Coroner Banks and Attorney Yarborough), according to the article, could clearly agree about the deaths being murder-suicide and yet they can't even agree to stick to the same information which, in my mind, creates a serious information conflict. The above-quoted information states that Malverda was shot three (3) times and yet Coroner Banks indicated on Malverda's death certificate that she was shot twice (in the chest and back). To me, this is also a serious information conflict. I believe that an investigation would determine if someone is lying.

Let's examine further the above-quoted information. Remember, Atkins is quoting Yarborough in the above-quoted information. My questions regarding that quote are as follows: (1) If Yarborough didn't go downstairs to the basement, how could he state so descriptively that he heard Malverda being shot in the chest, back and side by her husband without being on the scene and seeing Malverda being shot in the chest, back and side supposedly by Henry (her husband)? How can one hear shots without seeing the shooting and determine the location of the body where the victim was shot only by hearing shots and not seeing the body? (2) How could Yarborough state that the killed (probably meaning killer) staggered into the adjoining basement garage if he wasn't in the basement to see it? (3) If Yarborough wasn't downstairs to see for himself, how would he know that Henry staggered to the garage? (4) If Henry supposedly didn't end his own life until he entered the adjoining garage, why would he have any need to stagger into the garage? (5) Although I may sound redundant, how could Yarborough state so definitively and descriptively how Henry got to the garage if he didn't see him get there? Notice that nobody supposedly saw Henry shoot himself. Also notice the combination of Henry staggering to the garage and ending his own life. Notice that particular quote did not state how Henry supposedly ended his own life. Also, notice that there is no indication as to when Yarborough finally went downstairs. I am sure it took some time before the sheriff's deputies arrived. Even so, before or after the firing ceased, am I to believe that Yarborough didn't get his shotgun, rifle or pistol (if he had any one of these weapons or all three) and didn't do anything but stay upstairs and wait for the sheriff's men? I notice the article didn't state any actions that Yarborough took that most males in the South at that time would have normally taken to supposedly protect the sovereignty of their home either before or after calling the sheriff's men. Practically every home (white and black) had one or more shotguns/rifles. Aside from the sport of hunting, these small firearms were used to supplement putting meat on the table at that time by hunting rabbits, squirrels, deer and pheasants, etc. Although a shotgun was a necessity for reasons just mentioned, it was also a normal reaction to get the gun when anything happened that would seem to threaten the home. The first thing most men would do is grab the shotgun to protect the family. Chickens in the chicken coop would sleep very quietly unless disturbed. If they were disturbed late at night, they would make much noise to let the owner of the chickens know that a dog, fox, chicken thief or something was bothering the chickens and they could be heard in the house, which is usually some distance from the chicken coop. The shotgun is the first thing that most (men of the house) would grab at night when something was happening, even with the chickens. Having said that, would the news article have us believe that Yarborough did nothing of the sort? Are we to believe that instead, he did nothing but just waited for the sheriff's men to arrive to protect his home and to see what happened in his basement? To state the words of my dear late grandmother (Viola), "There's a dead cat on the line somewhere." In my common-sense analysis, the only way that I can perceive that Yarborough would know if Henry staggered to the adjoining garage would be if Yarborough were actually there and saw Henry stagger to the garage after Henry had been shot, which would be murder and not suicide. I truly believe that Yarborough is telling the truth **only** in a portion of information quoted above "staggered into the adjoining basement garage" because I sincerely perceive and believe that he was speaking from knowledge and not from imagination or speculation. Further, I believe that this same concept applies as well to Yarborough being quoted as to Malverda being shot in the chest, back and side. I believe that Henry had probably been shot first and then he staggered to the garage, which would explain why he staggered. One bit of important information surrounding this case seems to be that which was unforeseen in that referenced officials probably never dreamed or perceived that their actions and statements regarding the deaths of Malverda and Henry would ever be questioned or scrutinized sixty-eight years after 1939. I perceive that the mentality of the officials at that time was such that they were unable to envision their actions being scrutinized sixty-eight years later, especially considering racial conditions being what they were at that time. Let's continue on with the article.

"On the verge of going downstairs to investigate the door crash, Yarborough retreated when the firing began and telephoned for the sheriff's men." Being very conservative in my estimation, I would estimate at least ten or twelve minutes for the sheriff's men to arrive in my being presumptuous that the sheriff's men rushed to the scene as quickly as possible. After hearing shots fired in his basement without supposedly Yarborough seeing anyone being shot and for what reason(s) etc., ten or twelve minutes would seem a lifetime to be empty-handed without a gun and not doing some type of (human nature) investigating to see if anyone had been shot, especially after the shooting ceased. Don't you think so? Is it conceivable within what we perceive as normal thinking concept that Yarborough didn't take any action(s) to see what had actually happened prior to the sheriff's deputies arriving? Let's move on with the article. "Deputy Atkins and Joe Partin, the first to arrive, said they found the husband already dead and the wife breathing her last. Both were dead before an ambulance arrived, the woman lying on the basement stairs and the man in the garage." This quote also leaves some unanswered questions. If in Yarborough's call to the sheriff's office he explained shots being heard in his basement presuming that people had been shot, why wouldn't the sheriff's office summon the ambulance so as to arrive when they arrived? When was the ambulance summoned in relationship to when did the ambulance arrive? If we look at the scenario from Yarborough being quoted we hear a door crashed, three shots being fired and finally another shot but no mentioning of human voices such as screaming (out of fear), crying, howling or groaning by the person(s) being shot would appear to be highly unusual in my thinking pattern. Further, the lack of such appears to be somewhat abnormal in my perception. It is very difficult for me to perceive the quoted scenario under such violent conditions that would normally seem to provoke noise and other actions resulting from fear and excitement that is not mentioned. Certainly such commotion would seem to have had some impact upon nearby neighbors. There was no mentioning of neighbors.

Keep in mind that this was in the city of Raleigh and houses were not that far apart from one another in the city, even though there was more distance between houses in the city at that time than there is today. Certainly, the sound of a pistol being fired would be loud enough to reach the ears of nearby neighbors. Therefore, it would seem that such noise as a weapon being fired four times at that time of night would have been heard by nearby neighbors and would have had some inquisitive impact upon the neighborhood perceived to be white middle class. There was no mentioning anything about nearby neighbors and that seems very strange to me. I guess we are supposed to believe that only Yarborough heard the door being crashed and the shots. Let's move on with the article. "Attorney A.B. Breece said Yarborough spoke to him yesterday afternoon about drawing legal papers to prevent Riddick from molesting his wife while she was on duty." There is a lot stated in the foregoing quoted statement that is actually not stated in written form. The terms "on duty" and "molesting" in the conversation between Yarborough and Breece (both attorneys) about drawing up papers disturbs my spirit. Referenced conversations seems to imply that Yarborough had some difficulty about Henry seeing his wife at all and termed such husband and wife contact as "molesting." Again, there seems to be a dead cat on the line and the smell of romantic involvement with jealousy seeming evident. Certainly, I cannot believe or perceive of any black man at that time in Southern white society disturbing a white man's employee from doing her work in the white man's house, even if it were the black man's wife, as in this case, considering racial conditions at that time. In my observation and perception, it was the seed of respect for another man's home that had generally been planted in the black man's mind in addition to the race factor. From my observations and perceptions growing up in North Carolina, which I will discuss in another chapter, even if a black man and his wife had problems, the black man would still respect the white man's home even in dealing with his wife in the white man's home if his wife worked for the white man. Further, if a black man did disturb the white man's employee and it happened to be the black man's wife, the white man only had to tell the black man not to come to his house anymore or during what time frames he shouldn't come and it would have been obeyed in the South during that era, from what I clearly remember. Under the scenario just mentioned, black men in general felt and knew that there wasn't any justice in the judicial system for them if it were a matter between a black man and a white man. Also, should Yarborough have spoken to Henry himself or had he spoken to the sheriff or one of the sheriff's deputies to speak to Henry, such would have been more than sufficient at that time and Henry or any other black man would have complied, in my opinion. Therefore, drawing up papers as the article quoted Breece would not have been necessary at that time simply because of the racial conditions. Whether such was stated in order to serve as another "prop" to support the officials' conclusions, I do not know. The other portion of the quoted statement regarding "on duty" by Breece raises further questions in my mind. It implies that Malverda was still "on duty" per my perception and Henry being there at that time of night was disturbing or disruptive to her while she was still in "duty" status. The question that comes to my mind, "Was she supposedly still on duty in the servant's quarters at 10:30 P.M. Mar. 24, 1939 at the time of her death?" The statement by Breece seems to imply that had the papers been drawn up, Henry would not have been there and therefore the tragedy supposedly would not have happened.

Further, I question the duty status as to when did Malverda's duty day begin and end? From my perception, it seems to me that she was "on duty" twenty-four hours day. Let's move on to the term "molesting" in Breece's quote. I see no evidence as to the manner or frequency that Henry was harassing his wife in any way whatsoever. Further, I see no evidence of Malverda complaining of such. Also, I don't see any physical evidence of the door to Malverda's quarters being "crashed" in. In the absence of such, I can only conclude that Henry was in her living quarters because she let him in. If Malverda let Henry (her husband) in her living quarters, it would seem that she wanted him there. Therefore, how could such seemingly scenario be termed as "molesting"? Further, even if Henry had been "molesting" Malverda (his wife), she could have gone directly to her employer or to the appropriate judicial authorities (probably the sheriff) and complained and Henry would have been put in jail if he went anywhere near her again after such a complaint. Notice the quote by Breece didn't make any reference to Malverda complaining to anyone about Henry molesting her. Breece's quote, referring to a conversation that he had with Yarborough only refers to Yarborough's concern about the supposedly "molesting" factor. To use the word of the officials mentioned in the newspaper article, this "clearly" reveals to me who had a problem with Henry seeing his wife at all. Further, in the absence of any complaints from Malverda, it would appear that she still loved her husband, even though they were living in separate households.

In viewing that portion of the scenario presented to us surrounding the tragedy of Malverda and Henry's deaths, some of us are urged to question the actual relationship between employer and employee. Yet, we do not know if their relationship extended beyond the realm of what we normally perceive as an appropriate relationship between employer and employee. Even so, my sense of smell is very sensitive and "I smell a rat" so to speak. I say this because the conflicting areas that I have pointed out in the newspaper article and death certificates combined with the seemingly intentional omission of important information, as well as obvious deviation from normal standards by officials appears to me to have been done in a manner so as to support the "care-rack-ter" (character) of a white man (probably prominent) being protected. Again, I question the sheriff's failure to come to the scene of a major crime in that the deaths of Malverda and Henry represented a major crime scene. Wouldn't you agree? All roads of perceived protection by way of omissions and deviation from standards seems to lead directly to the need for Henry to be framed for something that he didn't do. This would seem to lend sufficient support to the officials' conclusion for those who would be supportive of the racial conditions that existed in the South at that time. I do not agree with the officials' conclusion about Henry and Malverda's deaths being truth. Considering the possibility that interracial romance which was in violation of Jim Crow laws in the South as well as being against Southern society, especially white society (ruling class) in the South at that time, such romance may have existed in this case and may have contributed significantly to the untimely early deaths of Malverda and Henry. Hence, I can easily see how the first law of nature (self-preservation) would or could have played a significant role in the omissions, deviation from standards and final conclusion in regards to their deaths, even though such may not have been the truth. Maybe I should briefly elaborate on what I just stated. While (romantic jealousy, including interracial) could contribute to any individual's death, it wouldn't necessarily create the need for those responsible to seek and reveal the truth about such death to conceal the truth about such death were it not for Jim Crow laws being against interracial romantic involvement. This created a scenario wherein the truth being revealed about such death(s) under such circumstances by those responsible to do so would be tantamount to committing political suicide. Therefore, if interracial romance had any part whatsoever in the deaths of Malverda and Henry, we can see how Jim Crow laws would or could have contributed indirectly to their deaths, and to the information conflicts regarding their deaths as well. While Jim Crow laws may have now been taken off the books, such laws still remain in the hearts and minds of many Americans. It seems so sad to see how mankind, through the ages, has interfered with the natural laws of nature as pertains to matters of the heart through legally establishing and socially maintaining barriers to support racial hatred. Now someone reading this might mistakenly misinterpret what was just stated to mean that I am an advocate of mixed racial relationships. "Matters of the heart" between two people shouldn't have anything to do with race, in my opinion. When it comes to matters of the heart, people should be able to be free to do as they desire to relate to one another in such matters without the color of one's skin being involved, and without interference from legislative laws being passed (by biased politicians) to prevent such. This is why, in my opinion, it is so important for people of all races, creeds, religions and cultures to be involved in the political process in this wonderful, beautiful country called America.

Yes, America has many blemishes in her history and still falls short in correcting many past and current wrongs. Even so, while the wheels of justice are still slowly turning, her banner yet waves high. If you noticed the photo of me (age 8) standing in the yard with our house (palace) in the background, the picture was taken on late Sunday afternoon on the last Sunday in January around the 27th of January 1946, just two days before Grandpa Dock (O'Hara Riddick) died January 29, 1946. The other photo of Malverda holding me as a baby was taken when I was a baby earlier at some point probably in 1938 when Henry and Malverda were keeping me in their home, as I am told. Anyone viewing the front cover of this book, seeing general housing conditions for African Americans during that time in the South (without voting privileges), should be able to understand that some improvements have and are still being made in America today for all of its citizens. Even though there is still a great amount of injustice being encountered by America's citizens of color, I still cannot symbolically throw America (the baby) out with the dirty bath water (her injustice). Truly I thank God that I am a citizen of America, whose foundation is built on principles and promises wherein we (America's citizens of all races) can slowly but surely hold America accountable to such principles and promises through our efforts to seek redress, thereby lubricating the wheels of justice to make them turn more smoothly and faster. I am hoping that one day America and her citizens will discover the value of the symbolic lubricant of love which represents, in my opinion, the greatest resource from God for equality. I am confident that many of you are now able to envision reason(s) why those who had the responsibility to investigate and provide the full truth about the deaths of Malverda and Henry failed to do so, in my opinion. This now leads me to share with you pertinent portions of my **perceived** theory as to why Henry and Malverda were killed in Attorney Yarborough's home on Friday night, March 24, 1939 and why the probable killer had to be protected.

My Perceived Theory

I perceive that Henry did not kill Malverda nor did Henry commit suicide. Therefore, I perceive that Henry and Malverda were killed by someone else. I perceive that the same person who probably killed Henry also probably killed Malverda. I perceive that it would have been shameful to the white society in general during that time to be publicly informed as to why the real (perceived white) killer had killed Henry and Malverda. Further, I perceive that had such probable killer been identified and brought to justice by the white officials, who had the responsibility to do so would have been symbolically committing political suicide to have done so in that white society (who had voting power to do so) would have, in all probability, removed such officials from office. I perceive that Malverda and Henry were seeing each other (husband & wife) even though they probably did so secretly when the opportunity was available for them to do so, as they both probably still loved one another. I perceive that Henry was in

Malverda's living quarters because Malverda wanted him there and let him in. It is conceivable that she and Henry probably didn't anticipate that they would be caught by someone else who might have been against them seeing one another and or performing their marital duties to one another. I perceive that Malverda and Henry were caught by some white man who was jealous of such in that he may have been secretly involved with Malverda romantically, which was in violation to Jim Crow laws at that time. I perceive that probably after some verbalizing by the killer, Henry was probably shot (in head) and staggered to the adjoining basement garage as previously quoted. I perceive that a white person who probably shot Henry also saw Henry stagger to the adjoining basement garage in addition to Malverda seeing Henry being probably shot and staggering to the adjoining basement garage. Conceivably Malverda, being in somewhat a state of shock, probably confronted the killer in a manner that revealed her true feelings for Henry. While I perceive that even though the probable jealous killer may not have desired to kill Malverda, he probably determined that she couldn't be left alive to identify him, notwithstanding the probability that an all-white judicial system and an all-white jury would never convict such killer for killing two "Nigras" during that time. Therefore, I perceive that after some anxiety verbalizing by the probable killer, Malverda was shot three times in chest, back and side as was quoted in the previously referenced news article. I perceive that when the sheriff's office was notified, the sheriff probably felt the need to distance himself by not going to the scene, and sent the two deputies, which possibly contributed to the omissions, deviations from standards, information conflicts and the conclusions that followed. I perceive that photos were purposely not taken of the crime scene or if taken, not released for obvious reasons. Certainly photographs would have provided a great deal of pertinent information. I perceive that pertinent information about the caliber of pistol, where it was found at the crime scene or what was done with the pistol including the pistol's whereabouts, were purposely not furnished. Why not, since such information would normally be part of a crime scene SOP? I perceive that the usual or expected requirement of an autopsy being performed (homicide) was purposely not performed. Again, if not, why not since such procedure would normally be SOP? I perceive that the investigative procedures normally required in (homicide) cases were purposely not performed. There are too many omissions, deviation from standards as well as a serious information conflict for me to agree with the conclusion of the officials, in the case of Henry and Malverda's deaths. Therefore, it is clear to me to conclude that Henry and Malverda were both murdered.

Pertinent Information Contributing to Above Theory

In order for me to have arrived at the forgoing theory, questions and answers had to be asked and answered. The questions that I asked myself may or may not be the same questions that you might ask yourself. Even so, it is my sincere belief that more of you as officials of the court of public opinion will agree with me as opposed to those who don't agree. Since I am not a detective by profession, I may or may not approach this in the same manner as a trained professional might do. Accordingly, my questions may not be in the same organized manner as those of a trained professional to arrive at a specific motive or motives for a particular action or inaction. Let's begin to seek some possible motives through questions and answers per my opinion as follows:

1. **Did the Coroner Roy M. Banks and the sheriff's people really believe that Henry shot Malverda with a pistol and then shot himself?** (My answer): I don't know but I don't believe so. Had they thought so, it is perceived that there wouldn't have

been any reasons whatsoever for the omissions and deviations from normal standards. Further, it would have been more logical to adhere to normal standards in order to honestly support their agreed-upon conclusion, if they honestly thought Henry was the real killer and suicide victim.

2. **Since it is perceived that the Sheriff normally would have personally appeared at the crime scene of a major crime had all parties (including the dead) been white, what perceived factors contributed to his not being on the scene or making any official statement(s) to the press that we could see?** (My answer): Being the sheriff at that time meant being a notable local white politician that carried social status within the white community. The sheriff probably desired to protect himself and couldn't allow himself to get bogged down in a "low-level echelon" matter that his white political enemies could use against him later on, since two dead Negroes would seemingly be a low-level-echelon matter in the eyes of a white politician at that time. Had he appeared on the scene and tried to do the right and honorable thing, his political enemies would have definitely labeled him a "Negra lover" and his political career would probably have been ended, in that area during that time. Therefore, I believe that he sent two supposedly capable white deputies to handle the matter since he could have easily claimed other higher priorities. Therefore, I don't believe that the sheriff's white political enemies would dare to publicly criticize the judgment of the sheriff for not being on the scene or publicly criticize the performance of the sheriff's supposedly capable deputies in the case of two dead Negroes, as any such political enemy would be committing political suicide to do so. Accordingly, I perceive that the sheriff distanced himself by not being on the scene or making any public statement(s) to the press as we can see.

3. **What motive(s) contributed to photos not being taken or taken and not released?** (My answer): I perceive that photographs would have revealed a great deal of supportive truth (in

detail) of how what happened really happened. I perceive that the officials knew this as well. The killer was probably a white man of professional status who may have been in a romantic relationship with Malverda and his identity had to be protected so as not to bring discredit upon a white male (probably professional), the profession and the white community at large by being in such unlawful relationship with a Negro woman, that was also against Southern (white) society in general.

4. Was an autopsy performed that we know of, especially of Malverda, since her death was homicide and an autopsy would normally be standard operating procedure (SOP)? (My answer): I don't know but it would appear not, considering the short time frame that their remains were released for burial. Further, autopsy results, notwithstanding that an autopsy was probably required procedure for a homicide, would have created too many questions that answers thereto may have revealed too much truth and possibly conflict with the conclusion of the officials.

5. Why wasn't any descriptive information given in the death certificate or news article concerning the pistol, the caliber, make and where it was found at the crime scene? (My answer): I perceive that to have provided this type information would put too many holes in the agreed upon conclusion by the officials. Further, providing such information, even though it most likely was normal procedure to do so, would have included ballistics testing, information concerning the confirmation of Henry's fingerprints on the pistol, etc. which would have revealed too much truth and would create a big problem for those responsible to seek and reveal the truth, take the appropriate judicial action(s) per their official responsibilities and expect to stay in good standing with white society in general. In my being redundant, providing such information about a weapon that had been concluded to have been used in a crime/homicide would seem to be basic crime investigative procedure but would have also created a problem to keep the truth supposedly covered up. Therefore, I question the intent of those who had the responsibility to follow basic crime scene procedures (where deaths were involved) and failed to appropriately do so, in my opinion. Under the same scenario, had Henry and Malverda been white citizens, I believe standard procedures would have been followed.

6. **Was the pistol officially retained as "official evidence" as would normally be required?** (My answer): I perceive that it was not retained and from an official perspective since no information was furnished about the pistol. However, I do perceive that the pistol that killed Henry and Malverda is still available. It would seem that not obtaining, securing and retaining such evidence (since it was available at the crime scene for officials to know that it was a pistol used to kill Henry and Malverda) seems to border upon dereliction of duty, obstruction of justice and tampering with official evidence by those responsible to have obtained and secured such pertinent evidence. Since there was no descriptive mentioning or information furnished as to whether the "pistol" was obtained and kept as evidence, in that doing so would be within the realm of normal procedure, I must again question the intent of those responsible to have done so but failed to do so. Henry's fingerprints would have been on the "pistol" had he used the pistol to kill Malverda and himself. Such information would be critical evidence to support the conclusion of the officials. Since such information would be so basic in collecting pertinent evidence, why didn't those responsible to do so failed to do so as relates to the "pistol?" If Henry had killed Malverda and himself with the "pistol" that we have no information about, wouldn't the "pistol" bearing Henry's fingerprints be critical evidence to support the conclusion of the officials? It seems so elementary to me for those responsible to have done so to have desired to seek, obtain, secure and reveal any minor or major bits of evidence to support or prove that Henry did what they concluded he did. Their failure to do so lends substantial support, in my opinion to my very "clear" and honest belief that Henry didn't kill Malverda or himself.

7. **Where is that pistol today?** (My answer): I don't know but in all probability, it was not destroyed. Shotguns and rifles (in many homes black and white) were common household items in the South, especially during the time in question. Pistols, however, in my opinion, were more common in white homes than in black homes. Even so, usually all of these items were handed down through many family generations. Therefore, the pistol that we are concerned with is probably still around now. It is my perceived opinion that some person still living today has knowledge of the pistol's whereabouts and probably also know that the pistol was used to kill Henry and Malverda, and know the person who used it to do so.

NOTE: We have already seen so many motives for the killer to have killed Henry and Malverda and some motives for the officials to lie and cover up the truth. It is easily perceived that had the elected or appointed officials properly carried out their responsibilities, their political careers would have been destroyed. The concocted lies, regardless of information conflicts, significant omissions and deviations from standards by officials would be sufficient to satisfy the white community in general, and the Negras could think whatever they wanted as long as they abided by the general white rule and kept their mouths shut about what white officials had decided. The whites who subscribed to truth and justice had to do as the Negras and keep their mouths shut as well. What the white officials and white community in general seemingly failed to realize is that the wheels of justice, even though turning very slowly, would still be turning sixty-eight years later when God would allow the little baby on the front cover of this book to present pertinent information through this book to America, setting the stage for a thorough investigation to hopefully be conducted and the full truth being revealed that could possibly clear Henry's name from what is

perceived to be the false accusation of him having killed Malverda and himself. What the officials and many whites in general probably didn't envision was the praying power of Henry's mother (Viola) when she would be talking to the Lord alone in my presence, as a little boy, planting the seed of "seeking the truth to be yet determined" in my mind. My faith in God allows me to feel confident that the truth, one day, will be revealed and justice will prevail. I truly believe that there may still be one or more white persons still living who know the truth about Henry and Malverda's deaths who are strong Christians and are anchored in God's love. Knowing the truth and withholding the truth, under these circumstances, places a heavy burden of guilt upon such person or persons. Therefore, I truly believe that such person or persons would be willing to come forth revealing what they know through a formal and thorough investigation being conducted probably at the federal level, thus relieving themselves of such heavy burden.

8. **Why did the real killer kill Henry?** (My answer): In my opinion, I perceive that it was jealousy because the killer probably (white man) was most likely romantically involved with Malverda. Further, the killer, possibly discovering that Malverda still had deep feelings for Henry and having probably caught Malverda and Henry (her husband) together in her living quarters, more than likely ignited the killer's **jealous rage.** What the killer failed to realize is that killing Henry not only probably brought focus upon Malverda's love for Henry, but also concurrently possibly diminished what romantic feelings that she might have previously harbored for the perceived killer. By the way, no door was crashed in by Henry to enter the house, in my opinion. Wouldn't it have been tremendous support for the officials' conclusion had they taken and revealed pictures of the supposedly crashed door, if in fact the door had been crashed whether or not

by Henry? In my opinion, Malverda, in the absence of any evidence of a door having been crashed in, in all probability, let Henry in herself. It really saddens my heart to think of the manner in which my Uncle Henry and Aunt Malverda departed this life and the last words that Henry especially heard probably were from the killer. I can imagine that Henry's only earthly comfort was from hearing his wife Malverda scream when he was probably shot (in that he was probably shot first) and realizing that even though she wasn't residing in the home with him at 1310 Poole Road, Raleigh, North Carolina, that deep down inside her heart she still loved him.

9. **Why did the killer kill Malverda especially if it is perceived that she was the killer's lover and if he supposedly loved her?** (My answer): Three reasons. (1) The first reason is probably because the killer was in an **insanely jealous state of mind** and may have had a few drinks in that it was Friday night and 10:30 was late at night in the South during that time. Being in that possible state of mind and now, seeing for himself that Malverda probably was still sneaking to be with Henry, her husband, may have infuriated the killer. (2) The second reason is probably the love and compassion that Malverda exhibited for Henry through her reactions or what she might have said in her reactions when Henry was probably shot (first) made the killer realize that she still loved Henry which also possibly infuriated the possible killer. (3) The third reason is very simple; she could not be left alive to be an eyewitness to Henry's death and thereby name the killer, notwithstanding the perception that an all-white jury (in NC or the South in general) during that time frame would not convict a White man for killing two Negroes, in my opinion.

NOTE: Someone reading what was just stated might ask, "Wouldn't the same insane jealousy scenario be sufficient motive for Malverda's husband Henry to have shot and killed her?" The answer would be yes indeed in most instances but

not in this case, as even the blind can see. Here are two major scenarios with supportive thinking points to support this concept. (1) The sincere love that Henry had for Malverda forboded such. From all the information that I have been furnished about Henry, including his ways, Godly Spirit, calmness and caring makeup along with his mannerisms were almost the same as his father O'Hara. He was a non-violent person in the worst of crisis. From all accounts I've received, Henry truly loved Malverda to the extent that he would rather see her alive even though not with him on a daily basis than to see her dead. I'm saying that his love for her was strong and tolerable knowing that he, as a Negro man, would definitely be killed if he brought about any type confrontation between him and the white man who Henry may have possibly known or perceived Malverda possibly being romantically involved with. I perceive that Malverda was still seeing Henry when she could get the opportunity as she probably still loved him (in her own way) and he probably still loved her even though he probably resented very much her possible involvement with such a man. She was a beautiful woman wherein her beauty was probably a ''curse'' to her as a Negro woman in the South at that time, conceivably with a white man having possibly fallen in love with her. Even so, I perceive her still loving Henry and Henry still loving her. (2) The omissions and deviation from standards by officials. Observing the contents of the newspaper article and the death certificates as to what was required, what the officials did combined with what they didn't do as opposed to what they should have done ''clearly'' lets me know that somebody wanted to cover up the truth and make Henry the villain. Therefore, instead of convincing me and probably many of you as well, that Henry committed the crime of shooting Malverda and then killing himself, the actions of the officials ''clearly'' convinces me that Henry is innocent and did not shoot Malverda nor did he shoot himself.

10. **How could Yarborough hear three shots and conclusively truthfully determine that Malverda was being shot in the chest, side and back (as he was quoted) without witnessing her being shot?** (My answer): I don't perceive such being possible. Keep in mind that although the article indicates that he started downstairs when he heard the "door crash," when he heard the shooting, he went back upstairs to phone the sheriff's people and from all accounts did not go back downstairs until after the sheriff's deputies arrived. I don't know about you, the reader, but as for me, I cannot accept or digest such. I don't believe that it would have been humanly possible for anyone to have heard three shots and by such hearing truthfully determine that Malverda was being shot in the chest, side and back without having witnessed Malverda being shot. Let's move on with another important question.

11. **Although there is a conflict between the news article and death certificate as to the number of times that Malverda was shot and what locations of her body were shot, what version should I believe (Yarborough being quoted in the news article or the coroner per the death certificate and why)?** (My answer): I believe the version quoting Yarborough in that I believe he is accurately being quoted and I believe he is telling the truth in the quote. Why I believe he is telling the truth I leave to your discretion. Maybe one day, we will all truthfully and accurately know which version is truth.

Although there are any number of additional questions that could be asked and possibly answered to shed more light on the obvious wrongful deaths of Henry and Malverda, I do believe that enough information has been presented to conclude the omissions and deviations from standards, to envision beyond a doubt that Henry did not kill Malverda nor did he commit suicide. Therefore, I truly believe that a thorough investigation would clear Henry's name from having been perceivably falsely accused of having killed Malverda and then committing suicide. The untimely deaths of Henry and Malverda in the prime of their lives is just another example of institutional injustice culminating from ignorance and fear that racial prejudice breeds. This was especially pertinent in the south in 1939. This is not to be misinterpreted to imply that racial prejudice has been eliminated in the South. Racial prejudice is still very much alive in the North, South, East and West and throughout the world for that matter. While much progress has been made, there is still much to be done in the hearts and minds of people. Many persons of any number of races have paid the supreme sacrifice in their contributions to this great nation (America) making progress toward living out the true meaning of the principles, upon which her foundation was laid, the Constitution. Even through the ignorance of racial prejudice with such meaningful principles in place, we can still see how the justice system, the Christian church and the pillars of our educational system in their individual and collective relationship to economics have contributed to the betterment of life in general in these United States. Even so we can yet see how that same ignorance of racial prejudice has also contributed not only to the shortcomings of these same areas in their association with the untimely wrongful deaths of Henry and Malverda, but to the obvious omissions and deviation from standards associated with their deaths as well. It is felt that some background specifics to shed a little light on what was just stated for the benefit of those in the writer's generation and those generations thereafter would be rather helpful. This might provide a clearer perspective of rural life in the South especially for ''Negroes'' as African Americans were referred to in the South during the 1939 time frame.

The Christian Church

Of course the Christian Church in the South, for the most part, was segregated in 1939 in that blacks and whites worshipped separately. This reminds me of a little story. A black man moved into a new neighborhood that bordered the black as well as the white neighborhood. However, the white church was much closer to him than the black church, so he decided to go to the white church to worship. Upon arriving at the front door of the church, an official of the church greeted him and turned him away, informing him politely that the black church was across town. The black man left but came back again the next Sunday deciding to go to the back entrance. A church official met him there also and turned him away again informing him politely that the black church was across town. He decided to try one more time the next Sunday but this time using the same entrance that the pastor used. In doing so, the pastor extended his hand and said, "Praise the Lord; Good morning sir." The black man responded, accepting the pastor's handshake and feeling that he would surely be able to worship there today. The pastor quietly informed him, "If you have a message or something to deliver to someone in the church, one of my aides here will gladly take care of it, and I hope that you all will have a great day praising God across town." The black man was rather despondent, having again been rejected and went to his home and fell to his knees to pray.

Within his prayer, he began to question the Lord as to what he had done not to be able to be allowed to go in that church to render praise unto Him. The response supposedly came from the Lord asking the black man, "Are you talking about the large white church on North Main street about three blocks from the railroad tracks?"

The black man responded, "Yes Lord."

The Lord supposedly responded, "Don't worry anymore about not being let in that church; I have been trying to get in there for fifty years when they first built that church and they won't let me in either." Again, the Christian Church was the center of most acceptable public socialization during the time focused upon in the South as I recall.

Although you will hear more about the church in a later chapter, the limited focus upon the church here is its relationship to Henry and Malverda's situation. It was the church, in reality, that brought Henry and Malverda together. Malverda was a close friend to a female first cousin of Henry, who lived across the field from Henry's parents (my grandparents—the late O'Hara and Viola Riddick). Occasionally Malverda would spend the night with referenced female first cousin, as I am informed (probably on Saturday night) and would thereby attend the local "colored" church (St. Matthew) on Sunday. Oh, "colored" was another label for African Americans during that time. I am told that Henry's bass voice was such that it could captivate even the wildest of animals. Henry sang bass in a gospel group generally referred to at that time as a quartet even though its members were more than four. His older brother Julius Riddick, his cousin Alpheus Jones, along with friends Carey Sanders, Johnny Coleman and Dave McCullers were members of that quartet, as gathered by piecemeal method.

One of the memorable songs that another cousin Mrs. Louise Goodson remembers so vividly today is one that Henry had a bass solo part that the quartet sang (New Jerusalem). I am told that when this group would be called upon to sing in church, they would start singing where they were seated without music accompaniment (a cappella) while walking to the front of the congregation. Although Henry would be singing, he would remain seated until it was time for his bass solo part, at which time he would rise and walk to the front (while singing his solo part) where the other members of the group were. It is perceived that such singing entertainment in the church was rather emotionally motivating bringing on "hand-clapping, foot stomping and shouting" throughout the congregation. I didn't know about the group until I was led to call a cousin (Louise Malone-Goodson) who remembered the group but could only remember Henry and the other two relatives, who were also her relatives (Henry's brother Julius and cousin Alpheus). Although she couldn't remember the names of the other members in the group, she knew that there were other members. I called another cousin (Almarie Jones-Caudle, Alpheus' baby sister) who was too young to remember but referred me to her older sister (Martha Jones-Utley). She vividly remembered the group but was unable to come up with the missing names. I was then led to call Viola Riddick-Jackson, Henry's baby sister whom I call my sister as well because we grew up together in the same household. Notwithstanding her not remembering anything associated with Henry's funeral, the year or month he died when I questioned her over a year previously, surprisingly, she remembered the group with her brothers Julius and Henry, her cousin Alpheus and she was able to provide the name of one of the unrelated members of the group (Carey Sanders). She was telling her oldest living brother Ivan Riddick, (who accepts me as his baby brother) of my dilemma trying to assemble the names of the quartet that Henry sang with. We all call Ivan "Bro." The Lord has blessed Bro in years in that he reached, eighty-nine in 2006 thanks to God. When Viola spoke to Bro, he quickly came up with the two missing names, Johnny Gaye and Dave McCullers. I'm sure you, the reader, have wondered why am I furnishing such detailed information about a singing group that Henry sang with. The reason is that I am now finding it so fascinating and spiritually moving to see how the power of God is moving to break what appears to have been a sixty-eight-year "mind-blocking yoke of fear" "thought reform process" among close family members having any remembrance of Henry's activities prior to his and Malverda's deaths after their deaths or even circumstances surrounding or associated with their deaths. It was parental wisdom of "Mamma" not to allow any talking whatsoever about Henry and Malverda's deaths by her children. Even as a little boy growing up, I remember that it was a "hush hush forbidden topic" implying safety because the justice system, for all practical purposes was seemingly administered by either members of a white supremacist group or sympathizers of such organization. Therefore, justice for "Negras" (referring to blacks) in the South at that time was what the white officials determined it should be to keep "Negras" in their place, so to speak, without any regards to the merits or facts involved with any particular case as history has confirmed.

When I first started researching certain information about Henry and Malverda, especially about the month and year that he and Malverda were killed, some relatives and friends that are still living today, who were old enough at that time to have remembered some aspects of such tragedy, i.e., the shock of their deaths, what year and month or some other aspect about the funeral that they should have remembered were legitimately unable to remember anything. Having some knowledge of "brainwashing, mind control, and thought reform process," it was my perception that such had been the case through parental wisdom for the families' safety creating "the yoke of fear" within most of the "Negroes" within the community. It was common knowledge and belief that any rumblings from "Negroes" about what the white officials had decided would very perceivably mean death *via* members of a white supremacist group for those "Negroes" who would be believed to have initiated such rumblings as "trouble makers" among the "Negras." Therefore, in my opinion, it is perceived to have been a stroke of genius by Mamma (Viola), Grandpa Dock and other parents in the community to institute total and "blessed quietness" about the case of Henry and Malverda at that time. In using one of the constant sayings of my mother's older brother, "Buddy," as I was informed by her baby sister Sadie, "We haf tu be rat quiet bout dees things;

can't talk about it too much roun heah." The Southern black community, from an individual or collective perspective, was not equipped politically, educationally or economically to challenge the decisions of those white officials who were perceived to have been either white supremacist group members or sympathizers. Mamma (Viola), through her wisdom from God realized then that "quietness" then would one day be "blessed" in that one day she knew or perceived that the time would come "to seize the moment." Although it may seem a little humorous, the irony of the "yoke of fear" previously mentioned that has been within me, her other children and other relatives' children was not from the white supremacist group at all. What we all feared most was Mamma. When she told us not to talk about something or to do something or not to do something, she meant what she said as it was her law. We didn't have time to think about fearing a white supremacist group for fearing Mamma. In my observations, it appears that once I spoke to Louise and then informed others of what she had told me about the quartet that Henry sang with, it seemed that others became more interested in obtaining the other missing information as opposed to being concerned with the "silence" that had been in place for so many years since 1939. In fact, it seemed to be desirous of relatives and friends to then offer "tidbits" of information about Henry and Malverda. Symbolically speaking, it would appear that the spirit of Mamma and other parents of her generation (from the graves) were beginning to speak among the relatives that were in the vicinity of Raleigh, North Carolina (St. Matthew) at that time, and informing them that, "It's all right now, you can talk about it." This would appear to be indicative of the "yoke of fear" being safely removed. There is no fear in love according to God's Word (I John 4:18).

During the 1939 time frame, the nation was recovering from the Great Depression. According to *World Book Encyclopedia*

Vol. 8, several agencies were established to manage relief programs. One such program was the Civilian Conservation Corps established in 1933 provided jobs for thousands of young men in conservation projects. I am informed that the setting for the Corps was similar to being enlisted in the U.S. Army. The workers enlisted into the CCC and they lived in the camp being provided with room and board. The CCC workers worked during the day. At the end of the day, they engaged in assorted fun activities such as sports, day-room ping-pong, etc. It is my understanding that they were paid fair labor wages at that time and they also made out allotments to their families, etc. "Jim Crow" laws were still on the books in North Carolina, and therefore whites were housed together in the white companies and coloreds were housed together in the few colored companies. I am informed that Henry, working in the CCC, had purchased nice clothes and he was a well-dressed young man when he came home on visits etc. and went to church as the church was the main socially acceptable meeting place. His being a handsomely dressed young man with a magnetic bass voice and Malverda's beauty appears to have been a drawing card that magnetically drew them together. It is my understanding as best that others, who are still living, can remember, Henry and Malverda were married and started their lives together as one. This leads me into getting back to the Church. Some of you may have read my first book, *Establishing a Board of Christian Education Ministry within a Local Christian Church,* (Vantage Press, 2004). There are areas in that book that may have been very helpful to Henry and Malverda had such Christian education concepts and perspectives been implemented and effectively functioning within the local Christian Church during Henry and Malverda's time. Specifically, had proper pre-marriage counseling been available from a learned and structured perspective, I am confident that it would have been very helpful to them. Also, when their marriage began crumbling, had structured marriage counseling been in place and effectively functioning within the local Christian Church, it may very well have saved Henry and Malverda's lives. I perceive that had the local Christian Church been structurally equipped from a Christian education perspective and effectively functioning to have addressed and met the spiritual, as well as other needs of Henry and Malverda that were directly or indirectly associated thereto at that time, things may have been different. At the same time it is not my intent to blame the church for what happened to Henry and Malverda. Henry and Malverda had the same opportunity to become more involved with church activities that were available (just as some other black couples did) and forget about the cares of this world and things may have still been different. At the same time we realize that we must accept crisis and situations as being part of the perimeters of God's plans while understanding that God has a "yes" in every "mess." Putting our thinking today in what would appear to be the proper priority thinking order, especially from a spiritual perspective, we might conclude that Henry and Malverda's priorities may not have been in the proper order so as to produce a union of oneness, being equally yoked and living a successful married life together with the Spirit of God in the forefront of their lives and their marriage. This in no way is to suggest that their deaths were justified because there wasn't any justification for their deaths whatsoever, regardless to what order their spiritual priorities were in from a human perspective. Yet, the togetherness through the marriage of his mother and father Viola and O'Hara, a role-model example of a marriage stamped with God's approval was very visible for Henry and Malverda to use as a guide. Finally, in regards to the Christian Church meeting the needs of its members, I hope nothing that I have stated within this section will be misinterpreted to imply that the church is a failure. God's Church, then and now, still rests on the solid foundation of truth upon which it was established by our LORD and SAVIOR, JESUS CHRIST. If we stop and carefully observe, we will find that the Christian Church has been under constant attack down through the ages with assorted abuse and corruption and yet the Christian Church still stands symbolically as a Soul Salvation Station and a spiritually healing hospital for sin-sick souls. Therefore, I conclude this area of the Christian Church with the assurance that God's Church will withstand any crisis and still be standing strong when all is said and done and the gates of hell shall not prevail against the church. I am confident that many readers have asked by now **"What will be gained now in bringing up the tragic deaths of Henry and Malverda?"**

I'm sure that there are many persons of different races, nationalities and religions that are probably asking that very question today. Believe it or not, some such queries have already come from members of Henry's family, which is my family also. Some of the readers of this book who have examined the material that has been presented thus far would probably be able to provide a very simplistic response simply because their emotions and feelings are in tune with my feelings and with the feelings of others who have lost loved ones under tragic circumstances comparative to the case of Henry and Malverda. Although I was less than two years old when this tragedy occurred and am now a senior citizen, it bothers me deeply that my uncle's wife and my uncle whom I accept as brother, both appear to have been brutally murdered per my belief and a supposedly system of justice within this great nation (America) seemingly condoned and covered up such brutality without any concern about such injustice whatsoever.

Realizing that some people are incapable of compassion in feeling the feelings of others and further realizing that the same people are often incapable of looking into the hearts of others, and seeing what they are going through emotionally, I find the reasoning behind the above question rather complex indeed and therefore requires a very in-depth, soul-searching response. Although any response that is provided may be insufficient to satisfy the thinking of some who would ask the question just asked a moment ago regarding what is to be gained in bringing up their deaths now, an attempt will be made to do so.

The United States Senate failed to ever pass an anti-lyncyhing law even though such law was desperately needed many years ago. According to an article in the *New York Daily News* Tuesday June 14, 2005, (late "sorry" for lack of lynch ban) the U.S. Senate apologized the day before for not having outlawed lynching. The article goes on to indicate that lynching between 1880 and 1960 took the lives of more than 4,700 people, most of them blacks. It would appear that "murders" other than lynching but otherwise "racial" would not be included in the statistics indicated above. According to *World Book Encyclopedia* (Volume 12) page 467 indicates that there were seven lynchings from 1957 to 1968. Considering that the late Andrew Goodman, Michael Schwerner and James Chaney were murdered in 1964 (Mississippi) when they were stopped by Klansmen and a local sheriff and shot to death according to an article (victim's mom to be at trial) in referenced article, such racial killings probably are not included in the lynching statistics. When we look at the sad lynching statistics and realize the racial killings or murders not included in the lynching statistics, is enough to make any sensible-thinking American (black or white) physically sick. Even more sickening is the very thought that some legislators still show no remorse regarding the racial lynchings and killings. Yet while we realize that there have been a number of laws enacted that have proven to be very helpful, we still must remember that legislators cannot legislate the hearts and minds of people. In addition to religion, ethnic origin and political idealogy, there are people in this nation and in the world that still allow themselves to be reduced to hating others for no reason whatsoever other than race, which to me represents a critical state of mental sickness resulting from brainwashed ignorance. I say this because there are people who allow themselves to be brainwashed to hate others while those doing the brainwashing and who encourage others to brainwash others to hate others, do so in many instances for economical gains.

Some people get rich through people hating others from the perspective of "racial hatred" ignorance. Even so, when we see how family members of the late Emmett Till pursued justice being done in that case after fifty years or so, it lets the world know that the wheels of justice in this nation may turn rather slowly; but they turn especially if a person or persons do what is necessary to make them turn. I am impressed with the attitude of Carolyn Goodman, the mother of the late Andrew Goodman when she was quoted in the *Daily News* article referenced above in part. "It's been a long time," said Goodman, a retired psychologist . . . Goodman said she feels no bitterness against the eighty-year-old suspect, ". . . The man is not a well person . . . What good is it to bear a grudge? I don't think my husband would have wanted it that way. Nor would my son." Although she is up in age, eighty-nine according to the referenced article, I along with many others have the utmost respect for such sound mental thinking, and yet possessing the determination to follow through in whatever manner necessary to insure that justice is pursued, addressed and prevails.

Although the officials, through omissions and deviation from standards somewhat delaying the full truth regarding Henry and Malverda's deaths may have passed on by now, the fact still remains that the accusation of Henry committing the crime and then committing suicide is a conclusion by the officials that appears to be untrue which is injustice to Henry and Malverda. Also, in my opinion, it would appear to be in violation of Henry and Malverda's civil rights. I don't know what some brilliant legal minds might see to be gained from a legal perspective in this case even though the fact remains that there is no statute of limitations for murder. My major concerns are (1) clearing Henry's name of having committed a crime that he did not commit and or suicide that he did not commit and (2) through an investigation (federal level) determine who killed Henry and Malverda with appropriate legal action(s) being initiated at that level. This would bring forth some emotional relief and closure as regards the emotional pain and suffering that our family, relatives and friends have endured for many years. It is believed that a thorough federal investigation would result in Henry being exonerated of Malverda's death and of his own death even though their real killer probably wouldn't be around to be brought to justice. Further, if there are any members of Malverda's family who may believe to any degree that Henry ended her life, the truth about Henry and Malverda's death would relieve them of any ill feelings toward Henry or the Riddick family.

Further, while the management and supervisory officials in the city of Raleigh, North Carolina in 1939 seemingly ignored omissions and deviation from standards thereby allowing such to stand in the case of Henry and Malverda's deaths, it is realized that the attitude of some of the officials in Raleigh and the state of North Carolina today are not necessarily the same as that of the officials in 1939, even though racial prejudice is still alive and well throughout our nation. In my opinion, the city of Raleigh, state of North Carolina and the federal government still bear the responsibility to reopen this case, conduct a thorough investigation with truth and justice being brought forth with redress for the possible Constitutional violation of Henry and Malverda's civil rights. Little by little, we can see the reality of the dream of the late Dr. Martin Luther King, Jr. taking shape. In many previously "Jim Crow" states, we now see highly educated blacks and whites in many of the official positions in Southern municipalities that were previously occupied, in many instances, by white men (some being educated and some uneducated) with some of both perceivably being either members of a white supremacist group or sympathizers of such organization. Also, we now see, in many instances, people of different races and origins worshipping together in the same Christian Churches. Further, the right to currently vote in local elections by blacks where such was denied years past has changed the hate *modus operandi* under which previous Southern white politicians could expect to be elected to public office without being challenged by a black candidate or black voters. The more race hatred rhetoric that a Southern white politician used in his election campaign in years past seemingly insured his election by the majority of white voters in that blacks were denied voting privileges during that time. That same rhetoric today would most likely insure one losing an election through the voting power of some white voters and the majority of black voters voting against such candidate now that blacks have voting rights and the right to run for political office. In line with what may be perceived as old-fashioned thinking, ''The journey of one thousand miles begins with the first step,'' we are now beginning to see that some first steps have and are still being taken throughout this great nation (America).

A copy of the death certificates of Henry and Malverda and a copy of the quoted newspaper article can be examined in Annex A herewith. I would hope that you, the reader, would carefully review these documents and after having read the material presented by the author of this book, be prepared to render a verdict unto your own conscience as to Henry's guilt or innocence. I am thankful to God that He has allowed me to write as I have written without any malice or hatred within my heart against anyone. I praise and glorify God for allowing me to approach writing this task with AGAPE love (brotherly love) in my heart knowing that there is no fear in love. I sincerely feel that I have complied with God's Will and with the spirit of Henry and Malverda by presenting this case to you, the reader, an official of the court of public opinion. I truly believe that when all is said and done, the whole truth will come shining through regarding Henry Edward Riddick and Malverda's untimely deaths.

Also, I look forward with the utmost confidence to the name of Henry Edward Riddick being exonerated and the name of Henry and Malverda's true killer being identified along with the appropriate legal actions being initiated by the appropriate authorities for the truth and justice, in this case after sixty-eight years (1939–2007), to finally prevail. Therefore, in my mind and heart, I truly feel that Mamma's spirit rejoices in that her vision many years ago that one day the process of clearing her son Henry's name would begin, is now begun through this book.

V
Growing Up with Grandparents O'Hara and Viola Riddick aka Mamma and Grandpa Dock and Several of Their Children

I have already explained the situation with my father being in the household because of his terminal illness. Bro, who was next to my father, maintained his residence there with us but he did not stay there every night. Edna Mae was still there for a very short while as I am able to remember. Thelma was there for a while after Edna Mae was married before she left with one of the older brothers (James) to live with him and his wife Mabel in Baltimore, Maryland. Thelma, also known as "Baby Doll" and "crybaby" was labeled by the other bothers and sisters as being Mamma's "favorite" and her "pet child" so to speak. I am confident that the reason for such labels resulted from Thelma's beautiful and loving personality, which caused Mamma to seemingly or probably give special attention to Thelma. Some people have the capability of stealing the hearts of others. Thelma was one of those unique persons who didn't have to steal the hearts of others; just being in her presence for a little while would be sufficient for them to willingly give their heart to her. That leaves Ruby, Viola and Clyde who I spent a lot of time with growing up. Our closeness developed into a relationship like that of brothers and sisters. This eventually extended to the children who had "left the nest" and were living on their own. I have already stated previously that this book is not intended to provide a full account of my life or my childhood. I am merely focusing upon certain events that have a special place in my memory. Yet, in my thinking process, this book is not all about laughter, tragedy or sadness. It's a mixture of all the foregoing and more. Among the children listed above, Bro and Viola are the only siblings still living as of this writing.

St. Matthew Elementary School
(My First Bout with the Love Bug)

The St. Matthew Elementary School is located just a stone's throw up the hill from the St. Matthew Baptist Church, south on Highway 401, Raleigh, North Carolina. The school is a historical building that is now owned by the St. Matthew Church. Be reminded that the time that we are about to speak of is during the mid 1940s just after World War II. Three teachers made up the entire faculty. Ms. Smith taught the first, second and third grades. She was the daughter of the late Rev. Smith who was the pastor of St. Matthew Baptist Church at that time. Her room was situated on the south end of the school building. There was an inside divider between her room and the room where Mrs. Atwater (the principal) taught the fifth, sixth and seventh grades which was the north end of the school building. Ms. Lane taught the fourth graders. Her room was on the front (western) part of the building facing Highway 401 which, at that time, was just Louisburg Road. On the northeast side of Mrs. Atwater's classroom and the southeast side of Ms. Smith's classroom were several large windows facing the playground (ball field) where baseball was the sport or game mostly played during rather long recess or lunch hours and in the morning before school officially opened. At the very southern part of Ms. Smith's classroom were a stage and blackboard across the wall the width of that portion of the room. Whenever there was need for Mrs. Atwater (the principal) to talk with the entire student body or if there were some type inside function that the entire school was involved in, the divider would be lifted up and all eyes were focused toward the stage (Ms. Smith's room).

Also, the stage served as prop during school plays or other performances, etc. On all such occasions if my memory serves me well, Ms. Lane would bring her students either into Mrs. Atwater's classroom or Ms. Smith's classroom depending upon what the principal determined, usually predicated upon the available empty seats. It often turned out that more empty seats would be in Mrs. Atwater's classroom mainly because her students were of the age and size category that they could be kept home to work on the farm during harvest season in the early fall. Keep in mind that most of the student body were children from families who were sharecropping. Having described a mental picture hopefully of the school setting scenario, you will probably be able to get a better view of the portrait of the dilemma of my little heart having fallen in love with one of the teachers. For the reader to really get a good view and understanding of this little boy's heartthrob, maybe I should describe the three female teachers from the position of an adult male. Mrs. Atwater, the principal, was the most senior in age probably in her mid-fifties or a little older at that time. Her height was average for female, not tall or short. She had very smooth dark skin, a lovely grade of semi-curly hair, and a rather normal physique. Her dress code was a dress, skirt and blouse or suit with high-heeled shoes and stockings each day. Yet she was conservative and professional in her dress. The firmness that she exhibited in her general decorum daily was that which would be expected of her as the principal at that time. She walked with a ruler in her hand mostly all day. The ruler in her hand could be referred to as the "officially established precedent" to encourage students to learn as well as a tool of discipline. Regardless to what teacher you were under, the word among the student body was that she didn't play nor was she hesitant to use that ruler as an "encouraging learning tool."

To my knowledge and recollection, the educational system had not progressed (so to speak) to the extent that "labels" such as "learning disabilities" had been developed. If a child didn't catch on in the time frame that would normally be expected, the child was "slow" simply because the child had an "attitude problem," didn't want to learn, wasn't studying enough or needed more encouragement from the "official encourager" the ruler. She also had another slightly heavier "encourager" that was taken from a tree, which was supposedly a "switch." In reality, it was a lightweight "stick." When one of the larger girls or boys whose voice was beginning to get heavier; got out of hand, Mrs. Atwater would get the "heavy duty encourager" and take the student back to the "cloakroom" for some private lessons in gymnastics as there would be some jumping around (by the student) going on. When she went to the blackboard, wrote and explained an area in a specific lesson a couple of times, the student should be able to go to the board and perform the same function using another given problem, per her judgment. Before some students could successfully accomplish such feat, the lightweight "official encourager" would be needed and used in such cases. Rarely was the heavy duty encourager used in such cases. When she smiled at a student or a group of students, it made them very happy. Likewise when she gave that certain look without saying a word, the student(s) knew that any minute the discipline tool (ruler) was about to take over. Through it all, she was an educator interested in the children learning. Now let's shed some light on Ms. Smith. She was just a little shorter than average but not exactly short. She was young, probably in her mid or late twenties or early thirties at that time, per my recollection at present. She always wore some type of necklace or pearls which really positively accented her neckline now that I can see from the perspective of an adult male, even though I am now in senior status. Her hair was cut somewhat short, but not to look as a male in my opinion. Her legs were extremely shapely and beautiful, also my opinion. Her physique would generally be considered rather appealing from the view of an adult male, per my view. She exhibited the most beautiful white teeth when she smiled. She too, like Mrs. Atwater, was a tough educator, in my opinion at that time. She also walked with a ruler and didn't hesitate to use it. It was my perception along with many others that she was walking in the footsteps of Mrs. Atwater. Now that I am able to look back over many years from a much larger zone of experience, Ms. Smith was a wonderful ''class act'' teacher. I guess you are wondering when am I going to explain the ''heartthrob'' of a little seven to eight-year-old boy (me). Soon, please be patient because it still brings back painful memories to me because I couldn't tell a living soul of my pain at that time. If I had done so, it would have created even more pain for me because Mamma would have almost killed me during that time for being so mannish and fresh plus I would have been the laughing stock of the entire school, church and community at that time. Even the teacher that I had fallen in love with and she broke my heart ''big time'' has never known anything about what I am about to reveal to the entire world. As far as I know, she and her husband both may still be living today even though they would be rather aged. So you see now that I must be rather cautious in revealing this information as it may cause a few people who were around at that time and still around now to experience heart difficulty or even failure. Now, let's shed some light on the final teacher, Ms. Lane, who taught the fourth grade. In my vision, she was a little taller than average but not considered tall, so to speak. I never saw her with a ruler. Although she was young, her hair was a mixture black with streaks of gray, as I remember. I remember her mostly wearing appropriate skirts and blouses and occasionally dresses and suits. She wore high heels. She constantly displayed a beautiful smile and a lovely disposition. Her smile could capture the most untamed male animal. Symbolically speaking, were she put in a den of male lions at that time, she would have been safe because she was too pretty for the male lions to harm her. In a female den of lions, however, she would have been torn to shreds (jealousy). She walked with such grace and dignity. She was Hollywood material and she had it all. She was one beautiful lady per my eyes and heart. Yes, you now know; she was my "heartthrob." I was in Ms. Smith's classroom in the second grade when I was around seven years of age. The first time I saw Ms. Lane was when she came into Ms. Smith's room to see her for something. Her beauty stifled me to the extent that I couldn't seem to catch my breath even as a seven-year-old boy. Of course, I couldn't dare to let anyone (absolutely nobody) know what was going on in my mind and heart. If anyone fails to understand that children seven to eight years of age have romantic feelings, maybe they should speak to me. There were no such thoughts about "social promotions" during that time. Either you were able to do the work or you would not be promoted (left behind for that year or years until you had gotten it right). In addition to fearing Mamma, Ms. Lane's beauty was enough motivation to help me to be sure not to be left behind in the second grade. I couldn't wait to finish the second grade, get promoted and complete the third grade in Ms. Smith's classroom and be promoted to the fourth grade so I could just swoon over Ms. Lane's beauty as I envisioned. Now, if I happened to have been (left behind) in Ms. Lane's classroom, I felt that I could take Mamma's whipping and still be happy. I was probably subconsciously planning to be left behind in the fourth grade. Getting to the fourth grade was my only concern. I did my work, studied hard and was obedient (which I had to do anyway) or be almost killed. I carried that silent torch for almost two years that seemed like 102 years.

My Most Memorable Breakfast Along with My First Experience of a Broken Heart

When I was promoted to the fourth grade in the spring of the year probably around May, I was the happiest child in the world. I was going to be in Ms. Lane's room in September when we returned to school, at least so I thought. Mamma, Ruby, Viola, Clyde and I were all working in the field of the farmland that Papa (Grandpa Dock) and Mamma had rented as we were beginning our first farm year out of sharecropping. January 29, 1946 was a very sun-shining day. Papa had gone hunting early that morning and killed a squirrel that Mamma cleaned and fried for breakfast with hot brown gravy and hot biscuits. Hot coffee was made for Mama and Papa. Being a child, coffee was not for children except every now and then. It was generally believed that coffee would stunt the growth of children.

To the best of my recollection, Ruby and Viola might have been working (domestic days) that particular day and had left early that morning while Clyde had taken the schoolbus to Dubois High School, Wake Forest, North Carolina, as Mamma had fixed his breakfast earlier. This left Mamma, Papa and me for somewhat of a late breakfast before it was time for me to walk to St. Matthew Elementary School just up the road. The fried squirrel with other country breakfast trimmings really looked appealing when Mamma had everything on the table. After we sat down at the table and after Papa prayed, the three of us were ready to enjoy that delicious-looking breakfast. When we tried to eat that squirrel, it was so tough that it became the table topic for the remainder of breakfast. Papa started talking about the toughness of the squirrel and he started laughing and started Mamma laughing and then I started laughing at Papa because he was so tickled that tears started rolling down his cheeks and that tickled me. That morning constituted one of the happiest memorable relaxing meals that I had enjoyed with Papa and Mamma, not realizing how important that breakfast would later become in my life.

One of Mamma's older sisters, whom we called Aunt Lovey, lived in Raleigh, North Carolina and she had been a little sick. Sitting at the table, Mamma decided to go see her while Papa was going to work on finishing putting the roof on the new storage log barn that had been put up by the barn raising method. After the logs had been cut and hauled to the site where the barn would be, a date would be set, usually at church, and the men in the community would come to help raise the barn. It was done by teamwork. There was a team on top of the barn to put the logs in their proper place; there were log heisters (so to speak) to get the logs up to that team; there were log trimmers who would be trimming the ends of the logs, etc. It was beautiful teamwork regardless of the different arguments and gossiping that would take place during such an event. Also, the wives would be in the kitchen preparing the noon main meal for the workers as well as gossiping. The center of the conversation for both groups would be about somebody in the church having already sinned, involved in sin or looking at someone's wife or husband in a sinful way. Also, part of the conversation would be about where the money in the church was going and the pastor's greed for money as well. Often it was implied that some of the people handling the church's money would seem to be crooks and lightweight thieves but highly spiritual. After breakfast, I went out happily to school; Mamma went out to Aunt Lovey's and Papa worked on the roof of the new log barn. When I returned from school that day, I was the only one home with Papa. I handed him items while he was up on the log barn. He came down as he had taken sick and we went to the house (on the front cover). I gave him a glass of water with Arm & Hammer Baking Soda but he couldn't swallow it. I went out in the yard and used the relay voice method of calling the next house for them to call the next house, etc., with a message for Mamma. The relay would go on until it reached the house nearest the location (the local store) that had a phone.

Most Raleigh residents, including Aunt Lovey, had a phone while we in the rural area did not have phones at that time. The message reached Mamma at Aunt Lovey's and her son Winsdor brought Mamma home in his car. Families with cars at that time were also few and far between. Per Mamma's instructions Clyde had bridled the mule and rode across the field (high-speed cowboy style) to see if a neighbor who had a car could take Papa to the doctor or hospital. For whatever reasons, the neighbor was unable to do so. Even if he had been able to do so, from all indications it was of little use by this time. The Lord called papa home to eternal rest. That happy breakfast was my last breakfast with Grandpa Dock. Later that year, we had the best crop of tobacco ever. As Mamma, Ruby, and Viola were gathering up the wiregrass, removing the large clogs of soil in the new ground after Clyde had plowed it up breaking up the land, my job was to take the bunches of wiregrass and make sure all the loose dirt was shaken from the roots and pile the grass up in a pile which was later burned.

Getting that area ready for a tobacco crop was a slow process but it paid off, as the soil was very rich. The work we did along with the rich soil produced one of the best tobacco crops that we had grown. Although I missed Papa that summer very much, my being in love with Ms. Lane and looking forward to being in her class provided some comfort and to be rather frank, some excitement. The closer it came to September when school would open, the more exciting it was to me, combined with my being very nervous. During that time, many described my voice (singing) as that of a mocking bird as God had endowed me with a wonderful talent. Having sung in the church (solos) as a little boy even before I started school, when I sang in church that summer, nobody but the Lord and I knew that I was really singing my heart out to and for Ms. Lane, notwithstanding that she may not have been in the audience. Just a few days before school opened in September, 1946, I received the most painful news that a nine-year-old boy who was deeply in love could have possibly received. It was knockout news rendered in one, two, three flurries of blows to me. Not only had Ms. Lane gotten married during the summer, she was having a baby and would not be back to teach at that school. I was so angry and brokenhearted that I had to find some work to do that wouldn't appear to be out of the norm and yet allow me to be alone where I could let out my frustration and just cuss everything and everybody out, except Ms. Lane, who was still Ms. Lane in my mind and heart.

It was time to start doing some usual and normal chores. I quickly grabbed the bucket of slops to go feed the hogs in the hog pen away from the house down near the woods where I could also throw some rocks at the trees and do some cussing. If Mamma would hear me using a curse word, she would have almost killed me. Therefore, I had to get away from the house, performing a legitimate chore that I knew I would be out of hearing range because I wanted to do some serious cussing. Although I had never seen the man that Ms. Lane married and have since forgotten his last name (because I didn't want to accept it), I started cussing him out, calling him an assortment of names in cussing language while pretending that he was one of the trees that I was throwing rocks to hit. During that time, I was so deadly accurate with a rock, I could kill a bird that would be sitting in a tree with one throw. Be mindful that I didn't kill a bird just to be killing it, my sister Ruby would clean and barbeque my kills for only her and me to eat because none of the rest of the family had any desire to eat birds at all. The particular tree that I was throwing to hit that evening represented in my mind the man that I had never seen nor would ever see who had stolen (in my thinking) the woman that I was so desperately in love with. I had gathered up some rocks and put them in a pile while at the hog pen. As I would be cussing him I would also be bending down to pick up one of my rocks to throw at the tree that represented him, while I would be saying, "Ya cornbread-eatin', no-good-lasses soppin, buckteeth, wooly-headed (expletives)," I would let a rock go and "Pow" bullseye right up side the head (the tree).

Over the years as time passed, the pain in my heart subsided but I can still remember very vividly how I felt during that time. I have not seen Ms. Lane since the third grade and I have never seen her husband. Of course I can see much clearer now through the eyes of maturity, experience and Christian love over a period of many years. Even so, it still feels good at last to be able to express to Ms. Lane and the world through this book what I wanted to express to her then, but couldn't dare to, but now I can tell her and the world how I felt about her many years ago. Oh, I no longer harbor the ill feelings about Ms. Lane's husband that I did as a third grade little boy going into the fourth grade. Wherever Ms. Lane and husband may be today, I hope they have and are still experiencing a wonderful marriage filled with love and Christian fellowship. If children resulted from the union of Ms. Lane and her husband, it is also my hope that these descendants, through what is stated herein will contribute to their being able to experience an even deeper love and appreciation for their roots than they may have previously. My love goes out to all of you.

Other than humor, if anything of value is to be gained from the foregoing event, it is my hope that parents, Christian leaders, educators and other professionals who deal with children will be able to view emotional pain of little children from a more enlightened perspective than they may have previously. To be more specific, I hope those mentioned will be able to understand the importance of the need to provide a forum, at all times, wherein children will feel free to vent or discuss their true feelings regarding any matter without fearing any reprisal or humiliation whatsoever.

The Tater (Sweet Potato) Story (St. Matthew Elementary School)

If you recall, we indicated that almost all the time people were called by their nickname, especially children growing up. The two central figures in this story are two young boys who were probably in the sixth or seventh grade at that time, but they were among the larger and older boys in the school. To the rest of us in the lower grades in that classroom where there were fourth through seventh grades, they were big boys. Willie Winston was commonly referred to as "Bay" or "Bigun" and he lived down from the school going south toward Raleigh, North Carolina. Tommy High, commonly referred to as "Rabbit," lived up near Millbrook which was southwest of the school. The children going up the road as we would say, walked about three-quarters of a mile south and then would go west toward Millbrook. So as not to confuse the reader, the school, at that time, was located on a hill. When the children going south left school in the afternoon, they would be walking down about a quarter of a mile on Louisbourg Road which is now 401 and then the road would go upward to Haithcock's store and New Hope Baptist Church, which was the church for white people during that time. The children would then turn on the dirt road going west toward Millbrook, North Carolina to go home. There was a sweet potato field along the route to school for the Millbrook children down from Haithcock's store on the east side of Louisburg Rd. The sweet potato harvest workers did not always dig up all the potatoes, as some would be left behind, but you had to look or dig for them. Keep in mind that the children did not refer to this food product by its proper name (sweet potato). Instead, it was referred to as a "tater."

Before I actually get into what happened, let me tell you a little about these two boys (Bigun Winston & Rabbit High). Bigun was known to be rather mischievous in the St. Matthew community. Even though mostly everybody in the community knew some of Bigun's bad habits, he was very respectful toward elders and they liked him very much, but not some of his bad habits. Bigun was somewhat tall in stature and a little taller and older than Rabbit. Bigun was also known as a great fighter and most of the boys in his age category didn't care to fight him. Oh, by the way, he was handsome, had black curly hair, and knew how to con some of the little girls.

His father, however, Mr. Tom, was considered the tallest and largest man in the community at that time. In my estimation, he was probably around six-foot eight to ten inches, which was very tall then in comparison to most other men which were probably on average around five feet eleven inches to six feet two inches. Mr. Tom Winston knew exactly how to handle Bigun when he did something wrong, which was most of the time. The other boy, Tommy High, was somewhat of a quiet boy and if I remember was a southpaw. I don't recall him ever being in trouble. However, everybody knew you didn't want to get into a fight with him because he was tough and wouldn't back off anyone, regardless to how large they might be if they riled him up. There were times when someone would cause him to fight, they would seemingly forget that he was a lefty and while they would be on guard looking for the right fist, the left would catch them right in the nose. When one's nose was made to bleed in most instances, the fight was already won. As best as I can remember, most of the few fights that Rabbit would get into was due to his little sister Laura Jean, whom most of the children viewed as a quick-tempered ball of fire. She was the type of fighter that people would probably pay a sizable admission price to see her fight. She was small in stature but she was tough. Now that I recall, she was very pretty and could handle herself in a fight regardless to how big the other girl was that she would be fighting. She wouldn't back off boys at all. If someone struck up her temper, she didn't wait for the other person to strike first. If she knew she had to fight, she would set out to win right away and she was as swift as lightning. To the best of my recollection, I don't recall her losing too often. Although Laura Jean had another older brother Melvin "Horse" between her and Rabbit, her main protector was Rabbit. Horse was my best friend at that time and he was more interested in being a lover than a fighter.

When a verbal feud was developing between two children inside school, it had to be settled during lunch or after school and/or on the way home if it were between two children going up the road south or going down the road north. Other children that needed some excitement would often urge fights on. Some busybody would draw a line on the ground and then pick up a hand full of dirt holding it in his/her one hand waiting for the pending fighters to come up to the line with one fighter on one side of the line and the other fighter on the other side of the line. Often the pending fighters didn't really want to fight one another for many reasons, but the friends of each fighter would be urging them to go on up to the line. When and if one fighter would intentionally hit the hand of the dirt holder knocking the dirt on the opposing fighter, a loud yell would go up from all the children gathered and the battle was on. I really believed that some fighters knew what the results would be and didn't want to go to the line. There were times when both fighters would be equally matched and have doubts about the end result and neither fighter would go to the line when urged to do so by supposed friends on their respective side. Instead, a fight would break out between the pending fighter and someone urging that fighter too aggressively to go up to the line of action. Sometimes there would be a more preferable opponent among those urging the fighter (especially someone the pending fighter felt that he/she could beat).

The dialogue between one of those urging the pending fighter would be thus, "Gon up dare; you sched?"

"Naw ah ain't sched."

"Yes you sched."

"I said ah ain't no sched ov dem an you neda; stop pushing me."

"Yeh you sched."

"Stop pushing me; ah ain't sched; 'pow!' "

Well, we now have a new main event and the other supposed main event would be either put on hold or forgotten about because the teachers would have been alerted. Fights didn't last too long on the school grounds because someone would tell one of the teachers if the teacher didn't know. Now this particular day on the way to school that morning, Rabbit had searched the field where potato harvesters had finished. Rabbit struck the jackpot and found a huge tater, which was to be a part of his lunch delicacy. When Rabbit arrived at school, he supposedly hid his tater lunch under the school but up on the beams. We could walk and play under the south end of the school in inclement weather. That's just how high it was from the ground at that end of the school. Bigun found out about the large tater that Rabbit had supposedly hid. Maybe Rabbit didn't really call himself hiding the tater because if anybody really knew Rabbit they wouldn't want to rile him up. Bigun got excused by the teacher to go to the outhouse. I believe the teacher was Mrs. Atwater. If not, it would have to have been her successor, Mrs. Sharper. Not long after Bigun had been excused, I asked to be excused to go also. When I went outside, Bigun was enjoying himself eating Rabbit's tater. Bigun had that special grin on his face when he knew he was doing something wrong. He asked me, "Ya wan-a piece?"

"Naw, it might hurt ma stumok."

I was really lying through my teeth. That tater looked so good before lunchtime and I wanted a piece so bad but I knew it was Rabbit's tater. Also, Rabbit's younger brother Horse was my best friend and I just couldn't be a part of anything against Rabbit.

Well, lunch or recess came and of course Rabbit went to get his tater. Bigun, being somewhat of a bully at that time, let it be known that he ate Rabbit's tater. Well, I don't know just when the first blow was passed but Bigun and Rabbit fought all during the recess. It was all the teacher could do to get them apart. Although Bigun was known to be one of the toughest fighters in the community and larger in stature than Rabbit, we all found out just how tough he was and how much courage Rabbit possessed that day. I said to myself, "Wow, ain't nevuh seen a tater cawse dis much stuf."

Almost anybody other than Rabbit would have disregarded the tater rather than fight Bigun. Rabbit had a different concept, his tater had to be answered for. After school was out that afternoon, Bigun and Rabbit started fighting again on the school grounds and continued on south down Louisburg Road toward Raleigh along the side of the road, in the ditch until Bigun reached where his home was and they still fought some more. The children who were supposed to go north (including me) delayed their really leaving by going out on the big rock on the side of the road where we could still see Bigun and Rabbit fighting. There was no decisive winner but that was the biggest fight event that I ever witnessed in elementary school, and to think it all started over a tater that was raw and not cooked. Believe it or not, from that point on they (Bigun and Rabbit) seemed to develop a great deal of respect for one another and never fought again to my knowledge. As a matter of fact, years later they both played semi-professional baseball on the same team (Millbrook Tigers). In my biblical studies, I have read or referred to the book of Ruth many times. Almost every time I review the part about Ruth gleaning Boaz's field (barley—corn), I think of Rabbit gleaning the potato field and finding that large tater and what happened thereafter even though it has been sixty or more years since it happened. It is rather amazing how both Bigun and Rabbit many years later would be working for the Lord but in different spiritual capacities. Bigun was associated with an internationally well-known religious leader possibly as an adviser/body guard, chauffeur or all the above, and traveled throughout the nation with the religious leader for some time. Rabbit, on the other hand, became a great baritone songster singing with a famous professional gospel group (quartet).

An Elementary School Baseball Game to Remember
(Boyland Chapel School vs. St. Matthew School)

If my memory serves me correctly, Boyland Chapel School was located a few miles south of St. Matthew School. Elementary schools for "Colored" usually were located near the church that they were associated with during that time. Boyland Chapel School was located next door, so to speak, to Boyland Chapel Baptist Church just as St. Matthew Elementary School was located next door, so to speak, to St. Matthew Baptist Church. I only remember the one occasion when St. Matthew competed with another school in sports. How and who engineered such competition is unknown to me then or now. I do remember a lot of hype being aroused even at our respective churches about the upcoming baseball game between St. Matthew and Boyland Chapel. Another one of my good friends, Aaron Holmes called "Honk," was a very good player as I was and we were the two smallest boys that would be on the team. The teacher allowed the larger boys to put the team together. Of course they put the larger boys on the team first, probably thinking that the larger boys would be more intimidating to the opposing team because of size, even though some of the larger boys couldn't necessarily play ball that well especially hitting and fielding.

"Honk" and I were exceptional players (at that time) especially hitting or fielding and we had good arms in throwing even though we were smaller boys. By this time, my mother was living and working in New York. She would send me boxes of clothes at certain times during the year, i.e., Christmas, Easter, birthday, Childrens' Day at church and September (school opening). Also, if there were special events and I needed something for that event, I would write her and she would send what I asked for in most instances. Although I did not know it at that time, this was during the time that my mother was somewhat sowing her oats in New York as a single woman. She was not a minister at that time nor had she accepted Christ as her Savior. However, she was somewhat fearful of my deceased father's spirit talking to her as she informed me many years later. She could fit me to a "T" in buying my clothes even though she hadn't seen me for months and sometimes over a year. Whenever I really needed something real bad in many instances, it would be in the mail to me. My deceased father's spirit would let her know, she states. I must detour from the baseball game between Boyland Chapel and St. Matthew in order for the reader to fully get the picture of the game when I return to it.

As I was speaking about my deceased father's spirit communicating with my mother, she would send something that I needed at times even though I had not written her to send it. Mother was dating a fellow (as she revealed) who worked on the railroad (Pullman car porter). When he had a trip to New York, they would get together. On this particular day when he was coming to New York, she decided to take off her job and get all prettied up to be waiting for him when he arrived for the party of two. While she was all prepared relaxing in "la la" waiting for her "ya ya," my deceased father Johnny's spirit came to her and began talking to her, as she states, "Here you are taking off your job getting ready to have a good time with some man and your child down in North Carolina almost barefooted needing shoes."

His spirit disturbed her so much that she completely changed her plans. When the railroad man arrived, she told him about her disturbing experience and they completely abandoned their plans as she went shopping and purchased me a pair of shoes. Instead of mailing the shoes, she called her job and explained her "emergency" to come to North Carolina. She caught the Trailways bus to Raleigh, North Carolina and went to her sister's house (Leora) and her brother-in-law (Garland) picked her up from the bus station. The next morning around ten or eleven A.M., I was out in the front yard facing the road (Louisburg Road, now Highway 401) throwing some rocks across the road hitting the "simon" tree. In order that I wouldn't have to lose my concentration by having to find a rock, I would gather up a pile of rocks before I started throwing. I was thinking to myself, *Sho' wish my mother would come down* simply because I just wanted to see her that particular morning. I had no expectations at all about seeing her that day. During that time, the Trailways and Greyhound busses' engines had a certain sound and one could hear them coming almost a quarter of a mile before they actually approached where you were located. Also one could tell by the breaking sound of the engine where the bus was going to stop to either pick up someone or let someone off the bus.

While I was thinking about my mother coming that sunshining early summer morning having begun to throw my rocks, I heard the bus (Trailways or Greyhound) coming north toward our house. Just as it passed the St. Matthew Church, the engine began to break, letting me know that it would be stopping around my cousin James "Jake" Malone's house or our house. Since I didn't see anyone standing on the side of the road waving a white handkerchief for the bus to stop, I knew someone must be getting off the bus. Just a little before reaching our path (driveway), the bus stopped and the door opened. Out stepped my mother with a box under her arm. I said to myself, "Dares my muther." The first thing I asked her, even though I had not previously written her about any shoes, was, "Muther, did you brang my shoes dat my daddy said you gon brang?" You can imagine how this frightened my mother even though she remained rather calm. The shoes fit me just as if I had been present when the shoes were purchased. I then asked, "Muther, you gon spen da night wid us?" Although I do not remember her exact response, I do know that she indicated that she would spend the day but had to go back to Raleigh so she could go to New York to work. Years later, she revealed just how scared she was and she wasn't about to spend the night out there in the same house that Johnny had spent most of his terminal illness days in just before he died.

Now, getting back to the ball game between Boyland Chapel and St. Matthew. I had written my mother a letter telling her about this special baseball game letting her know that I needed a glove and a few other baseball items. I felt very excited when I wrote her because I could just see myself with a new glove and other items. Each day after school during the week of the game, I was hyped hoping that we had received a package from Mother. I would ask Mamma (my grandmother) about the mail and she would inform me that no package from Mother had been received. The day just before the game the next day, I arrived home and was so disappointed and despondent that I didn't even ask Mamma about a package. Mamma was sitting on the porch shelling some green peas or butter beans to cook for supper. She knew exactly what was bothering me. I felt so let down because I felt that my mother had ignored my letter, which was very painful to me at that time. It was all that I could do to keep from crying even though I knew that crying would cause me to get a whipping because Mamma wouldn't dare to put up with no "pity party crying." She was tough. To make matters even worse, Mamma said something that didn't make any sense to me at all and, in fact, made me mad but I couldn't show it. Mamma said something to the effect of, "Why don't-cha write ya Mother anutter letter. She might send it so you can have it for tomorrow." Mamma was sitting in a chair on the porch with the pan in her lap. I said silently to myself, "I know Mamma knows that what she is saying makes no sense at all." I was sitting on the porch and when she spoke as just indicated, I got up and started walking slowly toward the smoke house knowing that Mamma knew I couldn't write a letter to New York and receive an answer the next day. I don't exactly remember what the chore was that she gave me, but she told me to do something or go get something for her. Whatever it was that she told me to do would take me out of her sight for a moment or so. While I was out of her sight, she went inside and brought out the box that Mother sent that was received earlier that day.

When I came back with what she had told me to do, I saw this big box that I had received from Mother. I still remember today the joy and excitement that filled my heart when I saw that box. When I opened the box, there was a baseball bat, catcher's mitt, catcher's breast protector, catcher's mask, cap, uniform, spikes, socks and a ball. That's when I found out that Mamma was really pulling my leg all along. I was so excited I could hardly sleep that night waiting for the next day to arrive. Boy was I the king of the hill when I went to school the next day, the day of the great game. I wore my baseball outfit including the shoes (spikes cleats) and I took all the other items to school with me.

When the game started that afternoon, they used my catcher's equipment, bat and ball. I remember Willard Taylor was catching for our school and the two smallest boys on the team were my classmate and friend Aaron Holmes ("Hunk") and myself. I was in right field and Hunk was in either left field or center field. I do remember that we were right behind one another in the batting order. Both of us had a base hit and boy was I happy. For some reason I don't recall either team scoring plus the game didn't last long because the Boyland Chapel team had to go back to their school and be released for the day if my memory serves me right. Also, I believe that the late Deacon (Bob) Rayford of our church (St. Matthew) played an important part in Boyland Chapel team having transportation to come to our school. I believe that Boyland Chapel School and church were situated on his property as he was perceived to be one of the wealthiest black men in the region at that time. That game will always be among my fondest memories at St. Matthew Elementary School.

My One and Only Time Being Expelled from School (St. Matthew)

From the time that I was a little boy, I didn't care too much about being around dead people or the graveyard. The church's graveyard was behind the church near the woods but not far from our home and even closer to the school. By this time, I was probably in the sixth grade. The new principal (Mrs. Sharper) had been there about a year as the Lord had called Mrs. Atwater to eternal rest. Mrs. Sharper was tall and she could sing. Looking back now I can see that she had an appreciation for music and especially for children who had musical talents. She was also a disciplinarian with a ruler in her hand and the "heavy duty encourager" at her desk. Near the end of the school year, she prepared us to do a school play and selected the students who would play the parts. The play was "Little Jack Horner." If my memory is correct, my cousin, who we called "Teen" was selected to play the lead role, "Mother Goose." I played the part of Little Jack Horner. This character had a singing part to it, which according to the teacher I could do very well. We, the students, were very excited and playful about this play because rehearsing during the school day meant no school work during that time as Mrs. Sharper and the other teacher would be involved with the rehearsal. Teen was very playful and comical in the role.

We were onstage by the blackboard rehearsing this particular morning. Mrs. Sharper turned her head for a moment or so and Teen was kinda playing around creating a somewhat playful scenario wherein Mother Goose, Teen, lightly slapped me, Little Jack Horner. It was funny to the other children but humiliating to me so I slapped her back. By this time and just at that moment Mrs. Sharper saw me slap Teen. Although there was no animosity between Teen and me, it obviously upset the teacher. Clementine "Teen," her sister Mary Elizabeth "Lip" and I loved one another very much as we were cousins and very friendly playmates outside of school. I tried to explain this to the teacher but to no avail. She suspended me for the rest of the week and that was on Monday. I knew I was in deep trouble then with Mamma. I wasn't about to go home and tell Mamma that I had been suspended. I might as well go down to the graveyard and dig my own grave. I gathered my books and went down behind the church through the graveyard to the woods down behind the old lodge building. That's where I stayed until school was out for the day. When the children came down the road that go my way, I came up from the woods and joined them on the road and went home just as I would normally do. In the morning, I would join them in going to school and play on the playground until Mrs. Sharper arrived and rang the bell for the students to line up to come to class. At this point, I would truck on down through the graveyard to the woods until recess when we would play ball. After recess, I would go back to the hideout routine. This routine worked well up until that Friday (the last day of my suspension). I must deviate so you can get a good view of the closing portion of this scenario as well as better understand some of the support and Christian love values that existed in a economically deprived black Southern community at that time. One of the upstanding Christian women of the community (Mrs. Dolly Winston) who was the mother of my "Sister Ruby's" husband (Eugene Brooks) had taken ill. When one would get sick, others in the community would rally to their aide to do their washing, ironing and other chores plus cook and take some food to them. This was somewhat of an unwritten law in the neighborhood at that time. Mamma could make "hog head cheese" or "souse" as many call the dish so tasty that it could symbolically make the preacher lay the Bible down and stop preaching. I loved her "souse."

Mamma was doing her Christian duty toward Mrs. Dolly this particular Friday by going to take her some things (including food) and to do some chores for Mrs. Dolly. Mamma had to walk by the school on her way to Mrs. Dolly and wanted to surprise me for my lunch by bringing me some "souse." Instead of surprising me, Mamma received the biggest surprise of her life by finding out that I had been suspended for almost a whole week. Needless to say that she was very unhappy about the teacher suspending me and she not knowing that I had been suspended. If my memory serves me correctly, she followed through with the recognized leader of the community, the late Rev. Millard Jones, whom I called "Cut-in Millard" who really loved me and I loved him. Although he had very little formal education (to my knowledge), even today, I still view him as a man filled with knowledge, wisdom and Christian love. Everybody in the community knew how he and I felt toward one another. He was the grandfather of "Teen" and "Lip." It is my understanding that he talked with the teacher about my being expelled from school and Mamma not being notified by the teacher of such. Again, to my knowledge that never happened again with any other students.

Now getting back to that awful Friday when Mamma found out that I had been suspended. When school let out that day, I came up from the woods as normal and all the children began to state in unison as if rehearsed, "Ohhhhhhh, Miss Viola is gon kill ya. She come by de school ta-day." I pretended not to be scared thinking that they were lying and trying to scare me. But they kept it up and wouldn't stop until I began to feel that there may be some truth to what they were saying. After a while we were able to see my pathway even though we were still a good distance away. Those in the front of the group of children walking along the road sighted Mamma standing in the pathway and they said, "See, Miss Viola is waiting ta kill you." Sure enough Mamma was standing in the pathway with a large switch in her hand. I perceived her being as mad as a raging bull. Finally I realized that the other students were right. By this time they also realized my fate and they stopped teasing me and began to feel sorry for me. Some of them wanted to slow down to witness my being punished but Mamma told them in a commanding voice, "Ya chiren go on home now to ya parents." I started praying under my breath, "Lord, please don let Mamma kill me, please." Talking to me from the front of the path on around to the back yard where my fate would be realized, Mamma was saying, "I'm ma tare ya up, boy" meaning, "I'm going to tear you up, boy." As I remember, she told me, "Put dem books on dat porch an come ere ta me." I put my books on the porch. Now here comes the surprise that I hadn't expected at all. She made me take off my top shirt, making me realize that she was really going to kill me. She stated, "I'm gonna teach ya a lesson dat you an never gon fogit." She started beating me with what she called a switch but I called a tree limb with just a few leaves left on it to justify it being called a switch per my perception. Now that she had started beating me, this brings forth the poor communication problem that we always encountered whenever she was whipping me.

"Ya gon do what I tel ya boy?"
"Yepem" meaning "yes Ma'am."
"Ya gon do it again boy?"
"Nome" meaning to "no ma'am."
"Wha'd I tel ya bout lying to me boy?"
"Ain lying Mamma."
"Ya callin me a lie boy?"

By this time, I realized that any response that I rendered would be against my better judgment, so I just cried and hollered while she beat me. When she realized that I wasn't responding to any questions that she was asking me while beating me, she made the dialogue start up again by saying, "Ya an anseng me boy?"

"Yepem, I mean nome."

By this time I was hurting and really confused. Whatever I would say would be wrong. Finally, she came back to herself and stopped beating me and made me get up on the porch and sit in the swing. I was still crying and she said, "Stop dat crying rat now or I'll give ya some mo to cry bout." Just how I was able to stop crying I really don't know, but I did. By this time welts were on my back. Being concerned, she went in the kitchen and fixed up some medical concoction that included alcohol/liniment to rub on the welts which felt comparative to getting another whipping. While I was enduring the emotional and physical pain, she brought me a extra big size piece of her "souse." That "souse" tasted so good to me that it made me wonder in my mind how in the world could she be so sweet in one way and beat me up so bad the way that she did. Please, please don't take a negative or angry view toward Mamma, thinking that she was mean. In her mind she was showing me love and saving me from future disaster and doing her Christian duty by teaching me a good lesson, so to speak. It must have worked because I have never forgotten that whipping. Under child abuse rules today regarding the above-described whipping, Mamma and other parents, grandparents/guardians would have been put in jail for years for such "child abuse," and the child/children would have been taken away and most likely put in an orphanage where they would have received little or no love and certainly not the continuity of Christian training that they received in the home, church and school. Anyway, I went back to school on Monday as my suspension was over and everybody was glad to see me, realizing that Mamma had put a terrible beating on me. They were still rehearsing for the play. The role of Little Jack Horner had been given to another boy who wasn't able to do the singing part to meet the teacher's satisfaction. After a day or so, the teacher gave the role back to me. Although at that time I didn't want the role back as I was still a little "warm under the collar" because I felt that the role should have never been taken from me nor should I have been suspended and beaten unmercifully by Mamma for no valid reason(s). At the same time, I was afraid not to do the role right because I would end up getting another beating from Mamma. I did the role but went home and told Mamma about the role being given back to me. Well, for a change, Mamma was on my side. She hit the ceiling so to speak. Even so, she sought advice from the community advisor as I now refer to him, "Cut-in" Millard and his advice was of course for me, as a child, to be obedient to the desires and judgment of the teacher. I did the part and did it right without any outward bitterness toward the teacher. From that time on, the teacher was very nice to me and we seemingly developed a special bond. Although she never said it, I truly felt that she felt sorry for the terrible beating that some of the other children told her that I had received from Mamma because of her suspending me. Even after I had finished high school and left NC to come to New York, I still maintained a somewhat frequent contact with Mrs. Sharper. She, too, loved me and wanted to bring out the best in me which I later realized. When I would visit Raleigh I would contact her by phone and on a few occasions was able, time wise, to go by and see her. She was a wonderful teacher and person. The one common attribute about the black teachers that I knew was that the teachers allowed themselves to get attached to the students comparative to being the child's parent when the child was under the teacher's jurisdiction. The teacher loved the students and was concerned about the students' upbringing and future. This is where the Christian love and caring continuity of the home, church and school were so closely connected during that time frame. Also, notwithstanding racial prejudice being legally practiced and being alive and well, black students (in segregated schools) during that time were still being taught to love our country, the United States of America and to take pride in being an American. To further illustrate the referenced close connection, I remember as a child learning and having to recite in unison with the class the "Pledge of Allegiance" during morning devotion before class was started along with singing a Christian song, reciting Scripture and prayer. Those among us who are old enough to remember can easily see that the Christian home (although a shack in the South in most instances among blacks at that time), Church and school were on "one accord." That special and close three-way connection referenced above no longer exists within our American society (public schools) today, in my opinion simply because of new laws passed that have directly or indirectly contributed to its destruction within the public schools.

My First Day Riding the School Bus Going to Another School (DuBois High School)

DuBois High School was located in Wake Forest, North Carolina. St. Matthew Elementary School only went through the seventh grade. Once I was promoted to the eighth grade, I would have to attend another school. The school that I would have to attend was DuBois High School. This would be my first experience riding the school bus because I had to walk to St. Matthew School. One of the boys from the St. Matthew community was the bus driver for the bus going to DuBois (the late Charles Thompson) whom by some relatives and close friends was called "Polly." Although he was a few years older than I, he was my good friend.

Some years prior to this, another cousin on Mamma's side, Millard Jones, Jr. whom I called "Buttermilk" who also referred to me as "Buttermilk Custard or Bullets" had come to visit his parents one Sunday afternoon just across the road from St. Matthew Church. Mamma had gone to another church and she told me to stay up at Millard Jr.'s father and mother's house "Cut-in Millard and Cut-in Anner," until she returned. In the interim, Millard Jr. put all the children in his car and drove us a few miles over to see a cousin on his father's side, the late Oras Thompson and his wife and family. Oras' brother Charles, named above, lived there. Oras' wife "Dorothy" was a very good cook and she made a dish that I had never eaten before "banana puddin." Even though it is too rich for me today, I still love it. While still over there and while the adults were talking, Charles "Polly" put me on his bicycle and rode me to a path in the woods by the cornfield that led to the road near their house. He then put me on the bike by myself and held on to one handle bar and the seat while explaining to me how to ride the bicycle. After he let me go by myself and I fell a few times, I was riding the bicycle by myself and boy was I one happy youngster. Some years later in high school (DuBois) "Polly" taught me how to drive the bus. After all the school children had been let off the bus in the evening, he would let me drive the bus after his verbal and physical demonstration driving instructions. This would take place on the dirt road at that time in the vicinity of Neuse River where there was very little traffic. He taught me how to "double clutch" in shifting gears, etc. He could have gotten in big trouble for letting me, a minor, drive the bus without a license and endangering the life of a child (me) and the lives of others (himself). I guess part of Charles' bonding and catering to me was probably connected to my being so crazy about his older sister "Mozelle" who had been another of my "heartthrobs" when I was a little boy. When she would come to the house with my big sisters Ruby and Viola after church services on a Sunday afternoon, she would let me stand in a chair and kiss her on the cheek. I would be on cloud nine in another world. Even today when I see her, that scenario is still a remembered laughing event by her, my two big sisters and others from St. Matthew who are still around that were around at that time.

Getting back to "Polly." He was truly my friend and I loved him dearly. Now, let's get back to that first morning going to DuBois. Almarie, who allowed the late Deacon Clyde Riddick "my brother" and me to call her "Sweetney", was on the bus as she was in her last year of high school. Again, she was Charles' cousin on her father's side (Rev. Millard Jones) and my cousin on Mamma's side. Although I was rather fearful, not knowing what to expect, when I arrived at DuBois for the first time, having her and Charles' presence provided some consolation to me. Even so, I can still recall the fear that was within me that first morning seeing what seemed to me so many children that I had never known or seen before. The fear became progressively worse when the school bus arrived at the school. I was totally lost and scared out of my wits. When departing the bus, many of the elementary students and high school students were familiar with the routine procedures. All of this was totally new to me. I was so scared that I literally felt like running into the woods and hiding there.

The Teacher Who Reached Out to Me Making an Unmeasured Contribution Toward Salvaging My Future to Be What It Is Today (Ms. Vivian O. Windley, Now Dr. Vivian O. Windley, Ph.D.)

The fear kept mounting when I was escorted to my new eighth grade teacher's classroom who was at that time, Miss Vivian O. Windley. I thought I would almost burst a blood vessel when she started asking academic questions to get a feel for what the students had been exposed to in order to further see what they had retained. Everything that she was inquiring about was totally the same as Greek language to me for I didn't understand anything that she was talking about. I would estimate that at least twenty-six to thirty students were in the class. Miss Windley did something that morning that I will never forget as long as I live. She was standing while the students were seated and she made eye contact with me. I felt that she saw and felt the fear within me. Her facial expression somewhat eased the fear within me. She could see that I wasn't a student with a learning disability or emotionally disturbed or anything of the sort. She could also see that the only difference between me and any other eighth grade student was my not having been exposed to the material that would place me at the eighth grade level. This is especially pertinent in that I was academically among the top students at St. Matthew in the seventh grade. Many other students, under the same set of circumstances, would have been removed from the eighth grade and placed in a lower grade at DuBois. Years later, my assessment of Miss Windley's actions that awfully fearful morning, allows me to have the utmost respect for her professional credentials, quality of her professional education and training, faith, courage, judgment and compassion. Instead of putting me in a lower grade, she put her professional credentials and possibly her teaching career on the line and kept me in the eighth grade. Symbolically she rolled up her professional teaching sleeves and said, ''I'm going to save this child.'' She made me feel that she was there for me and with me while also making it very clear to me that she would not tolerate any foolishness from me whatsoever. She let me know that if I buckled down she could help me meet the challenge ahead of me. I asked her for extra work in the areas that I didn't understand, especially math and after carefully explaining an example to me, I would do the others on my time and bring them back to her. With her caring and concerned attitude along with her encouragement and guidance,

I met the academic challenge within three to four months. She was also the director of the Glee Club and she was very impressed with my singing talent.

In order for you to fully appreciate the information that I am about to share with you about this teacher, a portrait of her in words will be very helpful. She possessed the type of physical charm and spiritual beauty when combined that made her a role model example of a proprietor of a charm school who could use herself to teach and train Hollywood models to bring into balance the very good, the good and the not so good to the extent that 99.9 percent of such charm school's models would be chosen for modeling positions. The principal, Professor L.R. Best, possessed a rather commanding and intimidating tone of voice, making teachers and students alike fearful of him. By the time I met Miss Windley, she didn't demonstrate fear of anyone. In her professional capacity as a teacher, she didn't feel second to anyone and therefore equal to her superiors in her areas of expertise. Often she would emerge as a respected and accepted leader among her peers and a compassionate mentor sought out by teachers and students. I learned so much about life in general from her in the eighth grade. She taught us something very important about the ignorance associated with racial prejudice that I will never forget.

During that time in the South, many white folk who were friendly (as much as the law would permit) with or toward black families would show their respect for the elders in that black family by calling them "uncle or aunt." Miss Windley explained to us that this was just an ignorant and phony way of whites not respecting the blacks by not addressing them as "Mr. or Mrs." which the whites felt would make blacks their equal. To prove her point, she told us the next time we had the opportunity to do so, act somewhat shockingly surprised and inform the white person that called their black relative "uncle/aunt"—"I didn't know that you were related to us.!"

In order for you to appreciate what I am about to tell you how I was able to test what Miss Windley had taught us, I must provide a general scenario of rural farm life (sharecropping for most blacks) at that time in the South. Black sharecroppers didn't have the ''up-front'' money to lay out to run the farm and buy other survival necessities associated with living. They had to depend on the kindness of a good old white plantation owner (probably descendants of former slave owners) who would provide such and the sharecropper would settle up with the ''white man'' when harvest time came around in the late summer/early fall. Of course there was a small fee tacked on for this kind and friendly service. There was one well-known white man who was wealthy enough in the general Wake County area who was kind and friendly enough toward many black families who would do this. In reality, he was a ''loan shark.'' He was probably in his late fifties. He had suffered a stroke at some point earlier and talked out of the side of his mouth as his mouth was twisted from the stroke. The black families who were economically tied to him didn't really have to go to his home to look for him; he was kind enough to periodically visit them to see if they needed anything and of course to check on his ''investments.'' Mamma was a hard worker and she was thrifty with resources and she firmly believed in paying her bills on time. Mamma would only get fertilizer and needed farm equipment (to my knowledge) from him. When the first load of tobacco was sold in the late summer/early fall, she would pay him off completely and wouldn't need anything from him again until around next spring (fertilizer for planting).

Now hopefully you should be prepared to better understand the racial test that Miss Windley told us to conduct. This particular day when I got off the school bus and walked up the path to our home (shack) on the front cover, I was there by myself as Mamma, Ruby, Viola and Clyde were doing some farm daywork for some other white man. When he drove up in the yard and stopped, his driver side window was down. When I opened the kitchen door and stepped out on the steps, he didn't give me time to greet him in that he immediately asked, "boy, wyhars" (meaning where is) "Aint Vi la?" To the best of my recollection, the first thing that came into my youthful, energetic mind was to show this redneck white man how smart I am in that I am going to the best school in the area that teaches us intelligence. I responded "good evening Mr._____; I didn't know that you were related to us!" The coloration on his face and neck immediately turned to an inderscribable red. With an expression that I had never seen coming from him previously, he again stated, "boy, wyhars Aint Vi-la?" I became frightened and told him where Mamma was located. After he had gone, I knew that I would be in trouble but I felt very good about what I had done knowing that Miss Windley would be proud of me. When Mamma came home (early night) as it was dark, the first thing she said to me was, "Boy, go get me a switch." I knew that I was in for a whipping but I didn't really care. I did as she instructed and brought the switch back to her. She took me in the sleeping area of our house/shack and explained that the white man, Mr._____ had come over to the field where she was working and told her what I had done. I am sure that he did it in a way that carried implied economic threats to her if she didn't straighten me out. I am also sure that she, somewhat frightened about our economic welfare as she was the head of our family, let him know that she would "tear me up" so to speak when she came home. As Mamma began to whip me with the switch just a very few licks (nothing like her normal whippings), she stopped whipping me and put her arms around me and began to cry saying, "Child, you just don't understand." I wasn't hurting from the switch at all but I was now crying too because I was hurting inside for Mamma. We sat down in two straight chairs at the foot of her bed with one arm around each other's back, and Mamma was somewhat bent over with her left elbow resting on her left leg with her face in her left hand crying. I spoke to her saying, "Mamma, yes I do; I understand." I could feel the glow of pride that came over her through her tears and then to me as well through my tears. By the way, that was the only whipping that Mamma ever gave me that didn't hurt.

Miss Windley monitored and mentored me all my five years at DuBois. Regardless of whose class that I was in, whenever she felt that I was headed in the wrong direction, she would pull me aside and sternly but with love, care and concern put me back on track. There was, there is and there will always be a very special place in my life and within my heart for Dr. V.O. Windley for she is a phenomenal person that happened to be among the best of my teachers.

Thomas J. Culler, (deceased) Agriculture Teacher at DuBois High Was Another Special Teacher in My Life

Mr. Culler was the official manner in how most of the student body and faculty approached him. T. J. was the name that most of the student body used when we were talking to another student in reference to him. In addition to his official title as agriculture teacher when I first went to DuBois, he had numerous other unofficial titles that would fall under the category of "other duties as assigned" by the principal of DuBois at that time, the late Professor L.R. Best. Only boys took the agriculture course when I was at DuBois. He supervised the maintenance and beautification of the school grounds using the students. This included male students who received punishment from the principal who were instructed by him to report to Mr. Culler for such work duty.

Negro Farmers of America (NFA)

This organization was associated with agriculture and seemingly designed (per my perception) to teach Negro boys graduating from high school how to be better farmers and breadwinners for their families. Again, graduating from high school was the pinnacle of the education ladder for most Negro boys at that time. Very few went on to college mostly due to family economics (no answers) in relationship to the following biblical Scripture: "A feast is made for laughter, wine maketh merry but money *answereth* all things" (Ecclesiastes: 10:19). To me, that Scripture is very clear. Agricultural students at DuBois were being prepared by T.J. to compete in the NFA competition in 4 categories (quartet, essay, individual talent and Parliamentary Procedure). As I recall, the competition was at 5 levels (1—within DuBois school; 2—local; 3—District; 4—state of NC and 5—National). I competed individually in three categories: essay having prepared such on "soil conservation"; talent by singing a solo and in Parliamentary Procedure by being able to answer correctly questions concerning same. I won first place in all three categories at DuBois, the local level I believe was in Raleigh and at the district level in Elizabeth City, NC. At the state level at A&T College, Greensboro, NC, I came in second place in all three categories.

Competition in the quartet category is something that I will always remember. T. J. formed a quartet to compete in the quartet competition. In doing so, he coordinated with Miss Windley who was the Glee Club director. The four individuals that were selected to be in the quartet were myself—second tenor; LaMonte Mitchell—first tenor; Coy Parker—baritone and Harold Peppers—bass. It seemed that there was something that sounded so special and musically beautiful about our voices blending together. Coy and I were classmates. LaMonte and Harold, "Pep" as we called him, were classmates. Our quartet won with ease all the way up to the state at A&T where we ran into some very stiff competition. At A&T College competition was conducted among groups for judges to determine the best three groups to compete at the main competition that night in the college auditorium. Let me regress momentarily. A list of songs, semi-classical, and Negro spirituals was given to T.J. by the NFA. Singing two songs constituted the competition with one song from each category. T.J. and Miss Windley (to my knowledge) selected the two songs. Miss Windley taught us our parts and coached us with both songs until we learned the songs to a fine-tune polish. Afterwards, T.J. coached our constant rehearsals. Although I don't recall the name of the semi-classical, I remember very vividly the name of the Negro Spiritual ''King Jesus Is a-Listening.'' Although we could be given the beginning pitch on the piano for each voice, the songs had to be sung a cappella. We always sang the classical first and then the Spiritual. When we were at our school rehearsing, we never had a problem with the pitch because we were not nervous and a piano was available with someone to give us the initial pitch. T.J. had constantly reminded us that if we started wrong and stopped in the middle of the song when we were in competition that we would automatically lose points with the judges and lose the contest. A teacher with one of the competing groups that had made it all the way to A&T college had promised T.J. that he would be there to give us the pitch that night on stage when competition would be between the three chosen quartets, as we had won the preliminary and would be one of the three groups competing that night. As I remember, he was so cocky and sure that his group would be in the final three. Well, his group lost in competition that afternoon and he didn't show up that night. We were very nervous with the auditorium full of people. I remember that one judge was on the front right side of the auditorium, one on the extreme left and one in the extreme back middle. Being very nervous, we started out without the pitch being initially given and boy did we sound horrible. Being the leader, I immediately said quietly ''stop, stop.'' Monte,

Coy and Pep stopped. T.J. was in the audience and I could see that he was disappointed. I took one step forward toward the audience while Monte, Coy and Pep stood still in their position. In a very clear voice, I asked, "Is there anyone in the audience who could give us the pitch on the piano?" It was so quiet in that auditorium that one could hear a pin drop. After not receiving any response from the audience, I turned and faced our group, letting them know what I was going to do. I told them that I would give each one of them their note (based upon my note) to hum very low and hold it until I gave each one of them their note (as I then blended my note). Our voices began to blend as required, seemingly with a special determination. I must say that our group did a wonderful rendition of the classical and then with even more determination really "tore up" so to speak—the Negro Spiritual even though we knew that we had lost points by stopping. Even so, we knew that we had to win at least third place and possibly second place realizing that "stopping" would probably prevent us from getting first place.

One of the competing groups was neck and neck with us from a harmony and voice for voice quality perspective but they did not sing the songs on the list (especially a semi-classical). When it was time for the winners of the quartet competition to be announced, we were feeling somewhat down. The three judges came together meeting in the front of the auditorium in a quiet huddle for a minute or so that seemed like an hour. After they had made their decision, the announcement was then given starting with the name of the high school of the third place winner, which was not DuBois. That gave us a little consolation for we knew that we would at least win second place. Then came the name of the high school that won second place which was not DuBois. Our eyes lit up almost like a Christmas tree and holding our breath when the announcement came "first place winner—DuBois High." We all grabbed and hugged one another with eyes very watery. I don't believe that I have ever seen before or after the expression that T.J. had at that moment on his face. For years, DuBois had been competing but had never won first place (quartet) at the state level. Well, here we were Monte, Coy, Pep and myself making history for DuBois. Also, for winning at the state level, the school received the first place large trophy and each of us received fifty dollars and a very colorful prestigious NFA jacket (yellow and black). When we wore our jackets to school that fall when school opened, we were indeed heroes and the DuBois population (faculty and student body) were very proud of us, even some of the boys who were jealous were proud. Although we didn't win first place at the National in Atlanta, I believe we came in second place and we were selected to sing on a local radio show in Atlanta. By the way, T.J. took us to and from Georgia in his car. He was so proud of our group that he and Miss Windley hand picked among the boys from the Glee Club and trained for the competition indicated above. By the way, 1954 was the last year for (NFA as such) as the U.S. Supreme Court rendered a landmark decision supposedly ending segregation in public schools.

Getting Transportation to and from School, Eventually Driving and Getting a School Bus Route

T.J. also supervised the school's bus transportation, which included selecting and supervising the bus drivers. According to my recollection, when the school zones changed during my sophomore year, two other students, Willa Mae Hunter (maiden name), the late Savonne Rucker (maiden name), and myself from our area were now in the zone of another high school. We chose to seek our own transportation so that we could graduate from DuBois. During that time, three other teachers (T.J., Mr. Pulley and Mr. Toole), who drove from Raleigh would come out of their way to pick the three of us up to and from DuBois. Willa Mae was in her senior year and graduated. For one more year that left Savonne and me to be transported by the teachers referenced above. When I entered my senior year, I had obtained my driver's license and had taken the school bus driver's test both during the summer prior to school opening in September. Although I was among the youngest of available bus drivers, T.J. still selected me to be a bus driver, giving me a bus (#40) and bus route. Because of the danger of making a blind right turn from my home to go to school, I bent the rules and went up near where Savonne lived to turn around and pick her up. Savonne was such a lovely young lady. T.J. and others knew that I was bending the rules but he didn't tell me to do it or not to do it in picking her up. So I did it. T.J. was a giant of a man in physical stature, deeds and accomplishments and yet he was so gentle. Long after I had departed DuBois, he became principal and accomplished much for the school and community. He touched the lives of so many people in so many positive ways. His name will always be in the annals of the historical legacy of DuBois High and within the boundaries of my heart.

Ms. Myrlin E. Skinner (deceased) My 12th Grade Homeroom Teacher Who Made a Great Impact on My Life

In addition to being my twelfth grade homeroom teacher, I was one of her students in two other subjects that she taught (French and typing). I never dreamed that both would be important in my life years later. This is especially pertinent in regards to my current literary works that weren't in my perceptive foresight at all at that time or that of any of my teachers. When I studied French under her in the tenth and eleventh grades, I never dreamed at that time that the opportunity would ever arise for me to go to France and obviously get the chance to use what little French that I had retained. Her voice seldom would be above a whisper. However, when she spoke, we understood her very clearly. This is especially so if she had to speak to a student directly in any way whatsoever regarding discipline. There would be any amount of words spoken but not outwardly just in the special look that her eyes could pierce through a student when she had to look at that student. Often just looking at the student and calling that student's last name would be sufficient for the student to get the complete message that she would be communicating.

My two best friends were my classmates Harold Winston ("Jack") and the late Buchanan Crenshaw ("Buck"). To me, Buck was the most comical person that I have ever met even to this day. Further, his humor was accomplished in such a quiet and unsuspecting manner in that Miss Skinner would seldom catch him. However, my uncontrollable laughter at his comedy (actions or communications) made me constantly a victim by my being caught. Even so, she was rather lenient with me because she knew that I wasn't a discipline problem student as such. My being addicted to Buck's humor was my major sin. Most, if not all of my classmates (twelfth grade) realized that there was something very special about Ms. Skinner as related to her true feelings toward us, notwithstanding her having to discipline us rather harshly (verbally) at times. Through it all, a lot of love would be lurking within her heart for us and likewise in our hearts for her. It was many years after graduation that I discovered her spirit being with me and somewhat guiding me along with the spirit of then-Ms. Windley. These two teachers, from an educational perspective, were the pinnacles of teachers in my life. In 1961 I was drafted into the U.S. Army about six years after graduating in 1955 from DuBois. Upon completing basic combat training at Ft. Dix, New Jersey, two of us in my company were selected to go to Ft. Benjamin Harrision for Military Occupational Specialty

(MOS) training with my being slated to receive secretary stenographer training. I felt elated and Ms. Skinner crossed my mind in that I felt sure that the major reason I was selected was my years of typing training under Ms. Skinner. When all the soldiers across the nation that had been selected to attend referenced training at Indianapolis, Indiana, there must have been more than forty students gathered.

The first two or three days consisted of classroom typing exercises to raise and test our typing speed in that a student had to type thirty-five words per minute (WPM) in order to meet the entrance level requirements for such training. Several students couldn't meet those requirements and were quickly reassigned to other locations throughout the world. On the last day of testing, I was the very last student to finally qualify (typing speed). The entrance level of thirty-five WPM was necessary in that a student had to type fifty to sixty WPM in order to graduate. The training pace was rather fast (in my opinion). We were in school from 8 A.M. until 5 P.M. (excluding lunch hour). After supper, we had mandatory study for two hours, 6 P.M. until 8 P.M. concentrating mainly upon typing and shorthand. I was constantly thinking about Ms. Skinner and I didn't want to fail. I would still practice after 8 P.M. in the barracks at times until the lights were out at 10 P.M. At times even then when I was on the verge of failing, I would go to the latrine (bathroom) and practice my shorthand. Believe me, it wasn't easy (at least for me it wasn't). To graduate a student had to type fifty to sixty WPM and shorthand ninety to one hundred twenty WPM. Each Friday morning we would be given a test in typing and shorthand. If a student failed, there was no possibility of catching up. Between the school administration, headquarters company and department of army, arrangements were immediately made after test results were completed between approximately 10 A.M. and by 12 noon to have that student processed, including orders being requested and received from DA, taken by staff car to the airport and put on a plane to his/her next assignment usually to Germany (infantry). Twenty-seven (27) of us graduated. Of the three blacks who started with the class, two of us graduated (my good friend J.L. Phillips) and me. Graduation day was one happy day in my life. Also, I was very happy that I graduated (the most improved in typing). I was so proud that I was now a school-trained qualified secretary stenographer which meant that I would most likely be assigned to a table of organization and equipment slot (TO&E) to be the secretary to a general officer (especially under field conditions). This also meant (as an enlisted soldier) that I would most likely go up in rank rather quickly (and I did) after reaching my permanent duty station, Orleans, France.

Although such an accomplishment would be considered routine in the lives of many others who may have started out to accomplish this and not a big deal, it was very significant in my life in that the choice was made for me plus realizing from whence I came and other variables related thereto. Additionally, now as an author, it has proven to be very significant for me to be able to do the bulk of my editing and all of my typing. Aside from my feeling that I had accomplished something in my life very significant that graduation day, I was also very sad during my graduation day from secretary stenography school. Many family and friends of numerous graduates came from distant locations to be there with their relatives (graduating soldiers) for this accomplishment. Many of the students were drafted and held prestigious professional positions in civilian life prior to being drafted. Accordingly, the financial position of the graduating soldier and that of his/her family/friends were far above that of my relatives and me. Although I would have cherished any one of my relatives being present for the graduation ceremony, I would have been exceptionally happy for my mother or one of my teachers from DuBois being there. However, I clearly understood the economics of my mother not being able to be there as well as other relatives in distant locations within the United States not being able to be there for the same reason(s).

I remember very vividly a situation that happened after I had been at my permanent duty station in Orleans, France. One Sunday morning when I was off duty, there was a requirement to get emergency supplies to an area that had been stricken with some type of disaster (I believe an earthquake). This requirement was obviously passed on to the Quartermaster (Brigadier General) where I worked. The Charge of Quarters (CQ) received the message to contact me and give me the message to report to my office immediately and not worry about getting in military uniform. I was in the barracks close by and did as instructed. When I trotted briskly across the front grounds the short distance to my office, the General and his staff were gathered near my desk where I had an electric typewriter. The General quickly explained to me that he had to get a TWX out very quickly and didn't have the time for me to take dictation in shorthand. I was to set up my typewriter and he would dictate it directly to me while I typed. I was saying to myself, "I sure hope the Lord and Miss Skinner are with me this morning." Even though I had exceeded the typing speed for graduation from secretary stenographer school, I had further improved my typing speed because every morning when I would go to my office, I would practice the practice typing phrase that Miss Skinner had given in typing class back at DuBois which is, "Now is the time for all good men to come to the aid of their country." At this time, my electric typewriter sounded almost like a machine gun when I would be typing. When the General started dictating to me and I started typing with my typewriter sounding similar to that of a machine gun, I saw the surprised look on the faces of his staff as they were in awe. I knew that the Lord and Miss Skinner were with me and that her untiring efforts to bring out the best in all of her students paid off for me that Sunday morning. When the General finished dictating, I asked, "Is that all, sir?"

He said, "Yes, son, that's all."

I pulled the TWX out of the typewriter for him to sign and it was errorless. The General, if my memory serves me correctly, immediately instructed Lieutenant Colonel Bull and Sergeant Major Chamberlain to see if I had enough time-in-grade to be waived and promoted to the next higher rank (E5). If so, the necessary paperwork was to be prepared for the General's signature. It wasn't long before I was promoted to E5. Over a period of many years, our student-teacher friendship has grown closer. When my first book was published, she purchased several copies from the National DuBois Alumni Association in that the association used the book as a fundraiser in 2004. She had me autograph all the copies that she purchased. On a very frequent basis we visited one another over the phone and continued to do as long as she was physically able. For several years whenever I went to North Carolina, my trip was not complete until I physically visited her. She was a dynamite teacher, mentor and good friend. She was excitedly waiting to see this book completed after I read to her the portion about Dr. Windley and T.J. and other portions as well. I told her that she would have to wait until the book was published to see the portion that I had written about her. The Lord called her home a few months before I finished writing this book. Again, Dr. Windley, T.J., Ms. Skinner and the other teachers that I have mentioned have made very significant contributions to the accomplishments that God has allowed me to attain. No monetary value could be placed upon such contributions in that they are priceless.

VI
Mother (Phase II)

The normal or what we perceive as normal love bonding between a mother and child is somewhat lost when the child is reared by grandparents or other guardians in my opinion. This is not to imply that love does not exist between mother and child. In my case, there was lots of love between my mother and me because my grandmother Viola took my mother under her wing just as if she had been one of her daughters. In doing so, she provided parenting and mentoring which included guidance in preserving her character and to prepare herself educationally, and otherwise to the extent that I wouldn't be ashamed of her to be my mother years later when I would be grown up. In the interim, many precious moments of "bonding togetherness" were lost.

Maybe I should elaborate just a little to provide more insight into what I am thinking. While it is true that Mother sent me packages and items of basic necessity which Grandmother didn't have the financial resources to provide, there were moments that I wanted, or better yet, needed my mother to be physically in my presence. An example: When I was four years of age and partially burnt up the barn and received the terrible beatings on that Sunday morning by my grandmother and then by my father (both of whom I loved very much), not only did I want to see my mother, in my mind I felt that had my mother been present, she wouldn't have allowed me to be beaten that way, regardless to what the consequences might have been afterwards for taking the stand that I perceived she would have taken. Certainly, while my grandmother seemed "out of control" and beating me, I dared not to mention the name of my mother as that would have probably incited her to be further out of control. Am I condemning my grandmother? Not at all, because she was burdened having to think about medically taking care of my father and not letting his contagious disease spread to other family members as well as feeding, clothing and housing the entire family. While she was probably in a state of shock, she didn't have the understanding or knowledge to think and act within a rational perspective. In my perspective now, this would have been a special time to administer love, counseling and teaching to the child as the child and others might have been harmed because of the child starting the fire. This would have been the time to let me, the child, know that love for the child and other family members as well as the protection of the mule and cow being part of the family's livelihood were much more important than the loss of food items, etc. as these items could eventually be replaced in comparison to the loss of life which could not be replaced. This type of love and counseling would seem much more effective at that time than the severe corporal punishment that was rendered to me as a four-year-old child.

Obviously, my grandmother couldn't provide what she didn't have or have knowledge of. At the same time, even though I wanted and felt that I needed my mother to be there with me, I can't condemn her for not being there. END OF EXAMPLE. My being a senior citizen now allows me to better understand the more we grow in God's grace, the more our spiritual vision expands, allowing us to look at any very disturbing situation and see the hand of God moving in a mighty way rendering blessings while preparing us for abundant blessings far beyond our view. Yes, there will be some suffering associated with life regardless to how much or how little we may have. As a child, when I looked at what took place between many parents and their children, I often longed to experience the love feeling associated therewith. At the same time, I would see those same parents under a given scenario desire their child to be like me or for their child to possess the talents that God had given to me. Even though these children were with their biological parents, I could feel the pain of the children when their parents thought such things. If the child was much larger than I was, I also feared for my safety if I was with that child out of the sight of that child's parents or my family members, who could look out for my safety against that child taking out jealous hostility against me.

Often such child (a boy) would pretend that he wanted us to play down by the field or woods where others couldn't see so we could have fun playing after an episode by that child's parent as that mentioned above. I wasn't stupid. My excuse to that child (boy) was that Mamma would whip me if I went out of her sight. In some instances, that child would still find snide ways to take out jealousy against me all stemming from the unwise action(s) by that child's parent of focusing (publicly) upon the child's limitations in comparison with praising another child thereby filling the child with enraged jealousy against the child being compared to, in this instance, me.

I'm sure there were times that my mother wanted to be with me. Now, I must admit that there were times that my mother could have been with me and wasn't. First of all, my mother wasn't saved during all of her adult life. She too, as many others, had her bouts with "sowing her oats" so to speak. During the years that I can remember while with my grandparents (from a baby to age eighteen), my mother wasn't financially able to come to see me in North Carolina every year. Even so, there were some years that she would come to North Carolina more than once. Therefore, during the years mentioned, it would probably average out to once a year that she came down to NC. When she came, she would stay at her sister and brother-in-law's house in Raleigh. She would come out to see me in the day and then go back to

Raleigh at night. Also, at night she could have fun with her peers partying. She couldn't do this had she spent the night with me at Mamma's house. She had conveniences at her sister's house in the city of Raleigh (running water, bathroom, electric lights, etc.) that were not available at our shack out in the country. Even so, since she and I only saw one another so infrequently, wouldn't it seem expected that spending the night with her child, even under conditions much more inconvenient than those she was accustomed to, would be the appropriate priority over not having such conveniences and over having fun with partying friends? I think so.

During my childhood from the time I can remember my mother until I was eighteen years of age, I never experienced my mother physically being with me during a birthday or at Christmas, even though she would have the gift boxes there. Obviously, I have never experienced a birthday party, which is rather important in the life of a child. At the same time, I'm not going to go through a "pity party" or trying to turn the world upside down at this stage of my life as a result of not having experienced this. I'm sure there are some who grew up with their parents and still never had a birthday party or some that were with their parents at Christmas and still experienced some of the worst memories of their life. Poverty combined with parents fighting and/or using alcohol as an escape route during Christmas season would be a terrible experience for a child to endure per my imagination. I didn't have to experience this because alcohol was not allowed in our shack or to be consumed by anyone who lived there. Now, please don't think that I am condemning my mother for any of her actions for not being with me when she probably could have done so. Even though there are certain scenarios where better judgment by my mother would have seemed more appropriate, I am still not condemning her. Who am I to condemn anyone, especially my mother? God's Word is very clear in this area. Also, as a grown man, I have made my share of mistakes as well combined with poor judgment at times as we all have done. While knowledge of the truth will take care of the condemnation process for us all, it will also remove the chains of bondage and set us all free if we can only accept the truth. I view the truth similar to cholesterol "good and bad" when both are balanced and closely monitored within the perimeter of necessity. While my mother never let me see her smoking or drinking, she engaged in these activities (somewhat extensively) for a time in her young adult life. Even during such times, she never turned her back on me as her child, in spite of some judgments that would have been better had she been exposed to education and training that would warrant such.

Some may look upon the actions of my mother and be ready to pass judgment upon her for not having me with her at any and all costs. This is very understandable from a human vision and emotional perspective. However, as humans we are not always able to have visible access to God's long-range plans and therefore unable to see what His plans for us in the future may be. Just as my father's bad decision not to let his older brother Henry and sister-in-law Malverda adopt me as a baby when my father wasn't providing any support for me, my mother's decision not to keep me with her at all costs was just as bad from a human nature perspective in my view. However, from my perspective and life experiences, it is clear to me that God took two bad decisions of my parents and stamped His approval upon them thus making them both very wise and Godly decisions. Yes, especially as a child, there were some good days, some hills to climb and some weary nights but God has still been good to me. What I am about to share with you will help you better understand (in my opinion) how God's involvement (when we allow Him to do so) in any crisis situation can take on an atom effect within one person splitting and spreading to so many others as in the life of my mother.

Although my mother was a hard worker holding down factory jobs that would normally have been done by men, she had not always been conscious of her spiritual life, i.e. soul salvation. Even so, she was a "path cutter" paving the way for other members of her family. When she came to New York, she not only sent me boxes but sent her mother, father, baby brother and two baby sisters boxes as well. One of her older sisters (the late Elnora), baby brother (Thadius), and two baby sisters (the late Mary) and Sadie resided in the apartment that she obtained when they came to New York. Also, two of her nieces stayed with her and she helped raise the two boys of one niece (during their earlier years on earth as both are now deceased). She purchased the first new suit that her baby brother Thadius had ever owned and mailed it to him. He was around seventeen as I am told. He was very proud of that suit. However, he was not the first one to wear his new suit. His father (my Grandfather Amos) decided to wear the suit without his son's permission. I'm told this caused much pain to Thadius. He cried all day and was unable to be consoled by his two baby sisters whom he was very close to. Yes, Grandpa Amos was a preacher and in my opinion, he made a human error in doing what he did. Yet, he was one of the best family providers that a family could ask for during that time. While that incident caused some problems with their relationship for some years, it is my understanding that it was cleared up between them. I really believe that love conquers all.

Getting back to my mother, she also sent her two baby sisters Glee Club outfits and their prom gowns. The gowns were such a surprise to them and a very heartwarming story. Getting a surprise when you need something and it seems that you are not going to get it, when in the rural area years ago has a very happy effect upon one when such surprise is received just as in my case with the baseball outfit. Mother turned her life around and completely dedicated it to God as she indicates and as it appeared to me once I came to New York to live with her for a while. She was called into the ministry in the early 1950s before I came in 1955. She was ordained in 1963. After receiving her GED she continued studying, receiving her AA and later her BA (elementary ed.), BA (theology) and later MA (Christian education). She studied piano under Octavia Morris and became the organist and choir director for Mt. Hebron Baptist Church, Bronx, NY for several years. Later on she started studying voice under Octavia Morris, approximately five years prior to being presented in "In Song Recital" at Carnegie Recital Hall, New York City, May 25, 1958 under the name of "Juanita Daniel." The recital was successful. Already being a preacher, she had promised God that if the recital was successful, she would settle down and do what God wanted her to do, which would probably be preaching God's Word. A promoter who had contact with Octavia's work and the students that she produced heard the recital. During the week after the recital, he offered Mother a contract. She states that while she was pondering whether to sign the contract, she was reminded by the Spirit of God what she had promised God. She did as she promised God that she would do which is do His work. In doing God's work, she taught a course for many years at the Leadership Training School, "How to Read and Study the Bible," which was sponsored by Congress of Christian Education, United Missionary Baptist Association.

My being a young adult man when I came to New York and living with my mother for a short period before she moved and gave me the apartment, we had a lot of bonding to do as Mother and son. Even though we were close and she taught me so much especially about the Bible, church and big city life, I had to finally realize that the daily bonding we lost by my being brought up by my grandparents could never be made up. Even though I was in a good Christian home, that missing link is still there not being with my mother daily. Yet, I firmly believe that I am much better off today by not having been brought up by my mother. Therefore, I "let go and let God." I now know that

God had it all planned out and He was looking out for my mother and me. Although I cannot state with authority what my life would have been, I truly believe that had my mother raised me under the same or similar circumstances that she was in, I would have probably been a drug, jail or graveyard statistic. I can say thankfully without any offense toward my mother whatsoever that I am glad that God's plan prevailed. My mother is a truly anchored servant of God. She has become my chief spiritual mentor (CSM) as indicated in my first published book *Establishing a Board of Christian Education Ministry within a Local Christian Church.* In her mentoring, teaching and counseling me together with the large box of biblical material that the Spirit of the Lord led her to give to me years ago were all obviously in God's plan, wherein He would reveal to me the need for above-referenced book and let me be His vessel to pen it. Resulting from positive educational and spiritual impact that the biblical material mentioned has made upon my life as well as that which it may have, at some point, upon many others in the world through me, I feel it necessary to identify these items. This is especially pertinent since it was the Spirit of the Lord that led my mother to purchase these items for me at an enormous cost for a birthday gift to me in my mid-thirties when I wasn't even interested in such material at all. The box of biblical material included (1) a large family Bible (2) a Paraphrased Living Bible (3) a Zondervan Pictorial Bible Dictionary (4) a six-volume Matthew Henry Commentary set (5) a two-volume World Book Dictionary set and (6) a World Book Encyclopedia set. When mother informed her husband, the late Rev. George C. Hoke, then Pastor of Mt. Hebron Baptist Church that she was getting me this material, he indicated to her, as I am told, that it was a waste of money to give me that material in that it was too advanced for me and I wouldn't be interested in it and probably wouldn't read it. She indicates that she responded to him, ''He'll read it one day.'' Pastor Hoke was partially right in that I wasn't interested in it at that time. Mother was completely right in that I did begin to read it one day many years later and I might add that I haven't stopped reading it since. The material stayed unpacked in the large box that it came in, collecting dust in the corner of the room for several years. Although I occasionally used the encyclopedia set and dictionary, I didn't bother with the other biblical material, until one day I casually picked up the Paraphrased Living Bible and slowly reviewing areas of it, I discovered something that really ignited my interest that I never dreamed would be found in the Bible. When Saul, first King of Israel, was talking to his son Jonathan, I saw in quotes, "You son of a bitch!" (I Sam 20:30). The rest is history.

That same box of material served as my major research items used in the first book, already referenced herein, that God allowed me to pen. Again, that same box of material is the greatest birthday gift that my mother could have ever given to me. Her obedience to the Spirit of God in giving me the material combined with her mentoring and teaching me how to use the material more effectively many years later warrants my first book being dedicated to her as it was and so stated in the Foreword of that book. Truly God's power is awesome. We especially realize this when we are obedient to His Will and allow His power to operate within us and through us. When I stop and look at the big picture of my mother's life thus far, seeing what God allowed her to do for me, her family members, many others and herself in the process, her life is already a legacy and I truly believe that her living shall not be in vain.

The Lord has allowed her to groom so many others at different age levels to put themselves in the pathway for God to call them into the ministerial vineyard. She is a minister's mentor to many ministers. The biblical course that she has taught for many years "How to Read and Study the Bible" is one of the most spiritually fulfilling courses that one could take. The kit that she prepared in conjunction with teaching this course is so helpful for reference purposes. Although it has been ten years since I took her course, I keep the kit near my bedside as I am frequently referring to it. When growing up as children, our perception of some things can be so strange depending upon what we have been taught or what we have not been taught. For instance, in growing up, I was in Sunday school almost every Sunday. Yet, while my perception of certain biblical geographical areas were a reality such as Egypt, other ancient biblical locations, at that time, didn't strike me as currently earthly locations such as Damascus, Babylon, Jordan (especially Jordan River and the banks of Jordan) and Antioch (where Christians were first called Christians). I feel very confident that I am not the only child at that time who had the same perceptions. Even now in the late stages of my life and the exposure experience that I have witnessed over many years in Christian churches, I seriously doubt if 30 percent of Christian congregations in the United States today know the names and what areas of the world today that were once known as ''Babylon'' and ''Antioch.''

According to accounting principles, land is a fixed asset that does not move. The name of a given area of land may change based upon an assortment of applicable conditions. Obviously, the major reason for Christian congregations not knowing where ancient Babylon and Antioch are located today is because they have not been taught this. I am not, in any way whatsoever, condemning Christian teachers. I am merely pointing out that I perceive biblical locations and what they are called today as being very necessary to include in Christian teaching and preaching today. This would give Christian students and Christian congregations a clearer concept of what has and what is taking place in these areas today in conjunction with what is being taught or preached about that took place in these same areas thousands of years ago. I can't speak for others but the above-referenced course taught by my mother put me on the biblical research road to arrive at the necessity of such teaching and preaching. If you are among those who don't know where ancient Babylon and Antioch are located and what their names are today, please read my first book referenced above. In doing so, you will also see the teaching concept advocated and the importance of an **effective Board of Christian Education Ministry** functioning as such in a local Christian church and not just shown on paper organizational structure or just for words-of-mouth purposes. I am led to believe that because God allowed my mother to be my chief spiritual mentor (CSM) and because He revealed to me the need for referenced book and allowed me to be the vessel to pen it feeling that the concept it advocates will one day have a major impact upon Christian education throughout the world, I sincerely believe that my mother's legacy in life will be centered upon her contribution to "Christian education" in carrying out the Great Commission given in Matt: 28:19-20. TO GOD BE THE GLORY.

Mother's Contribution Toward Further Developing My Musical Talents

When I came to New York in 1955, Mother had a piano. I had taught myself to play a little and practiced at the church in St. Matthew (North Carolina), after closing the windows and locking the doors from the inside so that I wouldn't be heard while practicing on the piano after I had finished cleaning up the church. This was on Saturday evenings when I cleaned up the church. I practiced once a week without anyone knowing that I was learning to play the piano. Although I was singing every Sunday in church, my North Carolina family or the St. Matthew congregation didn't have any idea at all that I was teaching myself to play the piano. When I started practicing on my mother's piano in New York, she didn't complain at all. Instead, she decided to put me in a music school (New York School of Music).

After learning the basics, I practiced on mother's piano but was very seldom practicing what I was supposed to practice. After the teacher discovered that I had been gifted with an ear for music and the talent, he and my mother or my mother concluded that she was wasting her money because I was playing anything that I heard and wanted to play. Since she had studied under Octavia Morris who had formed a Glee Club for her voice students, mother enrolled me in voice training under Ms. Morris as I called her. Her teaching methods including teaching the Glee Club a song, were so much like those of Ms. Windley, who was my eighth grade teacher at DuBois High and the music director for the DuBois Glee Club.

Ms. Morris loved my singing voice. During one of my visits back to North Carolina (home), most of the church congregation remembered my singing and of course called upon me to sing a solo. When I was growing up, I would sing *a capella* unless a musician was present. I will never forget the surprised expression on the faces of my relatives and the others in the church congregation when I was called upon to sing and I went to the piano to accompany myself with confidence. From that day forward, in addition to having already been accepted as "that singing boy from St. Matthew," I was now accepted as an accomplished musician by the St. Matthew congregation as well as by my North Carolina family. In New York, my mother was the official musician at that time in Mt. Hebron Baptist Church. She could only play by the sheet or book music. Being in a Baptist church from my years of experience, a musician has to be able to "pick up by ear" and Spiritually "git down" with an assorted quality of songsters who desire to sing, thinking that they can sound as good as someone they have heard (a talented songster) singing a particular song that they happen to like. When this happened and Mother was at the piano, she would look at me as I would usually be nearby and she would give me the nod to ease on over to the piano. She didn't mind at all; as a matter of fact, she encouraged it. This too, was bonding for us. Also, Mother was a well-trained talented songster with a beautiful voice. However, Gospel was not an area that she excelled in even though she loves to hear others sing Gospel, especially me and her baby sister Sadie who "ushers in the Spirit" so to speak when she sings Gospel. Although I didn't grow up with my mother, she has been "tons of blessings" to me. By her still being able to teach and preach at age eighty-nine, notwithstanding what might have been had she and I been together all of our lives and the pains that we both encountered by not being together, I can still truly say that God has abundantly blessed me by giving me my biological mother that He gave me in the person of Rev. Juanita Barnes-Hoke. Again, TO GOD BE THE GLORY.

VII
The Joy of Being Able to Search for and Recognize Blessings Even through Pain

If we carefully observe and recall to memory many conversations that we have engaged in with family, friends and strangers, we will often find that within three to five minutes of general conversation that something negative will emerge as the center focus of the conversation. This, in my opinion, sets the stage for the "blame game" or excuses to soon follow in justifying some form of our failure or "planning to fail" through shortcomings that we created ourselves by our own actions or inactions. Before you even ask the question, by "planning to fail" I am simply saying that if we do not "plan to succeed" we automatically "plan to fail." I have witnessed people making themselves sicker than they actually were by trying to be sicker than the person they are conversing with. Believe it or not, this often includes supposedly staunch Christian believers who wouldn't dare to be caught out of church on a bright sunny Sunday. Here is a brief scenario of two women who know one another and meeting each other after having not seen one another for a week or so.

"How you doing, sister 'C'?"

"Well, I tell ya; I haven't been doing too good; I've been having this old (some kind of ailment) that I just can't seem to get rid of. How you doing?"

"You won't believe it but I had the same thing. I had it so bad that it put me in the bed for a whole week; I couldn't even walk."

After they depart from one another sister 'C' would be saying, "I don't care how sick anybody is—she always got to try and be sicker. She ought to stop lying; she know she ain't been as sick as I was." End of scenario. Another important factor that I have often observed in even staunch Christian leaders is the extensive efforts that people will put into manufacturing excuses for something that they don't want to do. This includes using physical limitations to justify their excuse for not doing something that they can actually do themselves although it may be a little time consuming. The foregoing occurs, in my opinion, when positive and Godly thinking is not in the forefront of one's thinking process. Otherwise the first thing that would seemingly come to such person's mind is how blessed they are even though a bout of sickness wherein the major focus would be centered upon the hope, belief and expectation of being healed through the healing power of God. Better yet, instead of focusing upon what they don't have or limitations, it would appear from a believer's perspective that they should consider focusing upon what they do have and how blessed they are to have what they do have. I mentioned a short while ago about the "blame game" and excuses. We often find people blaming others for their failures and/or shortcomings instead of blaming themselves, which is generally where the blame belongs. Also, these same individuals will spend the major portion of their time manufacturing excuses for not doing what they know they could or should have done.

Blaming others for our failures or finding excuses often are the two main culprits that keeps us from searching for and recognizing the blessings that God has bestowed upon us, even in the worst of traumatic situations. When this happens, we are actually allowing the enemy to rob us of the joy that is right there for us if we could only adjust our thinking. It is my belief that regardless to how traumatic something may appear to be that happens to us, we can still find a blessing or blessings therein if we focus on searching for the blessing instead of allowing the lion's share of our focus to be upon the traumatizing situation. It took years for me to recognize that some of the worst things that happened to me turned out to be blessings in disguise.

I will share with you one such traumatic situation that was not only a blessing in disguise but was also a Divine medical miracle, in my opinion and as best as I understand from a medical perspective. In layman's terminology, I suffered a stroke in one eye in the early 1990s. Many of you are probably already wondering how in the world could a stroke be associated with being a blessing. While I know that some of you will be able to conclude such after reviewing the information that I am about to share with you, it is my hope that all of you will be able to recognize the blessing. I feel that I must give you a clear scenario of direct and indirect contributory events and circumstances leading up to the stroke. I was a federal civilian employee working for Department of Army (Dual-Status). This means that I was a civilian employee and a Reservist assigned to the same unit. The U.S. Army Reserve Unit that I was working for was the fourth Judge Advocate General's Detachment (Military Law Center). The Commissioned Officers were lawyers and a few judges. When I was first assigned as the Senior Civilian Administrative Technician and shortly thereafter assigned as an Enlisted Non-Commissioned Officer (E7) more than 50 percent of the enlisted personnel were lawyers also. Of course this was during the Vietnam crisis and I would imagine that some of the enlisted lawyers preferred to be in a Reserve unit as opposed to being vulnerable to the draft at that time; in that I believe that the draft lottery was in effect. The unit morale was high. I was very dedicated to the job both as the Senior Civilian and as the Senior NCO of the Command. I developed the habit of getting the job done working daily in my office after 1630 hours (4:30) over into the night.

When I arrived home I developed another bad habit of eating a heavy meal topped off with one or two drinks before eating and after eating. The drinks were supposedly to help me unwind.

Sometimes I found myself unwinding to the extent that I was really rewinding up. Of course you can see what my eating habit (late night) was doing to my health in general. I loved my unit and my work and I can state with clear conscience that my job performance was among the best and so evidenced by the ratings I received from my Commanders. My many years with the fourth JAG were tough at times but they were the happiest years of my life from an employment perspective. I might add that during the years that I was there, the fourth JAG was among the top rated JAG Reserve Units in the nation. Years later in my civilian status I was promoted to a position at the U.S. Army Reserve Command level. My years of experience, writing ability to draft directives at that level and knowledge of the training program (military school requirements, etc.) together with my administrative background (typing ability) placed me among those best qualified, or more likely the best qualified within the Command for the position. This meant nothing to some that didn't want me to have the position regardless to my having such qualifications. However, I needed to and did learn the computer aspect of the training program, which I was sent to school for. Although I continued the "job-dedication" *modus operandi,* it was rather clear that I inherited a mess. Obviously my being the new person in that position, I was the guy to blame instead of the one who created the mess or those above the one that created the mess who allowed the mess to be created. Within a short time, the Lord allowed me to see some of the major problems that led to the mess being created and what systemic procedures (which included my being allowed to train key persons together with physical help) would be necessary to be developed and implemented to put the professional school training train on the right track.

Believe me, there were enemies but there were also friends. Certainly some friends I knew well but there were other senior-ranking friends developed through my trying to do what I perceived to be the right thing to do. Some of these friends were professionals whom I have never seen even to this day would call me, thanking me for the successful efforts I had put forth in getting some of their personnel in professional schools that had been previously difficult to get either a quota or funding. Believe it or not, these friends proved to be very helpful in watching my back in that they knew some of my internal enemies. What my enemies didn't know and understand was that the power of God's love was with me and my enemies' arms were too short to box with God as the saying goes. Even so, there was a great deal of stress associated with cleaning up the mess that I had inherited. I was determined to succeed at all costs and I did. However, the stress combined with other factors previously described and my putting the job before my personal health led to (in layman's terminology) my having a stroke in one eye. I had noticed a red spot in my eye during the weekend that I thought would go away as it had done previously. Instead of going to the doctor on Monday morning, there were very pressing items to be addressed at the job and I said to myself that I would go to the doctor probably Tuesday after work if the red spot didn't disappear. However, (if my memory serves me correctly) I believe it was Monday night and Tuesday morning that I noticed the red spot had not disappeared plus I was constantly cleaning my glasses and rubbing my eye in that my vision was becoming more blurred in that eye. Instead of waiting until after work at 4:30 P.M., I decided to take off and go to an optometrist at noon. As soon as he examined my eye, he immediately instructed me to see an ophthalmologist immediately. I asked him if he could recommend one and he did. I went to see him and he put the diagnosis to me rather bluntly in language that I would understand indicating that I would be blind in that eye. The condition that he described should have been addressed within two hours or so for my eyesight for that eye to be saved. I was rather upset with his way of explaining it to me even though he gave it to me in a rather straightforward fashion. It was traumatic for me to come to grips with the thought of being blind in one eye after having enjoyed such good sight all of my life. To use a cleaner version of one of my late poker friends many years ago, my eyesight had been so good that I could "see from a distance two flies engaged in romantic intimacy on a cold and windy night." Observing that my vision in that eye was becoming more blurred, I was in a panic state. I called my regular medical doctor's office as he was closing and explained my situation to him. He instructed me to come to his office the first thing the next morning. I was his first patient the next morning and after examining me, he immediately contacted the ophthalmologist that I had seen the evening before.

Although I wasn't privy to the entire conversation, I could tell from a portion of my doctor's conversation that the ophthalmologist didn't seem to be providing any hope for my condition. After the telephone conversation ended, my doctor thought for a moment or so and then asked me if I would be willing to go downtown to Manhattan Eye & Ear Hospital if he gave me a letter. I responded by saying, in a grateful manner to him for his efforts and concern, that I would go to the Mayo Clinic in Minnesota if it would help to retain my sight. He prepared a quick letter and I was off to Manhattan Eye & Ear. My sight in that eye was slowly going. Several doctors examined me and they all agreed that my condition was too far gone for the normal medical procedure for such condition to do any good, which is my way of explaining their medical language as I understood the bottom line. The entire time that I was listening to the different doctors communicate in medical language, I was constantly praying. There was one doctor who was fighting hard for me to undergo the particular procedure and of course I was praying for him to win. Finally, there was a conference of approximately ten doctors with this one doctor pleading my case. He continued on to the highest level within the hospital as I could best determine. While all nine of the other doctors were gathered around me sitting in the examining chair, he requested that they look again at my eye and he stated words to the effect that, ''there is a trickle of blood there and that is reason enough to go through with the procedure and then hope for the best results in time.'' Observing that all nine of the other doctors were seemingly giving in to his plea, the final OK had to come from a certain doctor. All of a sudden, a very beautiful and strange feeling came over me as if to say ''everything is going to be all right.'' I knew and realized then that the power of God was ''in charge.'' I could hardly hold my peace in that I was swelling inside with joy and thanksgiving. It was seemingly as if fire was shut up in my bones. I was overflowing with thankfulness and joy inside. Finally the OK was received for me to undergo the procedure. Thank God I had one of the best medical insurance carriers. Only two doctors were by my side for the procedure (the doctor who had fought for me to have the procedure and the doctor who was actually going to do the procedure). Just before the procedure, I asked the two doctors, ''Gentlemen, do you all believe in the same God that I believe in?'' They both responded in the affirmative. I was standing between the two of them. I then asked if they would mind if we joined hands while I prayed. After praying, I had complete faith in God and in those two doctors and I told them to go ahead and do what they had to do. I was awake and my sight in that eye by this time was gone completely.

After deadening the nerve in that eye, a very long needle (it seemed to me) was inserted in (it seemed) the middle of my eye as if to go through to some portion of my head. Although I couldn't feel any pain, I could feel the pressure bearing down upon the needle or instrument being used that seemed to be a long needle. Although it was medically believed and hoped that I would regain some of my peripheral vision as time went by, it was doubtful as to whether I would ever regain any central vision in that eye. By this time I was happy to hope for any vision whatsoever in that eye in that I was totally blind in that eye. Of course I had a patch over that eye while the healing process was taking place from the procedure. As time passed and I was going back for follow-up treatment, I observed that a portion of my peripheral vision was slowly coming back. Obviously, I was thanking and praising God realizing how He had blessed me even though I only had just a small portion of my sight in that eye. After I had lost all sight in that eye even for a short duration of time, I could really be appreciative and thankful for any sight whatsoever in that eye. I feel that I had a good reason to be happy for some sight instead of complaining about that sight which I had lost.

As time passed, I wanted to see the doctor who had fought so hard for me to have the procedure. I wanted to let him know how much I thanked God for him and how much I thanked him for what he had done for me in that my peripheral vision was continuing to improve slightly. After about a year or so with much military experience, I went through the old G2 process and hunted him down. It wasn't easy, especially not knowing his first name at that time. It seems that when doctors began their private practice, their previous employer(s) don't seem too eager to release any information as to how to locate the doctor. I finally tracked him down many miles from me in New York and made an appointment with him as he was now in his own private practice. The reunion was one of much joy and still is as I go to see him at intervals on a yearly basis. He is and will be my eye doctor until. I discovered that the doctor who did the procedure is in Illinois. Several times over the years since I had the procedure at a given time during the year, a very sharp pain would come upon me in that eye. At first, I thought I was having a reoccurrence of that same problem and I would make haste to Manhattan Eye & Ear to make sure that this wasn't the case. Some years later, when this pain would come about, I would notice a day or so afterwards that a tiny little scab would seem to be working its way to the surface of my eye and afterwards I also noticed that my vision would be improved just a tiny little bit. After a while when I would get that pain, I knew what it was by now (per my belief) and could rejoice knowing that it was the healing process still in motion and that I could expect slight improvement in my peripheral vision.

As time passed, my peripheral vision kept expanding into my central area of vision (in my layman's terminology) and I could see a wider area. Are you getting ready to shout? I am. Believe it or not around once a year, I still feel slight pain but not as sharp as it once was and still I become joyful knowing what to expect. My expectation is usually valid and my own test method usually confirms that there is a slight improvement. Of course I bring this to my eye doctor's attention. Although I still cannot read with that eye, my central vision has improved or rather yet been restored to the extent that I can identify writing and any object and can tell what the object is. By having any sight in that eye whatsoever, I am convinced that such sight is a divine miracle from God. My medical doctor that sent me to Manhattan Eye & Ear often has medical students in his office, which is part of their medical training, as I understand. In giving instructions to some of the medical students on an individual basis, on a few occasions he has instructed the students to observe my eye very carefully in that they may never see such situation again in their medical career. My hearing such instructions let me know that my eye situation from a medical perspective would not be a common medical occurrence, especially considering that I have regained some sight and that normally if such condition had not been addressed in the first two to four hours the patient would be blind. This, together with other thinking processes leads me to conclude that my situation is a divine medical miracle for which I am eternally grateful to God and to the doctors that contributed to such success.

While I have clearly elaborated on the huge blessing from God of regaining some sight in my eye that many or most of you can concur with, there are even greater blessings derived from this situation that I haven't discussed as yet that I am about to discuss. In being very clear and blunt, the stroke that I suffered in one eye turned out to be great blessings in disguise to me. I feel that some of you may take great issue with what I just stated in trying to imagine, "How in the world could any type of stroke be a blessing?" Please, please before labeling me completely crazy as your final conclusion, please allow me to share with you my sincere reasoning how and why I was able to conclude that the stroke in one eye became blessings in disguise to me. I believe that I can best paint the picture that I need to paint by elaborating on two of the major areas of my life that I <u>know</u> have turned out to be blessings to me resulting from the stroke. I will deal with these two areas individually. Keep in mind that once you begin to realize that you've been blessed by a specific blessing, it tends to split and multiply into other blessings just as an atom splitting, and before you realize it, you are in the process of being bountifully blessed in so many ways. The two major areas are as follows:

A. **Spiritual Vision:** The stroke was an awakening factor to me seemingly broadening my spiritual view of other areas of life. I began to focus more beyond my needs and wants and began to see the needs of others more clearly and more importantly, see how their needs took priority over my wants. Not only did I see these needs but God allowed me to develop a stronger desire to analyze these needs to see how I could best go about making some type of contribution(s) to such needs which would, in time, make a difference in the lives of others, per my perception. Then my living would not be in vain. Although God gave me a "music ministry" throughout my life through an anointed voice and instrumental talents that He made me aware of, He was preparing me for a "writing ministry" for years that I was completely unaware of until just a few years ago after the first book that He allowed me to pen was published. Many believers are aware that God gives us one or more ministries and yet the ministry(s) given to us may or may not be a "pulpit" ministry. The book being referred to is *Establishing a Board of Christian Education Ministry within a Local Christian Church.* I am now thoroughly convinced that God, knowing my heart and what He wanted me to do, combined with what He prepared me to do, gave me the concept of the book, and chose me to be His vessel to pen the book that would ultimately, if implemented, be a great help to many people. This, now being included in the expansion of my spiritual vision, allows me to see beyond a doubt that referenced book is indeed "God's book." It is so clear to me now that referenced book will be around (for years to come) in making a great contribution to meeting many of the needs of others that God allowed me to contribute to the process for which I am eternally grateful and thankful to Him.

B. **Lifestyle Changes:** Certainly, it was the lifestyle habits that contributed to the stroke as I explained previously. Even though certain changes seem rather minor and simple to make, these important changes or better, yet lifestyle preventive measures should be taken rather seriously if one desires any quality of life as years pass. Therefore, I will treat the two major lifestyle changes that I made rather seriously and independent of one another because I personally feel that many people are experiencing poor quality health because of their weakness to one or both of these two lifestyle habits. Hopefully something that is stated herein will motivate them to seek the will power and determination to make the necessary lifestyle changes that will be supportive of good health and quality living. Now, for the two lifestyle changes that I made accompanied with moderate exercise (walking $1^1/_2$–2 miles 3 or four times a week).

    1. **Eating Habits:** The stroke in my eye was the motivating factor that made me desirous of doing something about these

habits in order to prevent a future more serious stroke. Eating late at night and laying down was bad enough in itself. Can you imagine the damage that I was doing to my health (late night eating) by knocking off a couple of ham hocks one night; a couple of pork chops the next night with rice and gravy, greens and potato salad or macaroni and cheese, two or three slices of bread and often a piece of "hog head cheese—souse" on the side and the next night a large tender T-bone steak with the same type trimmings? Of course a man-size shot of rum and sometimes an ice cold beer would be a regular part of such late night meals. It was a blessing that I didn't end up with a paralyzing or death stroke during that time. Not only did I cut out the late night full-course meal eating, I rarely eat the foods mentioned above even though I still love them very much. Further, when I do eat these foods very infrequently, I do so in very much limited amounts than those mentioned. For instance, I haven't eaten a steak in months and I haven't eaten one ham hock entirely since I had the stroke and only a piece of one in many months' intervals. Another important factor that went along with the poor eating habits is that (late at night) even before I tasted the food, I would grab the salt shaker and start sifting salt on my food to make it really ready for some good eating, all of which was leading me to an early grave. Now, I don't use regular salt at all (but rather a salt substitute). Even so, I rarely use any additional salt substitute. The salt substitute that is used in cooking the food is usually enough for me and I rarely need additional salt substitute. I do hope that what I have stated regarding the foods mentioned above will not be misinterpreted or perceived that I am stereotyping a people or anything of that sort. While I know that there are those in the world that love the foods that I mentioned just as much as I do, we must realize and admit the truth from a health perspective that these foods, especially consumed in large quantities and frequencies mentioned are detrimental to one maintaining good health, which is just plain and simple truth regardless to race, creed, religion, color or national origin. Now it is time to deal with the other culprit that I was using to supposedly wash the food down with, which is:

2. **Alcohol:** This includes beer, wine and whiskey. Before I start knocking alcohol (as I am going to do) and offend so many readers (drinkers) that will defend alcohol to the hilt, let me first tell you that I have never been classified as a drunkard, never been arrested for drunk driving or anything of that nature. The times that I did drive while under the influence, I guess I was fortunate in that I didn't drive recklessly or in an irrational manner after having a couple of drinks during the time that I drank years ago. My job in the federal government, church organist and military (reserves) occupied my time to the extent that I was only able to (so-called) drink sociably was after my obligations from any of the three above-mentioned areas would be finished for the day or during holidays or anytime when I would be free from all three obligations mentioned. Even so, I don't want to imply a false implication that I have never been drunk. Although cautious as I thought I was being by not having to have been disciplined as a result of drinking, I have been intoxicated or "drunk as a skunk" as the saying goes. However such times were very few during the years that I did drink. In all probability, if one drinks with any degree of frequency (social or otherwise), it is very likely that at some time during such drinking tenure, they too have been intoxicated. Certainly there were then and still are now social functions that so-called social drinking is not only accepted but in my observations, encouraged. This is especially observed and perceived so as to allow one to be intellectually and professionally viewed as being in the "in crowd or down-to-earth person" outside of one's professional obligations so long as one could "hold his/her liquor."

Preceding the main event of many functions (including business conferences) an "ice-breaker" period is included at which time alcohol (in many instances) will be available and drinking, in the opinion of some, helps people to gather the needed courage to be relaxed and unafraid to meet and greet one another including constituents within the same business entity, but strangers to one another in the sense that they don't know one another from a personal perspective. Yet, from a business perspective, they need to know one another. It appears to be a perception by the powers that be in many instances that alcohol is the main needed resource to bring this about. By the way, let me clarify the earlier implication that I would be knocking alcohol as a culprit or making it seem like a demon or condemning those who drink alcohol. Who died and left me in charge to render judgment upon others? Not a living soul. Therefore, I am not qualified or authorized, so to speak, to pass judgment upon alcohol or people who choose to consume alcohol. What I am qualified to do is to observe the actions of those who consume alcohol and compare their actions while they are under the influence of alcohol with their actions when they are not under the influence of alcohol if I have seen that individual in both scenarios.

Even now I have looked back at my own actions years ago while under the influence of alcohol, realizing that there were times my actions under the influence would have been much different had I not been under the influence of alcohol. Further, if you take a bottle of alcohol and put it up in the bar in the house or wherever, it would remain there harmlessly without bothering anyone. Alcohol doesn't bother people; it's people who bother alcohol. Likewise, some people are beautiful and fit the role of a model citizen until they get together with alcohol and symbolically form a partnership. That's when the trouble begins. Also, it's not necessarily a large amount of alcohol that is consumed by the individual, as would often be perceived that would determine the individual's behavior after consuming alcohol. In some instances after two, three or more drinks an individual's actions would appear to be rational or within their arena of normality while at other times just one drink could seemingly cause that same individual to go off his/her rocker and be ready to kill the person most close to them be it child, spouse, parent or best friend. As a matter of fact, there are times when alcohol can be rather beneficial from a medicinal perspective when it is used for that purpose and not for pleasure or a good time. The area of alcohol that I desire to deal with here is the drinking of alcohol by people for so-called social, relaxing, partying, fun and for supposedly having a good time. I have seen so many instances where alcohol, used in the manner just described, has unintentionally led the users to abuse resulting in so many untimely deaths, beautiful families destroyed, successful careers destroyed, friendships and relationships destroyed and flourishing businesses destroyed. We could go on and on and on. We therefore ask the question, ''How could one allow himself/herself to be unintentionally led to such self-destruction in the use of alcohol?''

Well, here is a portion of my input through self-experience and years of observing others that start out drinking just a drink or two and later become big drinkers, problem drinkers or alcoholics. Oops, I better explain this because even while I am writing I can seemingly feel the energy of some professionals with their professional guns pointed in my direction ready to pull the trigger on me for my making such seemingly accusatory statement. In my layman's perception, what I stated is not to imply that an individual who drinks alcoholic beverages will automatically become a big drinker, problem drinker or an alcoholic. So, please unload your professional weapons and put them away before someone gets hurt accidentally. We will leave the sickness/disease (alcoholism) for you professionals to deal with. We will deal here in layman's terminology and perceptions. Let's start by doing a little analysis and then asking a question. It is general knowledge that one of the main symptoms of the disease of alcoholism is the inability to stop drinking alcoholic liquors to excess. We further realize that alcohol in varying amounts can cause intoxication resulting in one being unable to be in good and complete control of his/her faculties which would allow one to cause harm to themselves or others unintentionally or intentionally that he/she would not normally do were they not under the influence of alcohol. With this knowledge and understanding why would one risk his/her life, the lives of others especially close loved ones, the destruction of their future or undermine and demean their unblemished reputation, professional status or their prior esteemed accomplishments, for the sake of being sociable or having fun through drinking alcohol in the first place? This question is especially pertinent since drinking alcohol for partying and being sociable and having a good time in this layman's vein of thinking is generally harmful causing organic deterioration damage to the body much sooner than it would generally occur without the contribution of drinking alcohol.

I perceive that good friends who drink alcohol contribute to leading their good friends that don't drink or that have never drank alcohol to drink it in order to be in sync with their good friend. Further, I perceive that good friends who drink alcohol generally pass on to non-drinking friends images that appear to be positive and rewarding that drinking alcohol presents when, in fact, such images are not positive and rewarding at all from a reality perspective. Often when one drinks a couple of drinks, the image portrayed is one that seemingly implies that his/her intellectual status is supposedly stimulated to a level much higher than it actually is. Also, after a couple of drinks, one's courage is seemingly stimulated in that he/she has the courage to start a conversation with someone that he/she normally would not normally initiate such conversation with for an assortment of reasons including the individual's high profile status. I guess that's why such social drinking is called "ice breaker" in some instances.

I guess that you have noticed by now that I didn't waste any time to compile any official statistics regarding the abusive use of alcohol and the addiction thereto by so many people. I am sure that you are already familiar with such statistics together with what I have described and with what you have heard, read or witnessed. I am also sure that you have watched the news on television and have seen how hard some people have strived for so many years going to school to build professional careers and suddenly allow themselves to be caught up in the abusive use and addiction to alcohol. They are exposed over the news because of their high profile status generally having done something negative that wouldn't normally be expected of one in their status. High profile persons falling from honor to disgrace because of their abusive use and addiction to alcohol usually becomes major news for the media and probably positively affects sales and/or ratings. It appears that the general public enjoys seeing the downfall of others who quickly destroy everything that they have worked so hard for almost in the twinkling of an eye. This, to me, is so sad. While I am not a medical professional, I truly believe, from a layman's perspective, that many people who have become addicted to the use of alcohol did so unintentionally initially through the "social route" which I have already described above. If we carefully observe some major tragedies where it seems that the real truth is initially omitted, we later find in many instances that the abuse of alcohol is the bottom line factor.

Many people who fall from honor to the destruction of alcohol abuse are individuals with high academic credentials from the finest of institutions of higher learning and not just uneducated individuals as some of us might think. Again, I perceive that some readers of this area pertaining to alcohol including high profile professionals who are alcohol drinkers or non-drinkers may disagree with almost everything that I have stated about alcohol. I don't suppose the alcohol industry will pay any attention to what I have stated whatsoever. They don't have to because most likely the individuals who drink alcohol will defend alcohol to the hilt. I dare one to start focusing upon the negative aspects of drinking alcohol in the presence of drinkers (professionals or non-professionals) as they will "light your fire." While many who read this book who happen to be drinkers may desire to discontinue drinking alcohol, the alcohol sales industry will probably not miss them because more new customers will probably begin drinking alcohol, which is a sad reality in my opinion. If we carefully observe how drinking alcohol, supposedly moderately, can be portrayed through assorted measures (including high profile persons who drink moderately) to be a "class act" thing to do being implied to be associated with success, I can easily see how some young people who have never indulged in alcohol are somewhat encouraged to drink, especially if they have reached the legal age feeling that it seems to be something exciting to do. On the other hand, just because something may appear to be exciting or the "in crowd" sociable thing to do, there is no gun pointed at one's head demanding that they must drink alcohol in order to climb the ladder of success. Therefore, if you are a non-drinker, please allow me to commend you for not starting to drink in that you may very well lengthen your life and add quality (health wise) living to your life that drinking alcohol may very well contribute to such being destroyed much sooner than it normally would from natural causes. In concluding this area, after the stroke in my eye, I took inventory of myself. I realized that **common sense** is not so common. Even so, in taking such inventory, I desired to use a little of it to aid me in such self-inventory. Although I didn't consider myself a big drinker, problem drinker or an alcoholic, in looking at the many alcohol-abuse-related tragedies previously mentioned, I couldn't find any reason that would be supported by **common sense** or health benefit to me for me to continue drinking alcohol for any purpose (social or otherwise) even in the smallest amount. Further, I really examined the blessings that God had bestowed upon me through the stroke and then, through God's divine miracle restoring a portion of my sight that medical science seems to view even today—years later—as a rarity. He allowed me to conclude after my inventory shortly after the eye procedure that I don't need alcohol as an ''ice breaker'' for social purposes or to have fun or for courage to do what I desire to do or for anything else whatsoever. Although I don't boast on myself at all, I can boast on the power of Him who resides within me, which allows me to be able to walk with kings and never lose the common touch. God's love, grace and power that are with me each and every day of my life represent the source through which any of my existing or occurring needs will be met. Hence I haven't consumed or had the need to consume any alcoholic beverages since the stroke around thirteen years ago, and I don't expect or perceive the need to ever consume alcohol in my lifetime even in the smallest amount. This includes not toasting with champagne at weddings. I will toast with juice or water but never with alcohol. Water is a very good friend to the human body. Now, I realize that there are those who will label me a fanatic in this area even though I and many others who don't drink anymore will disagree with such a label. It is simply a personal choice that I made in that I see no positive purposes for drinking alcohol at all. Yet I see plenty negative (health factors) and tragic situations that have been indirectly or directly attributed to drinking alcohol especially ''excessive/abuse.'' As for me, the negative risks factors outweight any positive aspects that I could hope to reap from drinking and I therefore choose not to drink alcohol. If you happen to feel otherwise, there is no need for any debate whatsoever, just continue drinking to your pleasure, satisfaction, your possible success or to your possible destruction whichever might result.

Now you know or should know beyond a doubt why I stated and do sincerely believe that the stroke in my eye that I endured approximately thirteen years ago represented two major blessings splitting into an abundance of blessings. Had it not been for the stroke, I might have continued with the same lifestyle agenda as described and not considering the damage that I was doing to my health and consequently most likely shortening my life span and quality of life. I am truly glad that God allowed me to see what I have shared with you and gave me the courage to make the choice not to drink alcohol again in my life. Someone reading this book may be encouraged to make the same choice. Again, I can say with thanksgiving in my heart "TO GOD BE THE GLORY."

VIII

The Planted Seed that Contributed to My Narrow Escape Provides Security As Well for My Soul Even in Times of Trouble

Many years ago when I was growing up with my grandparents, each day of my life during that time, they were planting a seed within me through their faith in God that, *"The soul that dwells in God is secure"* probably without them ever knowing the true knowledge and understanding of the 91st Psalm from which the foregoing concept is taken. "The Love Palace" (our home shack) was truly a powerhouse from a spiritual perspective. I hope that you (the reader) will take time out to read and analyze the real power that is given within the 91st Psalm (KJV) and then read the explanation that is given in the *Matthew Henry Commentary*. Having done so myself and looking at my life from childhood, I can now clearly see that God has kept His arms around me even through the worst troubles that I have ever encountered. The seed of faith, believing and trusting in God that Mamma and Papa planted within me allowed me to let my soul dwell in God from childhood, thereby being secure. Education and many years of training and experience together with seeking knowledge of God's Word allows me to better understand the concept that I just mentioned now in the twilight stage of my life. This confirms within my mind that God's love is there for us all the time and if we let Him, He will be with us through any kind of trouble. He loves us unconditionally. In looking back some twenty-eight years ago, I can see so clearly now how God allowed me to suffer and go through a stint of trouble. Although it was seemingly a miracle and definitely a narrow escape for me not to go to prison and destroy all that I had worked so hard to build, I know that God's presence was with me. God saw fit to come to my rescue through my best friend Francis D. Terrell then and now, who happens to be a lawyer and was also a Captain at that time in the U.S. Army Reserve, being promoted years later to Major General and now retired. My reference to him herein as "Frank" instead of the appropriate official military protocol is strictly for the purpose of accentuating our close personal one-on-one private relationship, which will allow you to see the powerful significance of what I am about to share with you.

Let's now continue with how I feel that "Frank" was allowed by God to come to my rescue. There was a time in my life that I felt secure by having a pistol in my car with me. Although I never shot anyone or attempted to harm anyone or had any intentions of shooting anyone, I just felt secure in having it in my car. Obviously during that time I thought I knew God when, in fact, I knew of God but didn't really know God as I later learned who He really is and what He is to me today. One night, instead of leaving the weapon in my car as I normally would have done, the crime-ridden neighborhood that I was in to sort of "hang out" and have a few more drinks, the few drinks that I had already had (coupled with tiredness and stupidity) encouraged me to keep the weapon in my physical possession for my supposed protection. This combination (the weapon and drinks) made me feel just a few feet taller than I really was and of course I felt protected. In case you feel the need to carry an unregistered illegal pistol, I hope by now that you are seeing how stupid I was in feeling such need and come to your senses to alter your thinking now so as to avoid making the mistake that I made. Yes, I was cited for being in the possession of a loaded illegal weapon, which at that time in New York, was almost certain to result in one being convicted and sentenced to two (2) years in jail. Although I had never been in any kind of criminal trouble with the law, I could have gone to jail for probably two years and my whole life would have been destroyed, and all the good things that I had accomplished would have been down the drain. This includes the fact that I would have lost my federal employment and my U.S. Army Reserve status resulting from the jail sentence that I could have received. Even though I was stupid being in possession of an unregistered illegal handgun, God was still with me. Although some of you may not yet see or feel what I am saying about God still being with me, I do hope that you are really getting the point about my being stupid about having the weapon and a few drinks and feeling that I needed the weapon to feel secure/protected. This is especially pertinent if you happen to be one that feels the need to carry in your possession or in your car an unregistered illegal pistol to feel secure and/or protected.

In spite of my being a Civilian Administrator for a military legal unit in the midst of many legal experts, the Lord allowed me to realize that not everyone was willing to make the sacrifice upon their legal careers that might have been required to rescue me from my having done something that they and I too knew was stupidity on my part. Certainly they would be justified in their thinking and actions if this were the way they felt even though several of them discussed several legal avenues of approach that I knew of. When all was said and done, Frank Terrell went quietly about tracking down one of his law school acquaintances to represent me. A day or so before I was required to face the judge, Frank called me and told me that he had finally contacted the lawyer who he had been trying to locate and informed me that the lawyer would contact me by phone. In late afternoon on the day prior to my having to be in court to face the judge, that lawyer called me. Since he and I didn't have time to meet face to face prior to being in court the next day, he was very specific in the areas that he discussed with me and what he instructed me to bring the next morning. This included him letting me know what color coat, suit, shirt and tie that he would be wearing so that I would be able to identify him in the area in the court house where he instructed me to meet him. He also desired that I tell him on the phone what I would be wearing to include suit, shirt and tie which was his way of telling me that I should dress as if I would be going to church in that I was a church organist and he would be able to recognize me. Although I was not completely relieved of the stress that I was obviously under, I felt a great deal of relief. The next morning after he and I met in the court house lobby and took care of our business I went in the part where I was supposed to be and took a seat. Frank was there with me. The lawyer representing me went upstairs to see some of the people that he once worked with in that he once practiced at that location. Of course, while he was gone and we (Frank and I) were observing other cases, I was silently praying under my breath. Shortly before the lawyer representing me returned to where Frank and I were, a sudden joyful feeling came over me making me feel as light as a feather as if a weight of three or four hundred pounds had been lifted from me and the tears began to roll down my face. Although I felt relief from the weight being lifted, I felt choked up because I couldn't holler out verbally, ''Thank You, Lord'' and disturb the court proceedings in progress. In the quietest manner that I could possibly muster with the tears streaming down, I thanked God. Shortly afterwards, the lawyer representing me came back and told me ''everything is going to be all right'' or words to that effect.

When the lawyer and I faced the judge, the judge looked at the information that my lawyer had given to the court which included the information that the lawyer had me compile and the judge made several positive remarks regarding my unblemished record. Not only did the judge treat me justly, he treated me in a humane and compassionate manner with dignity and respect almost as if I were a celebrity. By this time, I knew beyond a doubt that God was in the picture and His Spirit was in all the people (per my belief) who were dealing with me in regards to my specific case. My best friend Frank stood by me during that troublesome time. As the old song goes ''I never shall forget what He's done for me.'' Even now it is very difficult for me to find the words to express clearly my feelings when I walked out of that court house knowing that my life was still intact and my federal employment and military status were both secure, instead of my being put in handcuffs and escorted on to prison for two (2) YEARS.

I can't ever thank God enough for what He allowed Frank to do for me. Although Frank and I do not have any biological connections, I can still say and feel that we are ''blood brothers.'' I truly feel that the 91st Psalm clearly expresses what I have already witnessed and am still witnessing. I have already expressed my feelings about drinking alcohol ''socially'' or otherwise in the previous chapter. Now I will briefly express my feelings about possessing and carrying an unregistered illegal hand gun (pistol). Hopefully what I have to say about carrying a pistol may help someone to be enlightened to the extent that they may realize that carrying such pistol could very well be the cause of their own death or the death of a loved one instead of the pistol being their protection and making them feel secure. Although I do not have any supportive statistics to support my feelings, I truly believe that most people who carry unregistered illegal pistols have not been properly trained in the use and safety of carrying and/or possessing that pistol. This includes disciplinary training. The careless deaths resulting from this, serve, in my opinion, as sufficient proof. Also, innocent bystanders being shot who are caught up in crossfire gun battles with shooters shooting at random in all types of manner and directions except in the direction of the intended target as in a wild, Wild West movie shoot-out also serve as proof that illegal pistol carriers generally have not been properly trained in the use and safety of firing such weapon in that the safety of innocent bystanders would be considered prior to firing. Such shoot-outs in city streets over drug territories, etc. also serve as proof as seemingly described when reported by the media reveal that the shooters in such events have no regards for the safety of innocent bystanders. Persons who are authorized to carry such weapons generally receive extensive training in the use of such weapon and in the safety of protecting the innocent bystanders when the need to initiate gunfire arises. Children and adults being killed in homes by illegal handguns being carelessly or neglectfully stored have caused so many untimely deaths. From a personal perspective God has given me "love power" that is with me at all times which makes me feel secure and protected in any situation. Therefore, I have no need to carry or have in my possession or have in my car an unregistered illegal pistol for any reason whatsoever since the event that I just described.

Without seeming redundant but being very firm in my spiritual conviction, God's "love-power" and His Word are more powerful and more protective of me and my safety needs than any caliber of pistol that has been made. Therefore it seems to me that people who have the need for illegal handguns are concerned about the body and not their soul. They don't seem to realize that the body one day will go back to the dust in that the "human body is divinely designed dirt" (as my friend Pastor R. L. Mickens states). He further indicates that "the deteriorating body will one day become inadequate to house the soul which will go back to the Creator." God is my refuge and my soul dwells in Him making my soul secure. I called upon Him and He answered me; He was with me in trouble; He delivered me and He has honored me in allowing me to be His vessel to pen "His book" which is the first book that He allowed me to pen already referenced herein. I do believe that it will prove to be helpful to possibly hundreds of thousands and maybe millions of people as time goes on.

Some of you can see clearly that I was blessed by God not having to go to jail and lose everything that I had strived for up to that point. However, in my desire to be consistent or in sync with the title of this book, I am sure you have not seen the complete blessing(s) from God *via the love palace* through Mamma and Papa for my having had to go through the trouble that I did with the unregistered illegal pistol. I haven't yet told you. In growing up, I heard Mamma and Papa clearly warn their other older children about carrying any type of weapon (knives mostly because pistols weren't too accessible) for protection or to cause harm to others. During that time in the South, it was the social outlet of many African Americans or Negroes as they were called then to go to ''juke joints'' and be packing some type of weapon other than a pistol so as to let those, who thought they were bad know that you were just as bad as they were. ''Juke Joints'' were called such because a ''jukebox'' sometimes called a ''picalo'' provided the music. You had to put money in the jukebox and then select the record(s) you wanted it to play. Twenty-five cents during that time was a considerable amount of money especially for those whose total income was from farming and sharecropping at that. The jukebox would play five records and sometimes a bonus record for twenty-five cents. Often the clientele who went there had an attitude already, just waiting for someone to bump into them while dancing or step on their foot to or from the jukebox or anything to start a negative confrontation. Such would thus escalate to a fight where eventually knives would be pulled and someone would be badly hurt or killed. The type of fight was a determining factor as to how much prolonged enjoyable conversation was derived from that social evening about the fight for the next day's major news (usually Saturday or Sunday on church ground). Keep in mind if it was just a good old fist fight resulting in black eyes and bloody noses, it would result in great enjoyable and laughable news the next day. The violent reputation of some places was much worse than it was for others in that some were "not so bad," some were "bad" and some were "hell holes." It seemed that those which were called "tea rooms", had the worst reputation for violence. If my memory and understanding serves me right "tea" was the code word used in the South at that time for illegally sold alcoholic beverages including illegally made moonshine from a whiskey still—corn whiskey being available at juke joints. In the eyes of Mamma and Papa and the other church elders, all of such places were labeled the "devil's ground." Mamma and Papa were always telling their children if you needed a knife or some other weapon for protection in the place that they were going, they were going to the wrong place. I often heard Mamma and Papa (mostly Mamma) warn them that God was all the protection that they needed and that they should stay out of the devil's places. They told the children if you go looking for trouble, you will find it. In such dialogues with Mamma especially, the children wanted her to know that they weren't afraid of so and so person 'cause they could have a knife too. They missed the "love" point that Mamma was trying to get across to them. What they didn't understand at that time is that Mamma was not concerned as to whether they could or would be the winner in such fight, she didn't want them hurt at all in being in such fight because of her love for them.

Live your life so that God can fight any battle that you may encounter and trust in God, not in a knife, was what she stressed to them. Some people enjoyed their celebrity status of being viewed as the meanest of mean and a reputation of having cut up and killed or maimed so many persons in knife fights causing people in general to be afraid of them. This was their crowning success in life for such person as sad as it may seem. When we would hear about one of the real mean persons "knife fighters" being cut up, shot or killed, it was unspoken but seemingly general consensus that such person got what he/she deserved. By the time that I became a teenager and was going out, Mamma was the one who would reiterate to me what she had told those before me. So you see I had a double dose of her counseling and warnings. Yet she made it clear to all of us that she had put us in the hands of the Lord. Each and every day we were in her prayers and Papa's too, while he was living. Also, Mamma and Papa were not blind to the racial conditions at that time; their positive attitude and faith in God led them to believe that "love conquers all" and time would take care of that too. While such belief may be powerful and to some degree accurate (time-wise), it is also important to learn and know the system; know how and be willing to make the necessary sacrifice(s) to put forth the required efforts to force the system to do what the system advocates.

Years later when I had long left NC living in New York and got into the trouble previously described a few years after Mamma had gone home to be with the Lord, I had, in a moment of stupidity, strayed away from the basic training that she had embedded within me but yet through the seed of faith and trusting in God that she had planted within me was still with me. After the Lord saw me through the trouble, I started thinking, "Suppose through a confrontation while under the influence of just a couple of drinks of alcohol I might have shot someone and possibly killed them what a mess my life would still be in today if I were still among the living." So you see now the connection with the seed planted within me *via the love palace* and God being with me through the trouble described, not only am I blessed by God in that such has not nor will it ever happen again to me because I learned my lesson, it is also a blessing for me to be able to share with so many others through this book the lesson that I learned through my serious mistake and poor judgment. I truly believe that there are others who will read this book and be blessed by taking heed in seeing how God blessed me and it will be a preventive measure with them not to get into such trouble. Some parents who read this book will be blessed as well by escaping broken hearts in that one or more of their children will very possibly avoid an early grave or a life in jail by simply being encouraged to learn from what is being revealed herein and be blessed by God.

Just before bringing this chapter to a close, I desire to share a few perceptions and suggestions to those who are currently incarcerated for a few years, many years or a lifetime, some of which started from the same mistake that I made but escalated to a more serious level in that someone may have been seriously harmed or killed (intentionally or unintentionally) by one's mistake from poor judgment. I perceive that there are those incarcerated who have received the full benefit of the law that are justly paying the price for the crime that they committed who deserve to be in a controlled society for their safety and for the safety of others. Yet I also perceive and believe that there are many people in jail today and may have been in there for years who are innocent of what they are charged with and been convicted therefor. I suggest to the lifers that I perceive and believe that your life, even in a controlled society can still bear some good fruits by developing a personal relationship with God if you haven't already done so. Through this process, I truly perceive and believe that you will be led to develop a very positive attitude and spirit to allow the good yet in your life to be shared with your environmental neighbors in a positive manner within a controlled society, and with those still on the outside as a preventive measure so as to encourage them to make the same attitude adjustment **now** that you have made while they have time to do so to avoid coming to live with you and others in a controlled society. In the interim, never give up hope, especially once you have established a personal relationship with God in that your faith in God initiates the neverending hope process.

I perceive that many of you were brought up within the same scenario as I. Even while your parents or grandparents were experiencing the worst of economic conditions, yet you were probably taught to do the right thing and put God in the forefront of your life. Instead, you probably strayed away from your childhood teaching. Even so, I still perceive that many of you were wrongly convicted and sentenced due to the lack of money to provide the best legal representation. Hence, the lack of money would be among the major contributing causes for your current situation, which represents a major flaw within our judicial system. Now to those who **know** that you have been wrongly convicted and sentenced and are totally **innocent,** may I again suggest that you create a personal relationship with God if you haven't already done so. I believe that such will lead you to develop a more spiritual positive thinking foundation of faith and hope. In doing so, it is also perceived and believed that you will never give up hope and trust while you continue to learn the judicial system while being incarcerated within the judicial system that convicted you through miscarriage of justice. This will allow you to learn how to better use that same judicial system while continuing praying and working toward freedom within the process that this same judicial system provides. Instead of being angry with America as some of you may be, may I suggest that you render praise to God being thankful in that America is among the few nations in the world where injustice can eventually be overturned through the current Constitutional process that was designed for justice to prevail. I realize that some of you being of color may be feeling ready to pounce upon me. Hold it just a moment before you jump on me indicating that "the Constitution did not have blacks (slaves) in mind in that they were property" which is true per my understanding. However, considering my perception that the majority of the framers of the Constitution had no desire whatsoever for racial equality for blacks (slaves) during that time frame, imagine what the legal plight of blacks (slaves) might have been even today had the framers of the Constitution written in so as to provide for inequality for blacks (slaves) and had written the Constitution differently than they did so as to permanently exclude blacks (slaves) from ever being entitled to receive the benefits that the Constitution provides for its white citizens.

It is perceived that justice and equality for the same group mentioned would still be delayed many years more than they have already been delayed today. In my thinking, man does not have the capability to see far enough into the future and plan so as to compete with or alter God's plans. One important point for us to remember is that while the hands on the clock of justice may move very slowly, they move. Although you may or may not feel as I do, I believe that God's power supersedes the power of any legislative law or body of lawmakers. Therefore, I say to all of you, God can use His power for any cause through others, regardless to what their specific religious faiths may or may not be, to bring about the results that He desires (including seemingly miracles to man). Per my belief, embedded within a personal relationship with God is unlimited power in the power of positive thinking. Through the power of your personal relationship with God, your positive attitude and actions can make a significant contribution in bringing about perceived needed adjustments and changes to our judicial system that could possibly lead to your freedom in a miraculous manner. Keep in mind that even while incarcerated, you can still reside within the habitat of God, which provides security for your soul per my belief and further confirmed within me through my narrow escape.

IX

My Response to Two Important Questions Relative to the Title and Me

So often we look at others focusing upon a particular area in a manner so as to produce the vision results that we have already formed within our mind and heart, as opposed to having an open mind and heart and be accepting of what is truth. It is not easy for many of us to look within ourselves to see and accept the truth. General observation seems to reveal that it is rather easy for most of us to scrutinize others with a fine tooth comb but when we scrutinize ourselves we utilize the greatest degree of flexibility in our thought process. The application of this would seem to be more pertinent relative to "believers" than "non-believers" in that we can or should be able to better understand why "non-believers" would not desire to accept the truth about themselves. Yet, in the same vein of thinking, we should be able to unequivocally expect "believers" to be honest and sincere with self first and foremost. In my living and witnessing what the title of this book represents, it is my desire to share with you the simple truth that forms the foundation upon which my "care-rack-ter" (as my grandfather Amos would say) and my thought process were built upon or formed. This book is much more than being just about me. It represents life in that many older or younger than I will be able to identify with the lives and events indicated herein and, at the same time, it is representative of life that many older or younger have no concept of the life whatsoever as that indicated herein. To give you an even clearer view of the meaning of the title as it relates to me, I have divided it into two parts, as you will notice below. Hopefully, what is already stated herein combined with my response to the two questions below will provide an in-depth view and understanding of what the title of this book really represents. Further, it is my hope and belief that it will have a great positive impact upon many regarding the importance and power of God's love, our love for one another, "care-rack-ter" building, the power of positive thinking, faith and trusting in God.

1. **Why "Blessings Beyond View" as opposed to just "blessings"?** Most, if not all of us, realize that we are blessed daily by waking up daily and being among the living. Also, there are so many blessings that happen to us daily that we seldom take the time out to recognize them as blessings in that we take so much for granted being human. When certain things happen to us during a day or week such as being spared from a tragedy or accident or getting to the hospital in time to treat an illness when, in fact, had we been a couple of hours or an hour later, we would have gone on to our eternal rest. These are special blessings but blessings that we recognize rather quickly. On the other side of the coin, so to speak, there are blessings that it takes many years of life, education, training and experience before we are able to recognize them as blessings, which I categorize as "blessings beyond view."

Two good examples of what I am saying are (1) my mother not being able or willing to keep me as a baby with her at all costs or consequences, seems to me now a multitude of "blessings beyond view" in that I wouldn't have experienced the training and spiritual seed planting that I received with Mamma and Papa, and therefore couldn't have written this particular book even though I might have been able to write a different book.

Considering all the variables that I can think of, I have to conclude my being with Mamma and Papa as indeed a "blessing beyond view" and not just another blessing. Yet it took many years before I could arrive at this reality. Certainly, had I bonded with my mother as a baby to the extent that once I became aware of my surroundings and my mother was the first person that I knew and knew her as my mother, my preference would have undoubtedly been to be with my mother. It didn't happen that way in that my grandmother (Mamma) was the first person that I bonded with that I knew as Mamma. She was the central figure of focus within the family in that she was the chief operations officer, so to speak. Out of the goodness and kindness of Mamma's heart, she taught me about the person who was my mother so I would be able to know my real mother. She also taught me that I was supposed to love my mother. Hence, I would be able to develop a "love bond" with my mother when she came to visit once or twice a year. Resulting from Mamma's teachings, I developed a "love bond" with my mother in that I thought she was special and also rich because of the material things (clothes, etc.) that she brought to me and sent to me. I was in for a rude awakening probably almost a teenager when I discovered that my mother was not rich. Further, I was in for a real shocker when I discovered even a few years later that our family, from a financial perspective, was poor. Mamma's wisdom and teachings were such that instead of our feeling that we were poor, we sincerely thought that our family was among the well to do financially and otherwise. This was manifested even in our personal care of ourselves, concern for the way our clothes looked when we were in public, dignity in our walk and our conscientiousness when speaking correctly, especially in public. Someone, family or non-family, speaking incorrectly at church would be a laughing conversational topic when we came home.

Being in a home environment that nurtured the seed "I am somebody" planted by Mamma and Papa reflects tremendously upon their wisdom and spirituality. Getting back to "love bonding" Mamma especially knew how important it would be in years to come for my biological mother and me to have some "love bonding." Accordingly, Mamma reached out and took my mother under her wing to treat her as one of her daughters and counseled her as to the responsibilities of being a real mother and providing the type of guidance that would motivate my mother to conduct her life in a manner that I wouldn't be ashamed to call her Mother when I grew up. This was indeed a "blessing beyond view." Just suppose my grandmother (Mamma) had not liked my mother or didn't want my mother around me when I was growing up? My life and my mother's life would probably have been much different in that we wouldn't have any "love bonding" at all as Mother and Son. Instead of being as close as we are today, we could have been miles apart with little or no communication between us had it not been for Mamma's love and wisdom. So you see what Mamma did for me and for my biological mother by being obedient to God's Will allowed my mother and me to be blessed through the years. Yes, this was a real "blessing beyond view" for my mother and me. Considering how God has allowed my mother to be a blessing to so many others through her accomplishments in her walk with God after she came to know God and what He has also allowed me to do as well, especially as a writer, we have both been tremendously blessed by God. It all goes back to my grandmother (Mamma) being obedient to the Will of God. In being obedient, Mamma allowed God to direct her pathway during the first several months of my life when I was from "pillow to post" without being in a stable home environment until the Lord directed Mamma and Papa to take me in. This whole scenario is more than just a blessing, it is representative of "blessings beyond view" in that I wasn't able to see the whole "big picture" until God allowed me to see it years after I was grown and a much older man.

(2) Even though my mother felt that she couldn't work and properly take care of me as a baby and seemingly felt it best for my father's brother Henry and his wife Malverda to adopt me, my father Johnny wouldn't agree to it. Yes, I am confident that his reason(s) were very selfish in that even though he didn't have a pot to boil water in, he wouldn't agree to a plan that seemed best for my care and welfare at that time. Further, he didn't have any means to really support his decision in that I see no evidence from others that he was trying to prepare for my having a home and being taken care of during that time. Yet he still wouldn't agree for his brother Henry and his wife Malverda to adopt me. This too, in my opinion, developed into many "blessings beyond view." I don't want to seem as if I am focusing upon my father's wisdom or praising him for his decision because his decision wouldn't seem, from a human perspective per my view, to be in my best interest at all at that time. Yet I don't want to bash him for his decision in that he may have been unaware that he was being led by the spirit not to sign for my adoption. Although his decision may seem selfish to the human mindset in that he didn't seemingly show any concern for my health and welfare since he hadn't made any significant contributions toward my care nor was he making any current plans to take care of me, as I can see, he was obedient to what we can now see as "God's Will" by not signing for me to be adopted by his brother Henry and his wife Malverda. God is to be praised. Yet I am thankful to my father for not signing for me to be adopted in that many men in his position might have considered it a blessing to be able to get free of the responsibility of raising a child, especially if they felt that the child would be in good family care as he knew or felt that his brother Henry would care for me. My perception of my father's thinking relative to his brother Henry and Malverda adopting me is that—you can keep my son, feed him, do all the things required to rear a child but I can't give up "titleship" so to speak. It would appear that neither my father, my mother nor

my father's brother Henry and his wife Malverda, could see that God had different plans for me than they had because God knew what the future would be and they didn't, per my belief. Had I been adopted by Henry and Malverda, I could have perished along with them or I could have been left "homeless" for the second time in the almost two years of my life and may have ended up in an orphanage when the lives of Henry and Malverda were taken just two months prior to my second birthday.

During the short time while my mother and Henry were trying to catch up with my father Johnny to get him to sign for adoption, I was staying with Henry and Malverda. That didn't last long because Malverda was not wholeheartedly embracing this whole concept as I am informed. Malverda probably knew Henry's agenda and she had a private counseling session with my mother, as I am told by my mother. In a moment, I will share the results of that counseling session. While Henry loved me dearly as I am told, his major agenda might have been to tie his wife Malverda down with the main chore of raising me to keep her home, reducing her freedom outside of their home. I can understand Malverda's feelings of not wanting to be tied down with the responsibility of raising somebody's child when she knew that both the mother and father were alive and healthy at that time as far as she knew. I can also respect the counseling that my mother has told me that Malverda gave to her in that my mother should take me out to the "Riddicks" (disregarding what Mother's emotions might be) and let them raise me in that they had plenty of food and enough people in the home to properly take care of me and give me a good home.

Under conditions that we generally perceive as normal, such advice to a mother would generally be considered very bad advice in that a mother should, under the worst scenario of conditions, cling to her child as many of you would agree. Although Malverda's thinking was probably geared more to my father being forced to contribute to my being cared for by Mamma and Papa, I am confident that she didn't realize that her counseling would coincide with God's overall plans for me. Therefore, Malverda and her bad advice together with my mother following and executing Malvarda's bad advice all were, unknowingly to them, allowed by God to be included in the umbrella of His plans for me that became "blessings beyond view" as per my belief. While none of us is qualified to predict what the future might have been for me, those of us who are "believers" can truly see God's Divine Intervention in the given scenario. Therefore, I can only see that God allowing Mamma and Papa to step in when they did was in God's plans that truly became "blessings beyond view" for which I am eternally grateful.

2. **How did my childhood home (shack) develop into a "love palace" per my view?** This question, in the eyes of many readers, might seem rather simple and for others it may seem rather complex. My having witnessed and experienced love and pain in my life allows me to view this question from a simple viewpoint as well as from a viewpoint of complexity. Since it took me many years after becoming an adult and being on my own to really understand the reality of my childhood home (shack) being indeed a "love palace" notwithstanding the many difficulties that were encountered daily during my childhood, it might be best if we start with the viewpoint of complexity. In growing up as a child, it was not easy to look at some of the nicer houses, mostly owned by whites, and not wish that we could live in a house like they had. It wasn't something that I, as a child would speak out and say; it was just merely in my mind. In fact, it would be rather dangerous for me to speak out my thoughts about such in the presence of Mamma. I was taught to appreciate what we had and not to envy what others had regardless as to whether they were white folk or black folk. This concept, of course, came from one of the Ten Commandments in the Bible. During that time, if something was in the Bible and

the general interpretation or misinterpretation was that we shouldn't do it, it wasn't wise for us to do it around Mamma. Even if something from the Bible was seemingly misinterpreted, as was the case in some instances, it still wasn't wise for children or even teenagers to speak out with an opinion that seemed in conflict with the interpretation of the older respected religious leaders. Prayer, trusting in God and hard work seemed to be viewed as the general solution to desiring material items even basic necessities for living, etc. Although as a youngster I was aware of racial discrimination and some Jim Crow laws, I wasn't fully knowledgeable or understanding at that time of the side effects of such that resulted in economic depravity including economic injustice for most blacks, even those who thought that they were in the category of well-to-do. Mamma knew that there was injustice even at harvest time when the white man would take our cotton and tobacco to the market to be sold. She knew that we didn't get fair treatment in that being share-croppers (or working on half basis so to speak) we were being robbed in a manner that we didn't have the necessary resources (educational know-how, equipment, up-front money and political power) to do anything about it. Therefore, we had to take the "trusted" white man's word when he brought back the money from the cotton gin or tobacco market. It was **always,** as I remember, a sad story about the "prices being down" when the money was brought back. As a little boy, I remember Mamma's reaction at times to such after she was alone and supposedly talking to herself, "Lawd, have mercy; how long O Lawd, how long?" This would sometimes be followed by a hymn that she would start singing the chorus, "Love lifted me; love lifted me; when nothing else could help, love lifted me."

In some instances, she didn't realize that I was in her presence. When she did realize it, she would usually tell me to go and do some chore such as "pick up some chips from the woodpile to start the fire in the cook stove the next day or go to the well and get some water'' in that there was **always** some chore to be done at any hour of the day. It didn't take long for me to gain some smarts by being far enough from her so as to seem that I couldn't hear her when she was talking to herself but close enough so she could see where I was located so that she wouldn't give me any work to do. Sometimes this worked and sometimes it didn't in that she would still give me some work to do. She didn't want me out of her sight. The more that I started learning her assorted moods and conducted myself accordingly to get on her good side such as playing with my wagon but playing hard and sweating as if my playing hard was some form of working hard, she would look at me and it seemed that all of her parental love would come tumbling down. She would say to me, ''Come outa that yard boy and stop playing so hard; sit down on that porch and rest yoself fo you have a heat stroke.'' She would then find some goodie to give me, a biscuit with pear or apple preserve, a piece of candy that she would have saved in her pocketbook, a piece of souse (hog head cheese) or something to eat to show her love for me. Also, when others were not around and it was just Mamma and me, depending upon her mood, I felt safe to ask her questions that I wouldn't dare to ask her when anyone else would be around, especially when I knew it was something that I knew she wanted to hear and talk about. She would start talking up a storm. Sometimes she would start talking and go far beyond the answer, providing additional information that I didn't expect. When she did this, I dared not repeat such information or bring it back up to her as she had given it; I would put it in my head and keep it to myself knowing that she hadn't realized just how much confidential ''grown folk'' information that she had given me accidentally. This was one of the ways that so much information about her son Henry was given to me by her.

Looking back now, I can easily see that even though she loved all of her children, among her sons, Henry held a special place in her heart in that he wasn't "wild" and was family oriented (homebody) as his father O'Hara. Years later, such information allowed me to realize just how smart Mamma really was without her having obtained a significant amount of academic education.

Everybody in the household seemingly loved me to the extent that everybody wanted to boss me around especially if Mamma and Papa weren't around. Instead of my rebelling against them, I learned how to get on the good side of all of them to the extent that they were competing with one another to make me care more for one than I did the other. I loved all of them as my sisters and brothers especially those that were still home (Thelma, Ruby, Viola and Clyde) and I didn't want to show any partiality even though everybody knew that Thelma owned the hearts of us all. Even so, God endowed me with assorted talents that, as a child, I was able to capture their attention and love in some way or other.

Thelma, Ruby, Viola and I would be singing around the house and they loved me singing tenor. Also, I could mark any of the people who were in church, including their praying, singing out of tune, or shouting, especially some woman who would carefully select her time to shout and fall out, so to speak, when a certain man that she liked would be near so she could fall into his arms. Yes, this often resulted in mixed opinions among the church elders and leaders within their spiritual thinking process in that some would defend the shouting woman's spirituality while others would question the woman's motive, especially if any type of frequency or pattern appeared evident. Being a child, I would sometimes eavesdrop to hear "grown folk's" conversation when we would come home from church and hear them talking about the shouting event. It was indicated that the wife of one such husband who would catch a falling or fainting shouting woman in his arms told her husband when they arrived home from church, "Listen, lemme tell you supum, if the Lawd don't catch Sis. (woman's name) when she gits so happy and start dat ol put-on-mess uh falling, you better not catch huh any mo either.'' Of course this generated much laughter among the ''grown folk'' as I would be eavesdropping.

In looking back during those childhood days, there were so many complexities/hardships associated with daily living that were not seemingly viewed as such at that time. I guess the major reason for this was that such a lifestyle was the only life that we had known. It was the same for other neighboring families close by or some distance away on farms. Yet there was a great degree of happiness and love within the family. Gaining a reputation within the family and neighborhood as being a ''hard working'' individual was an honor and served as motivation to almost cause an individual with such reputation to work himself/herself to death. Some did just that and at their funeral it would be publicly expressed in reflections or in the obituary that the deceased was a ''hard working'' individual. It was very difficult to maintain that reputation almost twenty-four hours a day, seven days a week and 365 days a year. A couple of seemingly requirements were that one had to be the ''first out of bed'' in the morning and the ''last out of the field or barnyard'' at night. If one was seen just a few times momentarily sitting down resting while others were up working, the ''hard working'' reputation would be blown and replaced with ''I declare I jes don't know what happened to so and so who use to be a 'hard working' (man, woman, boy or girl); now dey jes as 'lazy as sin.' '' Although Mamma wasn't blind to racial hatred, she and Papa always taught and advocated ''love even for your enemies.'' She would refer to some known racist that happened to be the topic at the moment as ''that old so-and-so trash ain't nothing but trouble; don't pay em any tention; jes love em and gwone bout cha business.''

In the fall of 1954 or close to spring 1955, a hurricane/tornado (Hazel) hit Wake County, NC and I was driving the school bus. I had never been in such storm before. The wind was so strong that it seemed like it almost turned the bus over while I was stopped to let one student off the bus. When the child got off the bus, the wind picked the child up and just lifted the child through the cornfield and frightened me and the other students unbelievably. I saw the student arrive at home and I was afraid to let any other students get off. Even though I was not in an area that I needed what we called "bull gear" the extra pulling gear for a big load, I put the bus in that gear and just crawled along until the storm was over and then I let the children out. Although "Hazel" tore up many homes and barns, when I arrived home with the bus, our new cinderblock house (which wasn't finished) or our (shack) didn't suffer any damage at all except lots of rain. To us, that was a miracle and or an act of God that even though the storm came through our area, we didn't suffer any damage.

During that time, the church and school being the center of focus, there seemed to be some big event coming up in either the church or the school to look forward to. This embodied a lot of love, joy and happiness. Being as economically deprived (poor) as we were which took me years to find out, if we needed something, some way or somehow a way would be made to get it. Man oh man was it a good feeling to show off a new item of apparel at church or school. Now from a viewpoint of simplicity in looking back, it becomes rather simple in that everything associated with our entire lifestyle within the home was built upon a strong spiritual foundation in that the most important factor in Mamma and Papa's mindset was living a life and doing things in a manner that they felt would be pleasing in God's sight. This included rigidly training the children to do likewise even if Mamma especially had to beat the daylight out of us to insure that the rod was not being spared and that God was pleased. "Do something for the Lawd" was constantly instilled within us by Mamma and Papa. On every Sunday morning when the table was full of hot fried chicken, fish, country streak-o-lean (now slab bacon), fried rabbit or squirrel, sizzling hot biscuits, hot coffee for adults and lemonade for smaller children and the good-smelling scent from all that food would be making us so hungry and yet we had to go through the long drawn out scenario of saying Bible verses and Papa praying a very long emotional prayer. It took me years to really understand that this whole process was very simple in that it was spiritual love, appreciation, thanksgiving to God and obedience to the Will of God by Mamma and Papa. I can easily see now that Mamma and Papa felt that they were training us as children in the way that we should go through life and when we would grow older, we would not depart from such training.

When I think about all the burdens that Mamma and Papa had to bear and yet have somewhere to lay out heads and a table full of food and plenty in the smoke house under the sharecropping living conditions that we were living under, it was enough to arouse love and joyful feelings for one another while feeling blessed by God for the provision of simple basics that would be viewed as luxury by some others, during that time. It took years for me to understand fully the love-based foundation that Mamma and Papa established through their love for God, one another, us (their children) and for their fellowman. When we would be planting and harvesting food, canning food in the summer (spare time), raising hogs and taking corn to the mill to get corn meal and exchange some for flour, Mamma and Papa often stated the concept of having more than we needed so as to be able to share with some other family who might have fallen on hard times. This simple concept was all about love. Hate, especially when referring to individuals, was not allowed to be stated or we would risk getting a whipping. Love was instilled within us by Mamma and Papa. While it still remains a dark part of America's history today the way America (legally) allowed its citizens of color to be intentionally mistreated, I can clearly look back at my childhood days now and almost tremble at the power of love that Mamma and Papa demonstrated during that time, especially under the intentionally imposed hardship economic conditions that we were experiencing as a black family in Southern America. In reality, it was the same in the North, just a different form, per my opinion. While I am sure that Mamma or Papa were not biblical scholars, it was the biblically based love power that they both believed in, practiced and instilled within their children, even if by force, that ultimately proved to me to be the key to my being able to view our home (shack) as a "love palace." While I emphatically do not condone the intentionally imposed racial discrimination and economic hardships upon the poor (especially blacks) at that time, it is that same love power that was instilled within me by Mamma and Papa that allows me not to be angry or ashamed of where I came from yesterday and yet be appreciative of where I am today. I can convincingly say that it is my uncompromising view that "hate" destroys and "love" heals. Resulting from the foundation of "love" that Mamma and Papa laid for us through their Christian beliefs, our house, notwithstanding the physical eyesore that it presented, was indeed a house of royalty which made it a "palace" ultimately being viewed through my eyes as the "Love Palace." This, together with my Christian beliefs allows me to know and feel that I am of royalty without a doubt. Therefore, looking back from what the Lord brought me through and where He brought me from, I view the sky as being the limit for my descendants in that nothing can stand in the way of their success but they, themselves. Further, in spite of America's shortcomings in that many of its citizens have yet to enjoy total equality that is expressed within the U.S. Constitution), I still thank God that I am an American citizen who feels honored to have been privileged to serve my country, knowing that the wheels of justice are still turning, I can therefore say with pride, distinction and love, "God Bless America."

X
My Perceptions of This Book Being Helpful to Many People

I truly believe that the soul of those reading this book will be touched in some way, causing the readers to look deep within themselves to see and positively identify the truth therein. In order for the readers of this book to clearly understand how I arrived at my perceptions, my imagination concludes that I should let the readers know how writing this book has been a benefit to me even though jerking my emotions from one extreme to another. In symbolic language, my emotions have been on a "rollercoaster" experience. I wrote mostly with a towel around my neck in that tears would be flowing resulting from joy, pain, sadness and hilarious comical situations, many of which I personally relived. Yes there was some anxiety especially about my uncle Henry and Malverda's untimely deaths, and how the deviation from standards, which included the lack of a proper and thorough investigation to determine the truth as to whom really killed whom appeared to be intentionally allowed by officials in the city of Raleigh and state of North Carolina, in my opinion. Although it is understood that justice as we know justice to be was denied blacks especially in the South during the time frame in question, justice denied at any time to American citizens at any judicial level of government under the U.S. Constitution and allowed to exist by the officials who have sworn to uphold and enforce the laws at that level of government is injustice to such citizens. Further, it would appear that the judicial level of government responsible for the actions of such officials would be legally accountable for the actions/inaction of such officials until action(s) for redress would be initiated, concluded regardless to lapse of time and justice prevailed. Yet I dare not permit my stated anxiety to linger within my heart because I know that the Spirit of God and anxiety cannot co-exist within my heart. It is my belief that any degree of anxiety within me would make my temple (body) unclean. Realizing this and knowing that the Spirit of God would not dwell within an unclean temple, it was, is and will always be my desire to rebuke and remove the author of confusion and anxiety from within me so that the Spirit of God may dwell within me. I would then be able to deal with the issues that created my previous anxiety in a Godly manner.

Looking back over some events in my life helped me to better understand and appreciate the firm foundation upon which my life is built in that it is strong enough to support any level of heights that I might attain in this life without crumbling. Further, looking back also helped me to get a clearer view of the present and see just some of what is needed now for a brighter tomorrow. In elaborating on my perceptions, the following examples might illuminate my viewpoint.

America: Notwithstanding my having been born in poverty, grew up in poverty thinking that our family was among the "well-to-do" while being treated as a second class citizen. I was yet taught in the home, church, the former three-room St. Matthew Elementary School and the former DuBois High School, Wake Forest, NC to love, respect myself and others and be proud to be an American. In spite of America's many imperfections, the love-seed for my country that was planted within me many years ago still remains within my heart. I remember a large picture of Abraham Lincoln being in the three-room elementary school. By the way, after Miss Lane left, that room wasn't used anymore which meant that only two classrooms were being used for seven grades. I might be a little redundant in stating that there were no labels such as "learning disabled, special ed." at that time to my knowledge at least in referenced school. The teacher's ruler was used as the teacher's helper if a student didn't grasp what was being taught. While that corporal punishment may have appeared to be of great help more than sixty-plus years ago in many Southern area schools, it would probably create havoc in our society today even if it were legal to do so.

I vaguely recall a few students being helped by the ruler (licks in hand) for not being able to learn and recite the "Star Spangled Banner" (National Anthem) and "Pledge of Allegiance" when we were learning such in school. While these two items are very important parts of the foundation and infrastructure upon which America was built and stands that seems to be fading away, we must seek to regenerate love and respect for America in these areas. I have often observed when the National Anthem is being played and sung at public events, many (including educators) high school and college students don't know the words. Also, they don't know or don't desire to show common courtesy and respect by at least standing up and still (when physically able to do so), with right hand over heart (providing they have two hands) and refrain from talking, eating, chewing gum or smoking until the Anthem is completed. It is especially notable to me to see professionals who are city, state and federal officials and multimillionaire athletes enjoying the economic fruits of this great nation and yet show such little, if any, respect for the freedoms and opportunities that are symbolically represented by the playing and singing of the National Anthem. It might be helpful from a military perspective to increase the training emphasis in these two areas to include committing them to memory during basic combat training. Notwithstanding the fact that I am a retired Sergeant Major, looking from whence I came from childhood (sharecropping) and many obstacles (within the Army) that

I endured to reach that plateau, I still personally consider it an honor and privilege to wear the military uniform even though I was originally drafted. Accordingly, I feel that it should be worn with pride, dignity and honor. America is viewed as the "land of the free and the home of the brave." I am not convinced that Americans, in general, realize that "freedom is not free." I feel that there is a "human service" price tag associated with maintaining and defending the freedoms that America provides. While most benefit from such freedoms being defended and maintained, only a small percentage of America's total population pay the "human service" tab, in my opinion, which often requires the supreme human sacrifice through such service. It would seem to be more equitable if every able-bodied individual were required to pay his/her fair share of the "human service" tab to defend and maintain these freedoms. The "draft" (two-year military service requirement) with many considered adjustments from the previous draft might be one route to be examined to accomplish this. While it is realized that some segments of our society (including some religious groups) conscientiously object to being combat-trained to serve in the military, surely there are other areas of service that could be considered wherein members of such groups/organizations could be required to serve for two years in contributing "human service" toward the price tag of preserving the freedoms that America provides.

It takes a good deal of non-combat service support to house, clothe, feed, train and field a combat force. It is reasonable to perceive that the more of America's population from all walks of life contribute "human service" to preserve and protect America's freedoms, the more "thought process" could be expected to be given to the conditions and circumstances under which our elected officials would agree to dispatching our Armed Forces personnel into "harm's way." While many within America in my opinion feel that it is important to maintain a well-trained and disciplined military force and use such force as necessary to defend America's freedoms, they also desire that our elected officials be fully accountable to use every caution within our Constitutional "check and balance" system to insure that our forces are dispatched into "harm's way" as previously indicated and not for what might appear to many for the seemingly hidden economic and/or political benefit of just a few with special interests agenda. Further, in my opinion, if America is to remain a strong world power, those among us who love and cherish America must stand up to the forces outside and within America whose agenda is clearly to destroy America. This is not to be misinterpreted to mean that one has to be totally committed to only one political party's ideology in order to love and cherish America as some individuals seem to feel. There are fanatics in all walks of life. I don't believe that there is any government within the world that is without imperfections. The citizens of this great nation (America) being able to make continuous corrections, improvements and adjustments over the years of its existence, even though rather slow in some instances, as mandated by the people for the people makes America's form of government great. It is clear to me that there are forces within and outside of America who are doing all they can to totally destroy the foundation upon which America was built, per my belief and observations. It is very clear that there are those who are bent on removing the word "God" from all pillars of America's foundation while concurrently trying to destroy the government, the home family structure through steadily trying to destroy the marriage institution, the economy, the Christian church, the school and the military. All of these areas, in my opinion serve as support structures upon which this nation was founded giving birth to the Constitution.

I truly believe that one possible "thought process" of any enemy trying to destroy a more powerful foe is to randomly but yet systematically chip away at the foe's foundation of strength.

Such enemy's ideology is that once the foundation loses its stability, it will crumble and everything that is built upon that foundation crumbles as well especially political, economic and military power. The major key source of strength within the foundation upon which America was built, in my opinion, is the intended presence of the Spirit of God found in the Godly principles embedded in the Constitution. America's foundation has been tested since its birth over and over through several wars and has proven to be one of the strongest foundations within the world in spite of its imperfections, some of which are being slowly addressed. Yet, we can still see some of the areas mentioned previously being steadily weakened. In my thinking, America's enemies are well aware of this and are continuously trying to take the Spirit of God, Godly principles and the name "God" out of every major area of government which includes courts, schools and even in the military. While America itself has fallen short of living up to many of the Godly principles upon which it was built, American citizens must still recognize the fact that the design of the system allows for continuous improvements. Although improvements in some of the areas, where America has fallen short have been too slow and too few over the last 200 plus years, some improvements in these areas have and are being made. While many others and I may not be satisfied with the rate of progress in some areas, we cannot deny the fact that some improvements have been made. It is my hope that American citizens who allow themselves to be fooled by the outside enemy into helping the enemy to destroy our way of life will wise up and see the enemy for what the enemy really is to you. Such enemy is not your friend as they pretend. Instead they are your enemy who will destroy you along with trying to destroy America. In my opinion, any time your enemies can take a few areas of your dissatisfactions and enlist your assistance by fooling you to believe that they are your friends and make you believe that they are helping you to resolve your dissatisfactions while destroying the entire process that you benefit from should be sufficient warning that such persons are not your friends but instead your worst enemies. Such enemies, in my opinion, would never be able to trust you once they have achieved their goal of attaining absolute power because of your weakness and vulnerability to others that would become their enemies. Therefore, in my opinion, you would be among the first to be put to death once such enemies achieved absolute power because you were weak and vulnerable enough to help destroy yourself. Hence, I encourage working within the system by the system to improve and strengthen the system. One of the first steps that I perceive that Americans can take individually to put some strength back into America's foundation is to **remove all forms of hatred from our hearts and minds realizing the common fact that all Americans, regardless of race, creed, color or national origin have a stake in America's future and a responsibility to help protect the freedoms that America provides.** Our enemies will not help us do this; we must do it ourselves. Having done so, our future generations of Americans will be grateful for our having paved the way for God's Grace to be continuously shed upon America while crowning her good with brotherhood which will insure her remaining ''America the beautiful.''

Home: Symbolically speaking, the journey of a thousand miles begins with the first step. In this same ''thought process,'' a child's adult future is primarily shaped within the home during childhood. Regardless of how bad the surrounding environmental conditions may be where the home is located, the parents/guardians should strive to motivate and teach the child in a way so as to point the child in the generally perceived direction of life that leads to success. The first step in this direction according to what I remember being taught and shown is ''love'' and not ''hate.'' For those parents/guardians who believe in God—teach the child that God is love and that He loves us. Let the child know that he/she can be all that he/she desires to be if the child does what is necessary and apply himself/herself accordingly. In this same thought concept, the child should not be constantly fed with the negatives of that child's shortcomings. Instead, teach the child the "positives" of how he/she can turn shortcomings into assets through the power of positive thinking and positive actions. This concept, in my opinion, includes physical disabilities.

While I do not have any professional training or expertise in this area, I do believe that teaching such child to make the very best of what God has given is a step in the right direction in preparing that child to be all that he/she can be. Parents/guardians should provide proof of "love" teaching. The proof is letting the child see the example of love in the parent/guardian's life on a "one-on-one" basis within the home and not just only in the presence of others; putting up a defensive front for the sake of others not to be able to see the real parent/guardian. There were times when Mamma (my grandmother Viola) would beat the "daylight" out of me whether one-on-one or in the presence of others if she felt it necessary. Yet there were times when she showed me one-on-one parental love and its true parental value. Moral values, in my opinion, should be taught to the child as soon as the child understands what is right and what is wrong. This includes cultural values, teaching the child to love himself/herself. This type of teaching and love lays the permanent motivational foundation for the child's "care-rack-ter" (character) to be built upon to be with that child throughout his/her entire life. Further, this type of teaching and love within the home will be positively reflected in future generations as these positive factors will be passed on to them.

<u>Parents-Grandparents/Guardians Child Love & Trust Bonding:</u> While this area would begin in the home, I desired to focus on some important specifics in this area after the child has become an adult. Although love and trust bonding begins at an early stage, trust especially is very fragile and can be broken or destroyed at any stage, in my opinion. While parents-grandparents-guardians can force children to be obedient while in their presence in most instances, I perceive that children have to be motivated to desire being obedient to the parents' wishes while not in the presence of the parents. This process, as I view it, is the parent, through love building trust within the child and the child receiving such love and trust from the parent, is motivated to trust the parent through love. I guess by now that you, the reader, may begin to conclude that I am not keeping love and trust on the same level as I am led to believe that many people do. Let me carefully explain what I mean.

Let's say a parent who includes grandparents or guardians constantly stretches the truth in trying to control the children's thoughts to think as the parent thinks. If the child knows the truth or eventually learns the truth and believes that the parent knew the truth from the beginning, the trust that the child had for the parent may be severely weakened. Yet, depending upon the situation, the love that the child has for parent may not necessarily be lost in that the child's love may be adjusted to love the parent where the parent may be, symbolically speaking. This is especially so when the child has grown up to be an adult. The same concept applies to parents' trust in their children being damaged or destroyed when the child has grown up from beyond young adulthood to pre-senior citizen and the parent of an older senior citizen. Often such senior parent and pre-senior child could be solid Christians, in some cases, worshipping together in the same church and yet the trust dwindled to the extent the strong trust bond is missing when at this stage of life the parent and child/children should be able to trust one another with one another's "heart pills."

Believe it or not, outside spirit invaders, who desire to control the minds of others through "thought reform" process, are often the culprits. These invaders use one of the most powerful weapons in the enemy's arsenal which is "divide and conquer" in my opinion for the ultimate purpose of getting control of one's money and property assets. We see it happening all around us almost daily. In some instances, neither the parent nor the child is aware of how the origin of distrust between them originated. In my observations, it does not start out with money. It starts out with some other area totally unrelated to controlling one's money but seemingly proceeds along an agenda that is designed to eventually end up doing so. Often when such seemingly widespread distrust comes about late in years between parents and adult children, it is often the result of infiltration by outside spiritually masked influential individuals pretending to be friends possessing unclean spirits who invade the spirit of adult children and older parents by using divisive tactics that usher in distrust. If we carefully take a look at the daily happenings within our society, we see the serious side effects of such spirit invaders on a regular basis. One such notable side effect is that a previously close-knit and bonded family that loved and trusted one another is now divided and even though they still love one another must learn to love one another "where they actually are," having little, if any, trust in one another. The real sad part about this is that once that original "trust bond" is broken, it can never be restored back to its original position, in my opinion. We are living and functioning in spiritual warfare daily and we obviously need to be aware and knowledgeable of this reality and be able to detect and recognize the tactics of the enemy in any situations that we encounter. Therefore, in my view, it is extremely important for family members to be strongly bonded spiritually. Submitting ourselves to God strengthens that bond. This, together with studying, believing and applying God's Word to our lives will help family members obtain a clearer spiritual vision that will enable them to recognize any person(s) bearing unclean spirit(s) coming between them. Hence, through the power of the Spirit of God family members will be able to resist persons bearing such unclean spirit(s) at the very beginning.

One might ask how this concept would apply if parents of children are divorced? In my view, even though parents may have their irreconcilable differences that resulted in divorce, they should be united in their concerns in trying to provide the very best for their children under any circumstances. By this, I mean it is hoped that the divorced parents would be on the "same page" in their love, care and concern for their children. Therefore, even in divorce status, this concept has proven to be successful in many instances in that the positive way that many children of divorced parents, under this concept, turn out to be successful, productive, law-abiding citizens. We must remember that although satan is full of lies and deceptions, we must know the truth. We must also remember that there are many "two parent" homes where the parents are on separate pages and are not equally yoked. Often, in this case, we find one parent brainwashing the children against the other parent. Obviously the spirit of such parent is not of God. Even so, we can still look to the brighter side. God is to be glorified if the other parent's walk with God is unquestionable in such a household scenario. Mistakes are made in practically any given scenario. Yet, there are times, in some instances, when we are fortunate enough to use our past mistakes as "lessons learned" for future progress. I perceive that the following suggested three rules, if implemented and applied, will be very helpful to parents and children in strengthening and protecting the love and trust bonding throughout life.

(1) Walk with God daily in spirit and in truth. This includes being totally truthful and not stretching the truth. Ambassadors of God, which includes but is not limited to preachers, teachers and spiritual leaders should be extremely cautious to avoid the very appearance of implying a lie, intentionally telling a lie, condoning a lie or allowing their "care-rack-ter" (character) to be

such so as to be perceived as a liar. A liar is a liar regardless of what form or pattern one uses to lie or imply a lie. Further, included herein is that we shouldn't make up excuses to justify wrongdoings or use them as a defensive mechanism to avoid blame. If it is shown to us that we are wrong in a particular situation, we should be willing to accept it and make appropriate amends. We should avoid trying to show others how dirty their houses are and what they should do to clean them up when our own house is filthy. The items mentioned are just some of the items associated with this suggested rule per my opinion.

(2) Study God's Word to learn and know what is truth and apply this truth to your life on a daily basis. This will allow children and parents to be able to recognize when the enemy (person with unclean spirit) is trying to come between them. Thus the parents and children will have the spiritual power from God to rebuke/resist the enemy. I say person with unclean spirit because only such a person would desire to come between parent(s) and children.

(3) Parents and children should never, in my opinion, take sides against one another in public with an outside intruder coming between them. One would think that the bond between parents and adult children should have been nurtured from childhood to the extent that by the time the child reaches adulthood the bond would be so strong from love and loyalty viewpoint that parents and children would **never** take sides with an outsider against one another. Even if they disagreed with one another you would think that they would not publicly take sides with an outsider against one another. The strong bond of love and loyalty would seemingly mandate that the parents and children resolve their differences in private one-on-one. Yet we witness this rule being violated frequently. This rule seems to have a strong connection with Exodus 20:12 and further connects with the strong foundation upon which America's power was built. The cited reference is the only one of the ten commandments that comes with a

promise for children honoring their parents. Almost daily in our society we see this rule being violated. Instead of children honoring parents as the fifth commandment mandates, it seems that a serious increase of children dishonoring parents at an alarming rate is becoming the norm, including some teenager or adult children "cursing the parents out." While some parents may provoke such children to a "last nerve" degree, I don't perceive any provocation by a parent that would justify a son or daughter "cursing out" that parent. It doesn't take a rocket scientist to determine that such violation and non-adherence to honoring parents is contributing to the erosion of America's strong foundation. Parents and children should remember and never forget that decisions and actions bear consequences at some point in our lives. Even good decisions and actions may bear some emotional pain and suffering within the consequences. Even so, resulting from good decisions and actions, the comfort and joy that are coexistent with some pain housed within the consequences will prove to be dominant. I am a good example of what was just stated.

One of the best decisions that my mother has ever made, in my opinion, outside of accepting Jesus Christ as her personal Lord and Savior was to let my grandparents raise me. Surely there were some painful consequences associated therewith for her and for me. Even though there are some permanent painful scars within the consequences associated with my not being reared by my mother, since my father was deceased and I not being closely bonded with her on a daily basis in the early years and teens of my life, the overall love, joy and comfort that my grandparents and their children (seemingly as my siblings) rendered during those years overshadows the painful scars now. Yes the scars remain, but God's healing power is thorough and sufficient. Therefore, the scars without any current pain, serve only one purpose to me now. They allow me to pull back the curtains of my life and see what the awesome power and love of God has done for me, is still doing for me and will continue to do for me. He will do the same for others as well.

In our society today, many young and older parents and children (including teenagers and young adult children) are not closely bonded as parents and children should be, in my opinion. We personally witness, see and hear through media sources the disrespect that many parents and children show toward one another. Further, we can see that there are often so many issues between parents and children (teenagers and young adult children) that prevents close bonding. The invasion of drugs and destruction of moral values within a home contributes to the arrival of many issues between parents and children. These issues could seemingly be removed if the parents and children would come together, void of selfishness and allow the Spirit of God to dwell within them with the parents setting the example. However, these issues, not removed and becoming a way of life from one generation to another, seemingly leads to a frightening way of life within society that threatens the stability of our nation. We in America must never forget that the enemy desires to destroy our nation by any means necessary.

Let's amplify the frightening viewpoint. In many instances today, it is very difficult for parents who are legitimately trying to raise their children during the early school years in a manner so as to bring about close bonding, because they are fearful of the law; being afraid to use corporal punishment in that the child may hold the parent hostage with the threat of calling 911 on the parent. This seemingly leads to the child having no fear of the parent using corporal punishment and ultimately to the child being able to disrespect the parent without fear of being punished because the child can call 911 and the parent, in many cases, will go to jail. On the other side of the coin, the use of drugs by some parents destroying the parents' ability to utilize good judgment and contributing to the child being abused by the parent resulted in the arrival of the new weapon and yet a friend for the child against the parent by the child calling or threatening to call 911. While 911 is old and established as a friend to society, in my view, it can still be viewed as a friend to an abused child and yet a new weapon for a child in an otherwise good home where the child does not want to be disciplined and where the parent is concerned for the child's future. There are so many valid pros and cons to the use of corporal punishment within the home. While I don't agree with the need for every "whipping" that I received as a child, I do agree with the concern that my grandparents (Mamma, the enforcer) showed love and concern for my future. Also, the threat of a "whipping" served as a deterrent in many instances to what I did or didn't do that ultimately had a positive impact upon my "care-rack-ter" being built and molded. In essence, there are "side effects" positive and negative for the 911 friend or new weapon to a child. Therefore, in my opinion and experience during my childhood and later years as a parent, there are times and circumstances when concerned parents need to have at their disposal as a necessary "care-rack-ter" (character) molding tool the use of corporal punishment to be used in a positive manner at the parents' good judgmental discretion without being under the threat of going to jail at the discretion of a police officer, some of whose attitudes would already be against certain parents without any regards whatsoever for what the parent is trying to do positively for the child's future. This is not to be interpreted as an indictment of all police officers. Police officers are trained professionals and generally, many adopt a professional attitude desiring to carry out their difficult and often dangerous duties in a professional manner in accordance with the law(s). Yes, there are many exceptions. Instead of protecting these exceptions, the flaw in the system that allows such protection should be corrected to weed out such "unprofessional" officers for the benefit of those officers who are "professional," in my opinion. When the system allows the protection of those officers who are "unprofessional," it appears to me that the system needs serious review and legislative renovation that would support the fair and just removal process of such "unprofessional" officers in a much quicker time than it seems at present.

Getting back to the child being able to call 911 as a threat against the parent, one seemingly serious negative "side effect" is that the child grows up to be a teenager with the misconception of expecting the same protection of police officers as he/she did as a child and commits an infraction that a concerned parent might have prevented through the use of corporal punishment as a child and now that very same police officer who previously listened and took the position of the child and threw the parent in jail would not show that same (once) child any consideration whatsoever as a teenager, and in some instances have taken the teenager's life wrongfully. Many young poverty stricken teenagers are jail or death victims of what was just stated. Surely the drug crisis in our society today has contributed immensely to the foregoing scenario in that many close relatives are the guardians rearing the children of close relatives who are strung out on drugs. Although the bonding in such case will not be as biological bonding, it can still be strongly knitted through love, respect, understanding, compassion and good communication having been built upon a very strong spiritual foundation. By now, I hope that the main points that I have tried to convey regarding this major topic heading are well understood. Therefore, it is further my hope that you are encouraged to strongly consider and embrace what has been stated in that your consideration and your embracing such could very well make a positive impact upon the lives of many.

Church: The church has been a significant part of my life all of my life. The reason is very clear in that the church was the center focus for the gathering of families within the community on a weekly basis one or more times a week when I was growing up. Many major community functions were spiritually related and took place at our church (St. Matthew). During the infant years of America's growth, we can easily see that the church was a significant part of America's foundation, its growth and stability. The church, at that time, was seemingly viewed as a highly respected religious institution. It was indeed a rarity to hear or read of a minister being indicted and jailed for criminal wrongdoing during that time frame. Today, it is not uncommon to listen to news media or pick up a newspaper and see that a minister has been arrested and charged for criminal wrongdoing. This seems to suggest that the respect for the church and what it represents by the church leadership, to some extent have dwindled.

During my youth I observed that it was rather notable when children growing up in the church would go on to high school but only a small percentage would graduate. Among those that did graduate, an even smaller percentage of that group would go on to college. It seems to me that only a small percentage of this group graduated from college. Among those in the two groups listed that went to college in some instances (a non-Christian college), it seems that the larger percentage drifted completely from church during that time. Among those that drifted, the thinking concept seemed to suggest that the strong antichrist ideology within the non-Christian college environment (including) some of the faculty seemingly made these otherwise Christian students feel ashamed of their heritage and Christian upbringing as being "old fashioned uneducated thinking" that contributed to a few of these students embracing antichrist ideology. This is not to condemn the college environment or indict the need for a college education. On the contrary, a college education is extremely important in our society today. While some of these students didn't outwardly embrace antichrist ideology, some still seemingly abandoned their Christian upbringing ideology at that time. The few spiritually strong students that stayed with the church throughout college (some coming back to their home church) together with many of those who originally drifted from the church, and years later came back to the church, have made a significant contribution to the church, raising the intellectual level of the local church, in my opinion. Yet my having become more focused and observing the Christian educational level in the local church, it seems that Christian education training that would help the congregation better understand what is written in the Bible does not seem to be at a level we might expect in that more people in the church today have attained a higher level of education from institutions of higher learning than there were years ago. Therefore, one would think that Christian education in the mindset of those just mentioned would be a top priority for the Church in teaching the Word and preaching the Word concurrently with the "how to" process of applying the Word in our lifestyles. Further, it seems to me that knowledge of biblical history, what the Bible provides for us to guide us daily and the truth that it represents are extremely important Spiritual factors in the foundation of our belief to accept Jesus Christ as our personal Lord and Savior as well as why we believe in Him.

I have observed in many instances college-educated church members actively attending church weekly and diligently involved in the preparation and presentation of church activities, who have little knowledge of God's Word who admittedly seldom read and study the Bible at home or attend any Bible study at church or enroll in any biblical study courses. Sad as it may seem, this includes some that are in key powerful leadership positions within the church. From a Christian perspective, I am of the mindset that a college-educated individual has a soul to be saved just as a non-college-educated individual. It is my perception that when a strong Christian spiritual seed is planted within a child and nurtured up to the teenage level that many would go to college, such education helps them to be strong Christians and to better understand the need to seek biblical training for themselves and to spread or share such biblical training with others that especially leads more teenagers in the direction of college.

On the other side of the coin, I have witnessed that some who do not have such spiritual seed planted and nurtured during childhood and teenage years (even though they are from Christian backgrounds and don't embrace any other religion) who go on to college including post graduate level that don't demonstrate whatsoever any interest in **biblical training or salvation.** The spiritual seed planting and nurturing are just not there. Being a Christian, I truly believe that we are in spiritual warfare each and every day. It is as simple as can be that spiritual warfare training (to include knowing one's individual weapon) is therefore a **"must"** if you expect to defeat the enemy. My Christian beliefs together with my education, military training and biblical school training allows me to conclude that the Holy Bible and knowledge of its contents serve as an individual weapon in this warfare. From a Christian perspective, knowing how to use this weapon in spiritual warfare is our protection in battle. It appears to me that this is exactly what the Apostle Paul was emphasizing in his imagery of a tough, well-trained Roman soldier (Ephesians 6:11-18) in his instructions to Christians instructing them to put on the whole armor of God. If we carefully observe cited Scriptures, we find that Paul is figuratively telling the Christians that they are soldiers in God's Army. In that Rome was the ruling world power at that time, he comparatively associates the items on a Roman soldier's uniform and their military purpose in combat with the items that a Christian soldier must have and be trained to use that are in God's Word, making knowledge and application of God's Word in its entirety the Christian soldier's protective spiritual combat uniform to be worn and utilized daily in order for the Christian soldier to be victorious in daily spiritual combat warfare. Therefore, it seems to me that the most practical way to teach the believer in this area would be mainly through more structured Christian education within the local Christian church. Antichrist foes are well versed in their ideology and are also well versed and indoctrinated in their twisted and inaccurate version of the Holy Bible. In my opinion, that's why many untrained and uneducated Christians from a Christian education view point are not equipped to resist the antichrist foes and make them flee. James 4:7 of the Holy Bible (KJV) states "Brethern submit yourselves to God, resist the devil and he will flee." In that I have shared some of my observations with you, such observations might cause you to become inquisitive to the extent as to what, if anything that I have done about my observations relating to Christian education.

I am thankful to God and glorify Him in that He allowed me to pen a "how-to" book that will be a very helpful tool in this area especially for the local Christian church, *Establishing a Board of Christian Education Ministry within a Local Christian Church.* Referenced book helps the pastor and church leaders in better meeting the needs of the entire church membership beginning with the spiritual and Christian educational needs. Further, it suggests and recommends the development and teaching of structured biblical courses that helps the local Church membership and community residents to become more knowledgeable of the truth that the Bible represents thus leading those being taught to become hungry and thirsty for more of the powerful knowledge within the Bible. It is my hope that *Blessings Beyond View via The Love Palace* will serve to ignite an in-depth view and clearer vision within the local Christian church leadership, allowing them to see how desperately referenced book is needed as a training tool for Christian soldiers to be able to better utilize the conquering weapon (Holy Bible) that God has given us to defeat the enemy in daily spiritual warfare. In my view, structured Christian education is a vital part of the Great Commission (Matt 28:19-20). Let's examine what was just stated. Just before Jesus commissioned the eleven disciples, He let them know that He had the power to do what He was about to do in commissioning them in that this was after Jesus' resurrection "And Jesus came and spake unto them" (Matt: 28:18). Remember, Judas had already "hanged himself" (Matt 27:5) which is why there were eleven and not twelve disciples. By commissioning them, Jesus gave them the power and the duty to do what He was commissioning them to do. We see the word power written in the first cited reference just mentioned but not duty. Therefore, where does duty come into the picture? Here is what many of us perceive as being the answer. If we carefully look at the word "commission" and remove the prefix "com", we have another important word that requires action which is "mission." In commissioning them, He gave them the power to carry out the "mission" which now becomes an unwritten but clearly defined and understood "duty." Yet it would appear that He left the detailed preparation, planning and "mission-related" training and development requirements up to the eleven disciples. Hence, speaking in perceptive terminology, we have the birth of a Master Christian education, training and development plan, the New Covenant (New Testament). While knowledge of the New Testament helps us to better understand the origin, purpose and history of the Old Covenant (Old Testament), structured Christian education and training is a subsidiary tool to help us accomplish the "mission/duty" that Jesus gave that appears to be automatically interwoven within the Great Commission. Further, we now can see that Jesus intended for the Great Commission to be tied into nation's constitutions. To support what was just stated, the following quote is taken from Vol. V, Matthew Henry's Commentary page 446 beginning with "[1.] How far his commission is extended; *to all nations.* Go, and disciple *all nations*. Not that they must go all together into every place, but by consent disperse themselves in such manner as might best *diffuse* the light of the light of the gospel. Now this plainly signifies it to be the will of Christ, *First,* that the covenant's peculiarity, made with the Jews, should now be cancelled and disannulled. This word broke down the middle wall of the partition, which had so long excluded the Gentiles from a visible church-state; and whereas the apostles, when first sent out, were forbidden to go into the way of the Gentiles, now they were sent to *all nations. Secondly,* that salvation by Christ should be offered to all and none excluded that did not by their unbelief and impenitence exclude themselves. The salvation they were to preach is a *common salvation;* whoever will, let him come, and take the benefit of the *act of indemnity;* for there is no difference of Jew or Greek in Christ Jesus. *Thirdly,* that Christianity should be twisted in with national constitutions, that the Kingdoms of the world should become Christ's Kingdoms, and their Kings the church's nursing-fathers."

Therefore, it appears to me that America's Constitution includes the basic principles and Christian requirements that Jesus gave in the Great Commission. Now we can see how and why America has been able to withstand the many attempts by enemies to destroy America. The presence of the Spirit of God is in the basic plan, the "Constitution" even though some of America's actions within its history are not representative of the foundation upon which the plan was built. Yet, the plan in itself, containing the presence of the Spirit of God is solid, notwithstanding it being violated through the years by the nation's leaders and members of the governing bodies sworn to uphold it. However, we should also be able to see clearer that America's enemies are now aware of what makes this nation's Constitution so strong (God's presence) and we should now further see why the antichrist groups desire to remove any association of "God" from our Constitution seeking to make its foundation support weaker to eventually destroy America as a world power right in front of our eyes and believe it or not, with the willing help of some American citizens. Hopefully, the Christian church, as a whole, will be able to better see the vital mission that the church and each of us were given within the Great Commission when Jesus commissioned the eleven disciples. Further, it is also my hope that the Christian church will take the leadership role in giving more focus to the need of basic structured Christian education as outlined in the referenced book that God allowed me to pen. It is perceived that such focus will add spiritual strength to the Christian church, thereby contributing to restoring the originally intended spiritual support to the foundation of America's Constitution while carrying out God's Will as given in the Great Commission in His Godhead as God the Son, JESUS CHRIST our LORD and SAVIOR.

Public School: During my childhood, the general Christian viewpoint of the public school, as I have already mentioned previously, was once a continuing reinforcement agent of the home and church in expanding the academic educational level of a child from a Christian home. The public school once included the power of God and prayer being in the forefront of its daily teaching curriculum through "morning devotion" in many or most of the black schools during the era of segregation in the South to the best of my knowledge. Reinforcing within the child's mind and heart the reality of the existence of God and prayer were viewed as being very important during that time frame in building and molding the "care-rack-ter" (character) of a child to go through life successfully. Keep in mind that "success" during the early years of my life was not totally determined by one's personal monetary or material possessions from a Christian viewpoint. Yes, "money is important but it's not everything" as many believed then and now. The heads of Christian families i.e. parents who possessed strong spiritual and moral values taught those same values to their children while setting an example by demonstrating such values in their daily living. These same families whose children's conduct, for the most part, that reflected such values would be viewed as an "up to do" family representative of "success."

It's very clear to me that the antichrist forces saw how strong God and prayer actually carried over into strengthening this nation's stability and thereby set out to remove them from school. This may have resulted in a negative impact upon the teaching profession in that some very good teachers who subscribe to Christian ideology left the teaching profession voluntarily or felt forced to resign for seemingly the slightest of religious infractions. It is perceived that some good teachers being brought up on such seemingly frivolous Christian-related religious charges including "God and prayer" probably felt or feel forced to resign and go into another field of work, rather than go through a long and possibly stressful process of rebutting such charges. The "bottom line" effect of good educators (possessing Christian beliefs and moral values) leaving the educational system as mentioned above results in the antichrist forces being temporarily victorious. In using the word "temporarily" even though it may be years before the banner of our Lord and Savior is raised in final victory, we who are strong Christian believers **know** that it will happen. To symbolically view the frustration that some of the good teachers endure, especially those with Christian beliefs, during a typical school day within the classroom is like having to walk on ice without falling. It is very clear to me that Christianity is being attacked by antichrist foes from every perceivable angle. Knowledge of God's Word (the truth) is extremely important for Christian soldiers to be successful in fighting the daily spiritual war that we are fighting. I truly believe that the following suggestions will be very helpful to public school teachers who possess Christian beliefs but are not actively involved in the teaching process in a Christian church.

Teachers/Educators (Christian Backgrounds): Go back to the Christian church and get involved. Prepare yourself to help advance the Christian cause by taking some biblical educational courses so you will be better able to support the process of more Christian structured educational courses being brought to the local Christian church. Seek where such courses are being given and get enrolled being led by the Holy Spirit. After doing so, rather than wasting years waiting to go back to your home church to get involved, let the Holy Spirit lead you in getting involved in a Christian church where you are currently located where you can pass on to others what you have gained from the biblical courses that you have taken and get especially involved with the Board of Christian Education Ministry (BOCEM) if one is established. If a BOCEM is not established, let the Holy Spirit lead you in appropriately encouraging the Church officials and pastor to allow you to assist in getting one established and effectively functioning. My first book, already referenced, will provide some guidance in this area. This would include your involvement with a tutoring program with BOCEM in your local Christian church, streamlining and/or assisting in establishing a ''children's church'' within your church. This will provide more ''hands-on'' participation training for children to conduct worship services. This Christian training environment will perceivably teach the child at an early age what it means to be a follower of Jesus Christ. This will make the individual child stronger in Christian knowledge and principles as well as prepare the child in being able to spiritually combat antichrist grade and age peers in the public school. We must be clearly aware that children of antichrist parents and such environment are well prepared and trained to defeat a Christian child who is not trained and well prepared to fight against their antichrist grade and age group.

Public school teachers/educators being actively involved with the local Christian church, in many instances, would be involved with the child's spiritual Christian education within the church outside the public school after school hours as well as with the child's academic education in the public school. Although a teacher (public school/church) and child may not be in the same Christian church or public school, the conceptual process would still most likely produce the same positive Christian results. It is perceived that this concept would allow the Christian high school graduate who is about to enter college being spiritually prepared to utilize the power and authority (Luke 9:1) that is available for them over antichrist forces. Knowing how to use such power, more focus could be given to academic studies, resulting in academic success.

Teachers/Educators Must Seek God's Anointing Power: While the referenced public school teachers/educators (from Christian backgrounds) have the academic credentials and now biblical courses credentials to teach biblical courses within your church, seeking and receiving God's **Anointing Power** would be essential to effectively teach God's Word. In doing so, you would become a stronger fighting force in spiritually fighting the antichrist forces where you are professionally employed daily as a teacher/educator in the public school arena. Also, with such anointing it is perceived that a teacher, from a spiritual power perspective, would be better able to effectively communicate with students (including non-Christian), subordinates, peers and supervisors verbally or in writing, through your lifestyle, attitude and conduct without violating the law. A very good Scriptural example of this is the book of "Esther" in the KJV Holy Bible. You will not find the words "God" or "Prayer" in referenced book of the Bible. Yet you can feel the presence of God's power and the presence of prayer power. If you look up the words "Esther" and "Persia" in the *Zondervan Pictorial Bible Dictionary*, you will find that the absence of the words "God" and "prayer" from the book of "Esther" are probably by deliberate design and why. Also, you will be able to see and feel from the book of ''Esther'' how the spiritual courage and intelligence of one woman saved the Jews in Persia at that time.

Christian Teachers/Educators Should Consider Using Esther's Spiritual Courage and Intelligence as a Daily Guide at Your Public Schools: Your being a teacher/educator in the public school, you are encouraged to use Esther's spiritual courage, intelligence and willingness as a guide to stand up as she did, for her people and for the right thing. Such should be done intelligently and within the existing law(s). You will find that God's power within you will be far more powerful than any antichrist force or law designed to supposedly defeat God's Purpose and Will. I am confident that Esther was divinely inspired in doing what she did. I firmly believe that God's power supersedes any power that man can create even through legislative laws. Therefore, teachers/educators especially those brought up in Christian homes, churches, public schools (teaching Christian principles) years past prior to such being prohibited, private Christian schools years past and now, you are encouraged to get more involved in the Christian teaching process of the local Christian church. While it is clearly realized that when your duty week is completed as a public school teacher, the energy level of many is rather low and you don't feel up to getting involved with the church and seemingly increasing the stress upon you. I truly believe that envisioning the need for your participation through teaching in the local Christian church will increase your willingness and desire to teach in the church, thereby offsetting the additional stress transforming such into joy and happiness. Your influence as a public school teacher/educator combined with your teaching involvement in the Christian teaching process within the local Christian church will have a significant impact upon children's future whose lives are touched by your life. It is widely perceived that teachers do not go into the teaching profession for money in that as a professional, they could make more money in the business world with their professional credentials, generally speaking. It is fairly obvious that love and the joy of teaching weigh heavily upon their choosing the teaching profession. Therefore, I hope what has been stated herein will expand your thinking process much broader and even further beyond what has been actually stated herein to the extent that you will be able to envision and feel the collective and individual spiritual power that can be obtained from God through your teaching involvement within the church. In doing so, I firmly believe that you will become (collectively and individually) a vital positive spiritual power force to restore spiritual strength back into the public school which was originally established as a major support beam that supports this nation's Constitution. I believe that the presence and power of the Spirit of God and Christian principles within the Constitution represent the foundation upon which America is built and upon which its current status as a world power exists. While I do not desire to seem critical of non-Christian teachers/educators who may not necessarily be antichrist foes, my focus herein is upon Christian teachers/educators and the major contribution that they can make toward strengthening the presence of the spiritual power of Christianity within the public school, without violating the current laws. In doing so, these Christian teachers/educators would also be contributing to strengthening the local Christian church and lending support to America maintaining its status as a world power which is rooted in the presence of the power of the Spirit of God and the Christian principles embedded within the Constitution.

Money: Having discussed home, church and public school thus far as to how they fit into the scheme of my perception of this book being helpful to many, the question may be asked, "How does money fit into this scheme?" Money provides answers to many questions. According to the Word (Ecclesiastes 10:19) "A feast is made for laughter, and wine maketh merry;

but money answereth all *things.*'' Money can be used very powerfully both negatively and positively. It can be used as a tool to build and as a weapon to destroy or defend. Although money as a minted coin or as a printed piece of paper has no value to one who does not know what it is or what it represents, the actual power of money comes from one having the knowledge of how to extract the power from money by knowing how to use it to bring about the results that power produces. If many Americans would see crumpled up currency from different nations at a garbage dump and if we didn't have knowledge that it was valuable currency (large denominations), it would just be garbage as far as we would be concerned, not having knowledge of its value and of course its power. Although its true value could be worth hundreds of thousands or millions of dollars after being exchanged for American currency (dollars) which we understand, it would still be garbage in the mindset of one who does not have knowledge of such fact. Yet, in the scenario just presented about valuable foreign currency at the garbage dump, one's ignorance of its true value does not remove its true value at all. Only within the mindset of one who does not have knowledge of its true value makes it garbage in that person's mindset, per my perception for two reasons which are (1) lack of knowledge and (2) the foreign currency (money) was at the garbage dump and perceived as garbage in referenced person's mindset. The purpose of stating what I have stated thus far regarding money is to clearly let the reader see the ''value'' power of money (negative and positive) and how important it is to seek to be knowledgeable of the value and power of money, especially those of us who believe in God.

It is extremely important that believers in God be aware of the danger (evil) of falling in love with money. I Timothy 6:10 ''For the love of money is the root of all evil; which while some coveted after, they have erred from the faith, and pierced themselves through with many sorrows.'' Yet it is equally important that we as believers in God be aware of the great contribution that money can make toward spreading the good news of God's Kingdom through the concept of spreading God's Word in carrying out the Great Commission (Matt. 28:19–20). I am sure that many of us have observed or heard about how sudden wealth, in some instances, has served to bring out the worst in its benefactor while on the other hand it has served to bring out the best in others. It is perceived that money and power are directly or indirectly related to all wars.

I am sure that many of us have witnessed or heard about many families being torn apart because of money. The estate of a deceased relative has been the center focus on many bitter family feuds even though in some instances the estate has been rather small. Such feuds continue on through many generations. Believe it or not, many of the members of these feuding families sit right in the same church supposedly worshipping and praising God together. I perceive that many of such families fail to grasp the concept that families divided weaken the family foundation unit structure. This structure, per my perception, is extremely important as a support beam in this nation's structured foundation. Many believe as I do that everything in this world belongs to God in that He is our Creator. Therefore, the money that He has allowed us to be blessed with belongs to Him also. We, therefore are merely temporary "caretakers" in that we must leave it all behind one day regardless of whether our estate is worth just a few dollars or worth millions. If we believe in God, through our blessings from God, we incur an obligation to bless others in my opinion and belief. This, again per my belief, means giving or sharing with others through the church, charity or whatever way that the Spirit of God leads us to give or share. The bottom line is the requirement to give or share with others in need who are less fortunate than ourselves. To avoid misunderstanding what was just stated, this does not mean that one has to become an individual welfare center. I find that there is joy in giving.

Also, God loves a cheerful giver. The ninth chapter of II Corinthians supports what was just stated. In bringing the topic of money to a close, it is perceived that the concept of "financial generations investment" is very important. Teaching children how to save some, invest some, enjoy some and leave some for the next generation is extremely important in that it is a form of investing in the economic stability of the family tree and this nation per my view. Hopefully something that is stated herein regarding money proves to be a blessing to you and your descendants at some point in the future.

Love: According to Scriptures I John 4:8, God is love. Therefore, love, in my opinion, is the most powerful weapon in the world that God has given to man. I am confident that this word is one of if not the most misrepresented words in the world that has caused many much pain and suffering in its misuse and/or misrepresentation. While there are several types of love, the one that we will briefly focus upon is AGAPE (unselfish brotherly love). I truly believe that this is what Jesus Christ intended in His new commandment when He commanded us to love one another as He has loved us (John 13:34). This is the love that will last throughout our earthly life and the one that other types of love should rest upon if we truly seek and obtain brotherly love for our fellowman. I truly believe that AGAPE love helps other types of love to function in their true capacity. Also, from a biblical viewpoint, love is the most powerful defensive and offensive weapon that God has given to man. The more we learn about God's Word and how to apply it to our lives, the more and better we learn how to use the weapon of love effectively. In starting this book through the power of love and now bringing all of its areas to a close through that same power of love, it is my hope that many people in the world today, will be able to gain a clearer view of how the application of AGAPE love in their life would remove the reason(s) for them to hate others.

Further, it will hopefully help many to realize that hate is more destructive to the person(s) harboring hate in the long span of time than it is to its intended victim. In my view, it is a blessing to plug into the connecting power source of AGAPE love (God). The use of the word "hate" in its reference to a person or any group of persons was not allowed in our home when I was growing up unless the person using the word wanted to be "whipped" by Mamma or Grandpa Dock—mostly Mamma. I truly praise and glorify God for allowing me to be in the nurtured care of my grandparents O'Hara and Viola Riddick from childhood to a young adult even though from a child's view, I probably would have preferred to have been with my biological parents. Realizing now that God knows best, I praise and glorify God for my mother having turned her life over to God allowing Him to lead her in the path of righteousness preparing her to do His work. Her preparation studying God's Word through structured sources resulted in her being ready to initiate mother-and-son bonding and to pick up the reins where Grandpa Dock (until his death) and Mamma left off continuing to spiritually mentor and guide me through some difficult storms in my life after I came to my mother at the age of eighteen. This includes the major contribution that Mother made through biblical knowledge and spiritual guidance toward the first book, already referenced, that God allowed me to pen in that she is my chief spiritual mentor (CSM). Therefore, in looking over all the events noted herein and those not noted through a mixture of pain, joy and blessings while speaking from a child's desire and from an adult's knowledge and experience over a period of many years, I feel qualified to say, "while much was lost by my not being reared by my mother, much more was gained."

It is my sincere hope that what I have shared with you through this book, will assist you in being able to take a good look within yourself while allowing the Spirit of God to expand your spiritual vision and see God's love for you. This, I believe, will allow you to look back at some pleasant and unpleasant events in your life and draw similar conclusions as I have done many years after my childhood in that I can now better understand and visualize my *"Blessings Beyond View via The Love Palace."*

While I am thankful that the Spirit of God allowed me to hopefully make a deposit within your spirit through this book, I am also thankful to you for allowing me the opportunity to do so. I therefore conclude with **"TO GOD BE THE GLORY."**

Annex A

STANDARD CERTIFICATE OF DEATH

1. PLACE OF DEATH
County: Wake
Township: Raleigh, N.C.
City: Raleigh
Cambridge Rd

2. FULL NAME: Henry Ed. Reddick
(a) Residence: No. 1310 Poole Rd

PERSONAL AND STATISTICAL PARTICULARS

3. SEX: Male
4. COLOR OR RACE: Colored
5. Married
Husband of: Malvenda Strickland
6. DATE OF BIRTH: —
7. AGE: 28 years
9. Trade: Laborer
10. Date deceased last worked: 7-8-39
12. BIRTHPLACE: Wake County
13. NAME: O H Reddick
14. BIRTHPLACE: Wake County
15. MAIDEN NAME: Viola Malone
16. BIRTHPLACE: Wake County
17. INFORMANT: O H Reddick, Raleigh, N. C.
18. BURIAL: Wake County Date: 3-28-39
19. UNDERTAKER: Raleigh Funeral Home, Raleigh, N. C.
20. FILED: 3-28-39

MEDICAL CERTIFICATE OF DEATH

21. DATE OF DEATH: 3/24, 1939
22. Principal cause of death: Suicide
Where did injury occur: Raleigh
Manner of injury: Shot with pistol
Nature of injury: Shot in head

Henry Riddick Death Certificate, filed 3-28-39.

Malverda Riddick Death Certificate, filed 3-28-39.

PLACE OF DEATH
Township: Raleigh

2. FULL NAME: Malverda Riddick
(a) Residence: No. Cambridge Rd 320

PERSONAL AND STATISTICAL PARTICULARS

- **3. SEX:** Female
- **4. COLOR OR RACE:** Colored
- **5. Single, Married, Widowed, or Divorced:** Married
- **5a. Husband of (or) Wife of:** Henry Riddick
- **6. DATE OF BIRTH:**
- **7. AGE:** 22 Years
- **8. Trade, profession, or particular kind of work:** Domestic
- **9. Industry or business:**
- **10. Date deceased last worked at this occupation:** 95-96
- **12. BIRTHPLACE:** Wake County
- **13. NAME:** James Strickland
- **14. BIRTHPLACE:** Wake County
- **15. MAIDEN NAME:** Daisy Morgan
- **16. BIRTHPLACE:** Wake County
- **17. INFORMANT:** Daisy Scott, 324 Lombardy St., Richmond
- **18. BURIAL, CREMATION, OR REMOVAL:** Wake County, Date 3/27/39
- **19. UNDERTAKER:** Raleigh Funeral Home, Raleigh NC
- **20. FILED:** 3-28-39

MEDICAL CERTIFICATE OF DEATH

- **21. DATE OF DEATH:** 3/24/39
- **22. I HEREBY CERTIFY** That I attended deceased
- to have occurred on the date stated above at 3/24 10:00 P
- The principal cause of death: Homicide
- Where did injury occur? Raleigh
- Manner of injury: Killed by Henry Riddick
- Nature of injury: Shot or Chest Pain
- (Signed) Roy M Banks
- (Address) Raleigh NC

Negro Kills His Wife; Turns Gun on Himself

W. H. Yarborough's Basement Scene of Murder and Suicide

A basement in Budleigh was the scene of a murder-suicide last night when the husband of Attorney William H. Yarborough's Negro cook broke down the door of the servant's room and shot her three times before applying a pistol to his own head shortly after 10 p. m.

The dead were identified as Henry Riddick, 28, and Malveada Strickland Riddick, about the same age. The two had been estranged for some time.

Coroner Roy M. Banks and members of the sheriff's department agreed that the deaths were clearly murder and suicide.

Deputy R. L. Atkins quoted Yarborough as saying that he first heard the sound of the door crashing in, then three shots as the husband wounded his wife in the chest, side and back, and finally another shot as the killed staggered into the adjoining basement garage and ended his own life.

On the verge of going downstairs to investigate the door crash, Yarborough retreated when the firing began and telephoned for the sheriff's men.

Deputies Atkins and Joe Partin, the first to arrive, said they found the husband already dead and the wife breathing her last. Both were dead before an ambulance arrived, the woman lying on the basement stairs and the man in the garage.

The Yarborough residence is situated on Cambridge Road, beside the Boone's Pond dam.

Attorney A. B. Breece said Yarborough spoke to him yesterday afternoon about drawing legal papers to prevent Riddick from molesting his wife while she was on duty.

"He was going to be sure he made a good job of it," commented Deputy T. S. Rhodes. "We found an extra round of shot and a razor in his pocket."

Henry and Malverda Riddick news clipping (courtesy of the North Carolina *News & Observer*).

Annex B

This is Momma (Mrs. Viola Riddick) in the yard on a Sunday afternoon in 1966. Momma is the author's grandmother, who fulfilled her desire to give each of her children a parcel of land to build a home upon. In the author's words, "Momma was indeed a woman among women."

Deacon O'Hara Riddick, paternal grandfather of the author, carrying fireplace wood for the kitchen in the author's home (The Love Palace). The Deacon's son, James, tried to get him to take a picture but he refused, saying he wasn't dressed for a picture. This picture was taken two days before his death in 1946. The author says he was "a giant of a man in my memory."

In Loving Memory

Loved, remembered, and longed for
They'll be with each beat of our hearts.
Till in heaven, we're once more together
For eternity never to part.

Deacon O'Hara Riddick

Mr. Henry Riddick

Rev. Juanita Hoke, the author's mother, is an original member of Mt. Hebron Baptist Church in The Bronx, New York. Rev. Hoke's love, dedication, and contribution toward the spread of Christian education throughout the Christian community surely complies with the Mission given in Matt. 28:19–20. She celebrated her 90th birthday on June 17, 2007.

JUANITA DANIEL

SOPRANO

Juanita Daniel has studied voice under the supervision of Octavia Morris for the past five years, and deserves your attention.

She is currently the organist and choir directress at the Mt. Hebron Baptist Church, 1173 Hoe Avenue, Bronx, New York of which The Reverend George C. Hoke is the Minister.

The Artist of the evening joins hands with Octavia Morris in thanking you for your patronage and support.

Mrs. Juanita Daniel
Mother of Marvin O. Riddick

Picture taken Prior to her calling into the Ministry Vineyard. I truly wish that the world could have witnessed the melodious voice and beauty that Mother exhibited in song recital at CARNEGIE RECITAL HALL, New York May 25, 1958

In Song Recital

CARNEGIE RECITAL HALL

154 WEST 57th STREET

New York City

SUNDAY AFTERNOON, MAY 25th, 1958

At 5:30 P. M.

Song Recital featuring the author's mother, Juanita Daniel.

PROGRAMME

My Master Hath A Garden .... R. Thompson
Largo
When I Prayed To God .... G. Handel
Dido's Lament .... H. Purcell
Sento Nel Core .... Scarlatti
  My Heart Doth Languish
Comme Raggio Di Sol .... Caldara
  Like The Golden Ray's Of The Sun
Caro Mio Ben .... Giordani
  Thou, All My Bliss
Care Selve: (Atlanta) .... G. Handel
  Come, Beloved

ARIA

Le Nozze Di Figaro .... W. Mozart
  Non So Piu Cosa Son
  I Don't Know Any More Where I Am
  And What I Am Doing ....

INTERMISSION

Down In The Forest .... Ronald
Go Way From My Window .... J. Niles
Do Not Go My Love .... R. Hageman
Spirit Flower .... Tipton
I Talked To God Last Night .... D. Guion

Witness .... H. Johnson
My Lord What A Morning .... L. Dawson
I Want Jesus To Walk .... Boatner
Ride On Jesus .... N. Dett

OCTAVIA MORRIS
At Piano

Inside the Song Recital Programme.

Rev. Amos and Laurena Barnes, maternal grandparents of the author. This picture was taken around the late 1930s or early 1940s. Rev. Barnes was well-respected among Whites and Blacks, and he was a prominent leader in the Turner Swamp area of Uricka and Freemont, North Carolina during the early 1900s up to his earthly departure around 1950.

The author dropping soda around the corn as a young boy. Afterward, the dirt would have to be turned over the soda by plowing (mule and plow). The scene was across from The Love Palace on what is now Highway 401.

Rev. Millard Jones (deceased) was a pillar of strength in the St. Matthew community during the author's time growing up in that area. He referred to Rev. Jones as "Cut'n Millud." The author writes, "He has and will always be a strong figure in my life."

THE ORIGINAL CHURCH

HISTORY OF THE CHURCH

The initial start of the Saint Matthews Baptist Church came in December 1871, just six years after the Civil War, when some black men who were affiliated with the New Hope Baptist Church decided to establish their own church.

It is interesting, though difficult to delve into the history of Saint Matthews Baptist Church. Little is known of its early organization, however, we are able to establish the fact that the founders were men and women of great devotion. They gave of themselves and contributed to the development and growth of our church. As far back as we can recollect, Reverend Stephen Blake was the first pastor of the wooden framed structure that stood approximately one hundred feet from the present site. Church services consisted of a monthly conference held on Saturday and followed by preaching services on Sunday. Revival services were held annually.

Reverend Horton Pair was the second pastor of the Saint Matthews Baptist Church followed by Reverend Alfree Price. Under their leadership, the church continued to be the center of goodwill, fellowship, and love in the community. As the church membership grew, small additions were made to the wooden framed structure which stood as an edifice of worship for the Saint Matthews Baptist Church members until the late fifties.

Other past pastors included Reverend William Smith, Reverend Arthur Anderson, Reverend Levi B. Hockaday, Reverend Walter Egerton, and Assistant Pastor, Reverend Millard Jones. All of these great spiritual leaders along with many deacons, trustees and members envisioned a larger and better edifice for their worship. Thus, the building of the basement of the present church was begun. Worship services were continued in the basement from 1957 until Sunday, July 21, 1963

when the present sanctuary was dedicated for the worship of God in praise and prayer, for the preaching of the everlasting gospel, for the celebration of the holy sacraments, for the comfort of all who are tempted, as light for those who seek the way, for the promotion of righteousness and the extension of the kingdom of God. Organization of the church at this time consisted of deacons B. B. Basford, James Malone, Urah Jones, Calvin Hunter, Charlie Riddick and James Allen Watkins. Trustees were Reverend Millard Jones, Evans Jones and Luther Horton.

Since the dedication of our present sanctuary, just as before, much has gone into the preservation of human as well as material resources to keep Saint Matthews Baptist Church in the forefront of Christian endeavor. Many new officers were added, some include the following additions to the Deacon Board — Arthur Bunch, Luther Horton, McCoy Howell, George Hunter, Evans Jones and Clyde Riddick. Johnny Dunn was added to the Trustee Board. Other active organizations are the Deaconess Board, Missionary Circle, Lillian Jones, President; Senior Choir, Louise Goodson, President; Junior Choir, Harvey Jones, President; Young Adult Choir, Almarie Jones, Advisor; Tot's Choir, Ada Dunn and Clyde Riddick; Senior Usher Board, Ernest Rayford, President; Junior Usher Board, Ernest Rayford; and the Pastor's Aide Club, Viola Hunter, President.

Reverend John D. Lockley was installed as pastor of Saint Matthews Baptist Church in September, 1967, and continues to serve in that capacity.

As one stands in the vestibule of the Saint Matthews Baptist Church, one quickly recalls the struggles, the courage and the faith that have gone into the building of this sanctuary. One too, may realize the words of the poet who said,

God hath not promised skies always blue
Flower-strewn pathways all our lives through,
God hath not promised sun without rain,
Joy without sorrow, peace without pain.
God hath not promised we shall not know
Toil and temptation, trouble and woe
He hath not told us we shall not bear
Many a burden, many a care.
But God hath promised strength for the day,
Rest for the laborer, light for the way,
Grace for the trials, help from above,
Unfailing sympathy, undying love.

Truer words were never spoken — to the membership of the Saint Matthews Baptist Church past and present has realized that it takes much to overcome and rise to greater heights of Christian fulfillment. Now as we stand on the threshold of another century, having reviewed our past and looking to the future, let us join with the song writer in words of thankfulness and courage.

WE'VE COME THIS FAR BY FAITH
LEANING ON THE LORD,
TRUSTING IN HIS HOLY WORD
HE NEVER FAILED US YET —
OH, NO, WE CAN'T TURN AROUND
WE'VE COME THIS FAR BY FAITH.

Church history photos.

ST. MATTHEW BAPTIST CHURCH
136th HOMECOMING CELEBRATION

*"Uniting and Re-gathering Families
Through The Power Of the Holy Spirit"*

**Sunday, August 19, 2007
11:00 AM**

Pastor, Rev. Ronald E. Avery, M.Div.
5410 Louisburg Road
Raleigh, North Carolina 27616
Phone: (919) 872-7647

Sunday School 9:30 AM
Morning Worship 2nd & 4th Sunday 8:00 AM & 11:00 AM
1st & 3rd Sunday 11:00 AM
Bible Study Wednesday, 7:00 PM

St. Matthew School Preservation

This school built in 1922 is only one of a few of the smaller Rosenwald Schools in Wake County still standing today. The school with its characteristic banks of windows is a historic reminder of education facilities for African-Americans in America in the early twentieth century.

St. Matthew Baptist Church
5410 Louisburg Road
Raleigh, NC 27604

Rev. Ronald E. Avery, Pastor

St. Matthew School Preservation information.

Today the structures stand almost forgotten, scattered across the North Carolina countryside. Some are now houses, businesses or barns. Others – particularly those that stand next to churches as community halls – still retain the large banks of windows that mark them as school buildings. These Rosenwald Fund schools, landmarks in this history of Afro-American Education.

Conceived in the 1910's by Black educator Booker T. Washington and his Tuskegee Institute Staff, the Rosenwald program represented a massive effort to improve Black rural schools in the South through public-private partnership. The name came from Julius Rosenwald, President of Sears, Roebuck and Company.

–Thomas W. Hanchett
The Rosenwald Schools
and Black Education
in North Carolina

The family and community of the St. Matthew Baptist Church, 5410 Louisburg Road, Raleigh, NC, is proud to announce that we are in the process of restoring and preserving our Rosenwald school. Built in 1922, it was the center of education in this agrarian community. Long since abandoned as a bastion of education, it has served as a dwelling place for many of our members and community.

Recently, the Church, having recognized the importance of such a structure and its meaning to future generations, has decided to commit to restoration of this school.

Because of its significance not only to St. Matthew and its' community, we invite and solicit any financial or human resource that you are willing to make toward the completion of this project. Its restoration will be completed by the community, Wake County, and North Carolina because it is a part of a larger history.

Fundraising information from St. Matthew School in Raleigh, North Carolina.

References

Holy Bible (KJV)
Zondervan Pictorial Bible Dictionary, 1967
Matthew Henry's Commentary, Vol. V
World Book Encyclopedia, 1976
News & Observer, Raleigh, NC (March 25, 1939)
New York Daily News, June 14, 2005
Establishing A Board of Christian Education Ministry within a Local Christian Church by Marvin O. Riddick, Published 2004 by Vantage Press, Inc. NYC

About the Author

Brother Marvin O. Riddick is a retired Department of Army Civilian (DAC) employee and also a retiree of United States Uniformed Services (US Army Retired—Sergeant Major). The "Legion of Merit" is among the awards he received for exceptional outstanding Military Service. By Proclamation, The Borough President of Bronx, New York, proclaimed October 26, 1996 "Sergeant Major Marvin O. Riddick Day." In addition to attending Bronx Community College, he is a graduate of the Adjutant General's School, and has completed other military schooling (college equivalent). He is a graduate and former Instructor of the (NYC area) Leadership Training School, Congress of Christian Education, United Missionary Baptist Association. In addition to being currently the senior Church Organist at New Tabernacle Baptist Church, Bronx, New York, where he has been humbly serving for more than forty-two years, he is also Chairperson, Board of Christian Education Ministry (BOCEM).